INDO-US STRATEGIC RELATIONS

PROSPECTS AND CHALLENGES IN THE 21ST CENTURY

INDO-US STRATEGIC RELATIONS

PROSPECTS AND CHALLENGES IN THE 21ST CENTURY

By
MOHAMMAD SAMIR HUSSAIN

National Center of International Security and Defence Analysis University of Pune

Neha Publishers & Distributors
4832/24, Prahlad Lane, S-207 Ansari Raod, Daryaganj, New Delhi-110002

Published by
Neha Publishers & Distributors
4832/24, Prahlad Lane, S-207 Ansari Raod, Daryaganj,
New Delhi-110002
Tel.: 011-43570976, 23278261
Email-nehapubdistributors@gmail.com

First Edition : 2014

ISBN : 978-93-80318- 29-5

Price : 1550/-

Laser Typesetting by : Vinod Bhardwaj

Printed at: Nagri Printers, Delhi

PRINTED IN INDIA

Published by Neha Publishers & Distributors, New Delhi-110002

PREFACE

Unlike in the past, the relationship between India and the United States since the Cold War end has witnessed a sea change. Both the domestic and international factors have contributed to this change. Many new developments have emerged since then that had never experienced in the past. The multifaceted relationship has witnessed significant improvement in every aspect of India-U.S. bilateral relations including political, economic, defence and security. The main basis of this booming relationship are the convergence of interests such as promoting democracy, combating terrorism and ensuring regional and global responsibility. As we all know that the relationship with the United States is one of the most important among the many relations that India engages with other countries. Given this fact, India is fully committed to transforming the relations in a way that is beneficial to both countries and also for the international community. The recent upsurge in the relations between the two countries has inspired me to carry out study on the topic entitled, **"Indo-US Strategic Relations: Prospects and Challenges in the 21st Century."**

The disintegration of the erstwhile Soviet Union was the major turning point in the strategic relationship between the two world's largest democracies. The disintegration of erstwhile Soviet Union and the emergence of the United States as the only super power in the world opened up new opportunity for a productive and prosperous strategic relationship between the two countries. Both sides, after having realized the advantage of working closely together, without any concerned about the past events was fully ready to capture the opportunity that comes their way.

The expanding relations between India and the United States should also be looked at in the context of changing international scenario. Today, both sides need each other to meet their increasing interests and objectives. High-level official visits from India to the United States and vice-versa has become a routine work that is aimed at strengthening the newly gained relationship. The visit of the then U.S. Defence Secretary, Mr. William Perry to India in 1995 and the reciprocal visits by the then U.S. President Mr. Bill Clinton in March 2000 was a turning point in the history of India-U.S. bilateral relations. In a bid to strengthen the close understanding between the two countries, former Prime Minister of India, Mr. Atal Bihari Vajpayee visited U.S. in 2001. Such visits paved the way for further improvement in relations between India and the United States.

Indian Prime Minister Mr. Manmohan Singh and the former U.S. President, Mr. George W. Bush started moving from where the previous leaders of the two countries left. The turn of the twenty first century and the terrific events of 9/11 attacks in World Trade Center have only brought the two countries closer to fighting the menace of terrorism. Since then, there emerged significant developments in the military relationship between the two countries. For instance, military-to-military ties have strengthened a lot that there has been a non stop Malabar exercises between the two countries. Also, the security understanding between the two countries has improved a lot.

The transforming relationship reached a strategic level when both sides after a long discussion signed the 'Next Step in Strategic Partnership' in January 2004. The year 2005 was a memorable year for both the countries because it was on this very year both India and the United States came forward to initiating two landmark agreements- one, the Defence framework agreement of June 2005 and the second one being the India-United States Civilian nuclear cooperation agreement of July 2005. The defence framework agreement replaced the first defence accord signed in January 1995 named 'Agreed Minutes on Defence Cooperation', which will lasts for ten years. The distinctive feature of the civilian nuclear cooperation agreement is that of an end to almost four decades of technological denial. Secondly, it would open the way for nuclear commerce between India and supplier countries.

However, the ever expanding strategic relationship between India and the United States is not aimed at any third country or restrict India from having close relationship with other countries such as Russia, France, China and Iran. India is free to have close relations with any major powers. India will continue to enjoy close relations with all the major powers. This is in response to what many had projected when India is moving closer to engaging the United States in every aspect. The recent developments should no doubt guide the way for further improvements. No one would have expected that India and the United States would engage in a nuclear cooperation. This way we will find that in the coming years there will be more scope for cooperation between the two countries.

At the outset, I would like to thank *Allah,* the Lord Almighty for his immense grace which was bestowed on me in every walks of my life and in particular during the course of my research work. I would like to express my deep gratitude to my supervisor Dr. Abdul Khadeer Taj for his expert guidance, suggestions, encouragement, and moral support. I am also thankful to other faculty members - Dr. Shrikant Paranjpe, Dr. A.S. Dalvi and Dr. Vijay Khare for their help and encouragement at different stages of my research work.

I am extremely thankful to Dr. Altaf B. Nadaf, Senior Assistant Professor in the Department of Botany, Pune University, Dr. Abdur Rub, Assistant Professor, Jamia Milia University, Mr. Rizwan, Mr. Mohsin Bhatt, Lecture in the Chemistry Department of Kashmir University, Mr. Shaheen Showkat and all my friends for their innumerable favours that I have received from them both in my academic life and in my personal career.

My sincere thanks are also due to Indian Council for Social Science Research (ICSSR) for providing doctoral fellowship for two years that had facilitated me for the collection of the research material. I extend my heartiest thankful to the members and staff of the Jayakar Library, University of Pune, YC-NISDA Library, Centre for Advanced Strategic Studies (CASS), Pune, Jawaharlal Nehru University, Institute of Defence and Strategic Analysis, United Service Institution, Indian Council of World Affairs, India International Centre, Observer Research Foundation and Teen Murti library, all located in New Delhi for extending me with the valuable resources for the completion of my research work.

Last, but not the least, I must be thankful to my parents, sisters and in particular to my beloved brother Mohammad Amir Hussain for taking out time from his busy schedule whenever I needed technical support. Finally, I express my gratitude to Kalinga publisher and its staff for making it possible to bring out this book. I hope this book will serve as a source of information to academics, researchers, scholars and policy makers.

April 2013

(Mohammad Samir Hussain)

April 2012

Mohammad [illegible] (Hussain)

CONTENTS

INTRODUCTION

"We have an ambitious agenda with India. Our agenda is practical. It builds on a relationship that has never been better. India is a global leader, as well as a good friend. . . . My trip will remind everybody about the strengthening of an important strategic partnership. We'll work together in practical ways to promote a hopeful future for citizens in both our nations."

–Former U.S. President George W. Bush

Relations between India and the United States of America started improving steadily ever since the end of the perennial cold war that lasts for almost five decades. India and the United States, the two world's largest and powerful democracies respectively, have to hang around for almost five decades for the disintegration of Soviet Union and the end of bipolarism to start a new, better and a more robust strategic relationship. The end of cold war freed some of the major irritants to the strategic relationship. However, the end of cold war does not mean the disappearance of all the major irritants, but definitely the decades following the cold war era has been marked by close understanding to transform the relations for the mutual benefit of both sides that would have regional and global ramifications.[1]

The disintegration of the erstwhile Soviet Union and the resulting end of Cold War brought about a tremendous shift in India's foreign policy. Since then, the United States occupies an important place in India's foreign policy and vice versa. The post cold war India-U.S. relations are at the threshold of unprecedented developments. A remarkable change in the relationship between the two countries after the end of cold war era can be perceived in the nature, content and the scope of the evolving relationship. Thanks to the changing international strategic environment and the bilateral efforts on the part of the two countries that makes it possible for the relations to prosper better than the past.[2]

The improving relationship between the two countries is also a reflection to gaining understanding and convergence of views on major regional and global issues. Unless there is a better understanding, there cannot be a better and a mutually beneficial relationship between the two countries. In response to India's emerging stature in the new world order, the U.S. was ready to expand the multi-faceted relationship with the former spanning political, economic, defence, culture, science and technology, strategic and security realms. More than one factor has brought a discernable change in the speed and direction of India-U.S. relations in the 1990s. One is the disintegration of the erstwhile Soviet Union and the end of cold war. Second factor is that of the decision taken by Indian Government to liberalize its economy. Third one is the Indian nuclear tests of May 1998 and fourth one is the landmark visit of former U.S. President Bill Clinton to India in March 2000 after the gap of twenty-two years. Moreover, the role of Indian-American community in cementing the evolving bilateral relationship is not less insignificant.[3]

The demise of Soviet Union brought a huge blow to India because it had lost a close and a reliable strategic partner, Soviet

Union. Russia, after having succeeded Soviet Union, made it very clear that it would not be able to provide the security guarantee against India's adversary state like China. It was also reluctant to supply arms and equipment to India under the exceptionally favorable cold war terms. America, on the other side, emerged as the sole economic, military and technological power in the world, forcing India to think of improving relations with the former without any perturbing about the past events.[4]

Improving the relations is in the interests of both India and the United States. Both the countries are very keen to recapture the lost opportunities of improving the relations. There are very good reasons as to why the US would want to engage with India in the changing world scenario. India's assets and resources became more relevant to a wide range of American interests.[5] The U.S. perception of India's role in the challenging international security environment has changed. Today, the U.S. considers India has a significant role to play in fighting terrorism, preventing the proliferation of weapons of mass destruction and ensuring peace and security in the world.[6]

The tremendous shift in the relationship between India and the United States could not have taken place had the two countries showed firmness to alter its previous policy. Combined effort to evolve a new partnership did borne fruit. Otherwise, the relationship would remain where it was with no sign of improvement. The main basis for this evolving relation has been the common values and the strategic interests that both the countries share.[7]

Although the relationship has marked a significant improvement but no such significant changes have occurred in areas such as nuclear non-proliferation and disarmament issue and its related technology transfer. Nuclear non-proliferation and disarmament issue are the cause of disagreement between India and the United States. Had there been no controversial issues such as NPT and CTBT, the relationship during the first decade after the end of the cold war would have been much better. India and United States signed the first landmark defence agreement named "Agreed minutes on defence cooperation" in 1995. Defence cooperation between the two countries was not expanding up to the expectations due to proliferation concerns.[8]

Thereafter, India conducted a series of nuclear tests in Pokhran on 11 and 13 May 1998 to meet its security concerns. According to Mr. Brajesh Mishra, former National Security Advisor of India, "One either changes the policy to suit the environment or changes the environment to suit the policy". The Indian nuclear tests helped changed the environment. The nuclear test was important for India in that it forced the U.S. to consider India as 'a part of the solution' rather than 'a part of the problem'. Besides this, it also compelled the U.S. to reconsider changing its stand on issues such as nuclear non-proliferation and defence technology transfer.[9]

By the end of the twentieth century and the dawn of the twenty-first century, there was a significant change in the U.S. strategic thinking towards India ranging from Pakistan issue to nuclear issue to Kashmir problem and even started realising India as an emerging major power in the international system. With this, U.S. seeks to maintain good relations with both India and Pakistan based on their own merits and not to repeat the same mistake of allowing India-U.S. relations to become a hostage to Pakistan. As far as Kashmir is concerned, the U.S. has shifted its stand from direct or indirect intervention to bringing the two countries closer to engaging dialogue for resolving the dispute and if need be intervene given the consent from both countries. In Addition to these, Washington has decided not to allow the long pending nuclear issue to continue to disrupt the relations.[10]

In an effort to strengthen the relationship, former U.S. President Mr. Bill Clinton visited India in March 2000. The visit was a landmark visit because it came after a long gap by any U.S. president. Both the countries signed a number of agreements indicating the mutual desire to move the relationship toward a closer, lasting and a qualitatively new partnership. The March 2000 Joint statement between former U.S President Mr. Bill Clinton and former Indian Prime Minister Mr. Atal- Bihari Vajpayee provided the roadmap for building an enduring and a mutually beneficial relationship.

When the then U.S. President Mr. Bill Clinton was replaced by former U.S. President George W. Bush, he was more determined and committed to increase the level of the present India-U.S. relations. On the very first year of his presidency, George W. Bush waived all nuclear related sanctions imposed during Mr. Bill Clinton tenure without any reference to CTBT[11] and allowed the sale of spare parts for India's Navy Sea King's helicopters.[12] In his National Security Strategy of 2002, former U.S. President Mr. George W. Bush has referred India as "a growing world power with which we have common strategic interests." In response, India without any hesitation, announced its support to President George W. Bush national missile defence program unveiled on 1 May 2001.[13] It was a significant move in terms of clearing the way for expanding the relations further.

The incident of 11 September was a turning point in India-U.S. relations in that it brought the two countries closer than ever before to meeting the challenges of terrorism, which poses a serious threat to international community in general and security of both countries in particular. It gives an ample opportunity for the U.S. and international community to understand India's concerns regarding terrorism. It is only after this catastrophic event, the U.S seems to acknowledge India's concern over the terrorism arising from both within and beyond the border.[14] India, without any concerned about the past U.S. stand on India fight against terrorism, took the opportunity of offering support to the U.S. fight against terrorism by providing access to air bases, refueling and maintenance support, over flight rights, intelligence support and lastly but not the least port facilities for the U.S. warships. Despite of immediate Indian support, former U.S President George Bush went for Pakistan as a staging area for operation in Afghanistan due to its close proximity. That does not mean the United States have no faith to India.[15] Security understanding between India and the United States has improved after the 11 December attack on Indian Parliament (pillar of Indian Democracy).

United States has created a history by concluding a civilian nuclear cooperation agreement with India who is not a member of NPT regime. It has sent a clear message to the world that India is an important country very hard to be ignored in the twenty-first century challenging world. With this both sides had created a platform for a vibrant partnership. The intention behind this agreement was to assist India in achieving its vision to become a major power in the twenty-first century. This step would ensure that India to integrate itself strategically, politically, economically and technologically into the international system.[16]

Economic relations between the two countries would also play a key role in stabilising and strengthening the strategic relations. Since the implementations of economic reforms in India in 1991, economic and trade relations has improved. Former U.S. President Bill Clinton announced in a press conference that "our commerce department has identified India as one of the biggest emerging markets around the world". Since then America's investment towards India has increased manifolds. Today United States remains India's largest foreign direct investment partner and second largest trading partner.[17]

Closer India-American relations and the sharing of common interests and strategic objective in the regional and global affairs do not mean neither India has entered into an alliance nor the relationship is targeted at any third country. The evolving relationship would not pose any problem to India's relations with other countries like Russia, France, China, Japan or even Israel. If any of the American moves is against India's interest then India would not favor them. For instance, India did not endorse and not agreed to send its troops to join U.S. unilateral intervention in Iraq. While having a relationship with United States, India will maintain a close cooperation with other countries like Russia, China, Iran, etc.[18] The major questions that a researcher seeks to answer during the study were as under: How important is the relationship between India and the United States for international peace and security? How India is going to benefit by expanding its relations with the United States? Does the relationship with the United States pose any implications to relations with other major powers such as Russia, China, etc.? Does the growing India-United States relationship mean an end to Pakistan factor? Does the expanding relationship between the two countries aimed at containing China? What are the obstacles to India-U.S. strategic relationship? Which areas hold the key to future India-U.S. prospects?

1.1 Role of Strategic Dialogue in Regaining the Lost Relationship

Strategic dialogues between India and United States started since the end of the cold war. Lt. Gen Claude Kickleighter took the initiative in the late 1991. Since then, both the countries had engaged in strategic dialogue at the regular intervals. Without the strategic dialogue, whatever developments that we have seen today during the last almost decades could not have taken place. Strategic dialogues have given way to joint military exercises, security understanding, high-level exchanges, etc. Thus, the strategic dialogues have played a key role in helping to reduce the differences that existed between them even after the end of cold war and thereby bringing the two countries closer in a single platform.[19]

India and the United States entered into a longest ever dialogue after the former conducted the series of nuclear tests in May 1998. The strategic dialogue started on June 1998 between Mr. Jaswant Singh of India and Mr. Strobe Talbott of the U.S. In all, both the countries held eight rounds of talks between June 1998 and February 1999. The focus of the dialogue besides nuclear issue was on how to increase the level of the bilateral strategic relations. The dialogue was instrumental in bringing back the lost understanding, thereby resulting in the positive improvement of the bilateral relations. This was evident during the Kargil conflict between India and Pakistan in the summer of 1999 when unexpectedly the U.S. came out strongly in support of India and pressurizes Pakistan to withdraw its troops from the Indian territory. However, the dialogue was not able to grant India the official nuclear status.[20] It was a victory for India due to the fact that since then Washington recognized that its policy of "rolling back" of India's nuclear program was not a viable strategy.[21] Thus, in the absence of such a fruitful dialogue, the relations between the two countries would have been totally different.

1.2 Defining the Concept of Strategic Relationship

Today, strategic analysts and thinkers of international affairs are quite familiar with the term strategic relations.[22] The term strategic relations have increasingly been used by the authors, strategic analysts after the cold war era, when there emerged a tremendous shift in the relationship among the states. That does not mean that the term has not been used during the cold war era.

There are no such permanent definitions on strategic relations. Different views have been given by different analysts on strategic relations. It would also differ from one country to another country. How the Indian strategic analyst perceive the strategic relations would differ from those of American strategic analyst.

In the American parlance, the term strategic relationship implies little more than mutual respect and long-term cooperation in selected areas of mutual concern, and is not synonymous with the identity of views.[23] While in Indian parlance, the term refers to a situation wherein the two countries agree to raise the level of their regular interaction from the lowest to the highest, to deal with the great variety of issues that concern each of them in a cordial manner seeking cooperation and understanding and to make a long-term commitment for the mutual benefit and furthering their respective goals.[24] From the above Indian and American perspective, one can conclude that strategic relationship is meant for mutual benefit that would work together to meeting the common concerns for the long-term partnership and does not lead to alliance against any third country. Both sides will enjoy distinctive flexibility to chase respective interests and not come under the pressure of the partner.

There are some Indians who suppose that strategic relations means identity of views or military alliance. Strategic relationship between India and the United States does not mean identity of views or entering into a military alliance because, India and the United States have a divergent of views on a variety of issues.[25]

The term strategic is primarily concerned with the ways in which the actors make use of the military power and capability to achieve political goals.[26] In the international affairs, it refers to a global, long-term and comprehensive relationship between the two countries. In a narrow sense, it refers to a security relationship including the military cooperation.[27] The substance of any strategic relationships depends on the closeness and depth of interactions, the convergence of interests and the devotion of the two countries to accommodate the other's concerns.[28]

Strategic relationships between the two countries have to be founded on a sound and resilient security and military partnership. It doesn't mean that the other elements of the relations such as economy, trade and technology are irrelevant. These elements would also play a key role in shaping and strengthening the strategic relationship.[29]

The strength or weakness of any strategic relationship will be measured by the understanding shard by both countries. Any form of strategic relationship is aimed at enhancing the strategic understanding between the two sides. Strategic relationship should not be construed with strategic alliance. Strategic relationship is different from strategic alliance in the following way:

a. Strategic relationship is driven by common goal of ensuring peace, security and development rather than by common threat.
b. Strategic relationship is broader in sense and gives more room for having partnership with other countries at any given time.
c. Strategic relationship does not provide security guarantee to its partner.
d. Strategic relationship allows a partner to decide their own course of action.[30]

1.3 Background History of India-U.S. Relations (From 1945-1990)

Since the focus of the study in on the post cold war relationship between India and the United States, but I felt the need to highlight the historical underpinnings of India-U.S. relations for it helps us to understand the reasons why the relations between India and United States remain strained for almost five decades.

Relations between India and the United States of America during the cold war era have been characterized by mutual irritation, misunderstanding, and distrust of each other intentions. The estranged relationship between India and the United States was due to the conflicting policies adopted to protect and foster their respective national interest. After the end of World War II, the United States was very much concerned about the containment of the erstwhile Soviet Union, for which it seeks to draw the attention of other countries into a system of alliance. The United States want to have India as a partner in its effort toward achieving this objective. However, India on the other side, was reluctant to join any of the two power blocs, was focused on bringing an end to colonialism. As a result of which, India adopted a policy of non-alignment.

The United States after failing to secure India as a partner in its fight against communism turned to Pakistan. American started supplying military equipment and weapons to Pakistan as part of its effort to bring the relations closer and even included Pakistan in a military regime such as SEATO and CENTO.[31] On 19 May 1954, after a months long negotiation, Pakistan and the United States signed a Mutual Defence Agreement. The agreement had a profound impact on India-U.S. relations because under the agreement, the United States has agreed to supply weapons and equipment to Pakistan. This move forced India to turn to Soviet Union for military assistance.[32] With this, the relations between India and the United States started deteriorating. This is further worsened by the statement made by the U.S. secretary of State, under the Eisenhower administration, Mr. John Foster Dules, "They who are not with us are against us."[33]

During the Korean crisis in 1950s, India and the United States took a different path whereby India refused to send any troops, but it dispatched an ambulance unit.[34] The relations were further deteriorated over the issue of Indo-China. India was against the French activities in Southeast Asia whereas the United States supported French activities.

Despite of a continuing difference, the relations between India and the United States improved when the Indian Prime Minister Mr. Jawaharlal Nehru paid an official visit to the U.S. in 1956. In his public statement, Mr. Jawaharlal Nehru called Mr. Eisenhower a man of peace. The better relationship continued even after Kennedy assumed office in 1960. However, the high points in India-U.S. relations came in the latter part of 1962, when India came under the severe attack from China in the Northeast Frontier Agency and the Ladakh section of Kashmir. The Kennedy administration responded positively to Nehru's appeal for a military support. Very soon the relationship suffered a serious setback when India-Pak war broke out. What angered India most during the war with Pakistan in 1965 was the American failure to prevent Pakistan from using the weapons which they have supplied. And United States even suspended the aid which it promised to provide before the war. The strained relations were further worsened by the issue of Bokaro steel plant project, when the U.S. withdraws to support India in the project. Later on, Soviet Union replaced the U.S. in the Bokaro steel plant project. Thus, the relationship between India and Soviet Union improved at the cost of the United States.[35]

At this very crucial juncture, India and Soviet Union entered into a landmark treaty of Peace, Friendship and Cooperation on 9 August 1971. The treaty further complicated the relationship between India and United States.[36] However, the lowest point in India-U.S. relations came in 1971, when the United States without any reliable evidence charged India of attacking first to Pakistan. The United States dispatched its naval task force of the seventh fleet spearheaded by the nuclear powered aircraft carrier Enterprise to the Bay of Bengal in support of Pakistan. The U.S. tried to defend its aggressive move by ensuring India that it was meant for the evacuation of Americans residing in East Pakistan. Whatever may be the reasons, it has done enough damage for the rest of India-U.S. relations.[37] Further damage was done by the underground nuclear tests of India on 18th May, 1974. The US Government criticizes the tests[38] and even refused to supply nuclear fuel to Tarapur civilian nuclear installation. They even coerce the other nuclear advanced countries to bring an end to nuclear trade with India under the aegis of Nuclear Suppliers Group (NSG).[39]

The situation changed after the Soviet military intervention in Afghanistan in 1979. India seeks to open up its relations with the U.S. and Washington responded positively to it.[40] When Ronald Reagan became the president of the U.S, efforts were made to improve the strained relations between the two countries. It was justified when the U.S. Secretary of State Alexander Haig instructing the U.S. embassy in Delhi to "respond favorably to any arms purchase requests the Indians might bring up." However, efforts was not able to succeed when the Indians request for the purchase of F-5G aircraft were not met. It was the lack of understanding that didn't allow for smooth technology transfers.

Very soon, the two countries came up with the ideas of signing the Memorandum of Understanding on transfer of defence technology, including dual-use technology to India. The MoU was signed on 29 November 1984 and operationalised in 1985. With this, more than five thousand licenses were approved for dual use technology. It also opens the door for collaboration on night vision devices; LM 2500 gas turbine engine and Light combat Aircraft (LCA).[41] However, the implementation of Missile Technology Control regime (MTCR) in 1985 prohibited the transfer of technology suitable for satellites, space launcher and missiles.[42]

Despite of all this, United States was eager to have closer military relations with India. In an effort to strengthen the defence supply relationship, the U.S. Defence Secretary, Mr. Casper Weinberger visited India in October 1986 to discuss more about on the transfer of defence related technology for India's Light combat aircraft and electronic equipment. In the year 1987, the U.S. published a *Blue Book* that gave a list of technologies that could be released to India in order to allow the US firms to participate in the LCA programme.[43] Thus, throughout the period of cold war, both India and the United States were geographically, politically, economically and strategically on the opposite sides.

1.4 Transforming India-United States Relations

The end of the cold war period had seen an unprecedented transformation in the relations between India and the United States that is characterised by more understanding, trust, commitment and cooperation. The two countries have come a long way to transforming the relations from the estranged nations to the engaged ones. The transforming relations between India and the United States would not have taken place had the two countries remain uncommitted to transforming the relations. Numerous commitments were made by India and the United States to transform the relationship that would accrue benefit to both countries. As such the transforming relationship is based on the common values and interest and the understanding reached to meet the challenges that come on their way.

The leaders of the two countries from time to time have played a very significant role in helping the two countries to transform the much-needed relations. The contribution of Mr. Atal Bihari Vajpayee, former Prime Minister of India and Mr. Bill Clinton, former President of the United States was highly respectable. It was Bill Clinton, who laid the foundation for transforming the relations between India and United States. Before the end of his tenure as President of the U.S, Mr. Bill Clinton paid a historic visit to South Asia for five days in March 2000. It was during his landmark visit to South Asia, Indian Prime Minister Mr. Atal Bihari Vajpayee and himself announced their "resolve to create a closer and qualitatively new relationship between India and United States."[44]

The transforming relations can also be seen in every aspect of bilateral India-U.S. relations, but one area that has shown dramatic improvement is the defence cooperation. During his visit to India in February 2002, U.S. General Richard B. Myers contended that Defence cooperation between India and the United States would lead the way in continuing transformation of bilateral relationship.[45]

The transforming relations were speeded up by the turn of the 21st century. According to David Mulford, former U.S. Ambassador to India, "Over the past few years we have witnessed the beginning of a transforming that will open up the new opportunity for our two countries that would have been unimaginable a few years ago. We have taken important steps forward to bridge previous mistrust and lay the foundation for what I believe will be crucial partnership for the twenty-first century." Ambassador statement was followed by the statement of former Indian External Affairs Minister Mr. Yashwant

Singh, who said that, "The vision of the two largest democracies, placed in different situation but linked by strong bilateral ties, bringing diverse perspectives to address their increasingly common challenges, represents an exciting possibility in global affairs." The above two statement reveals the potential role that India and the United States need to play in the 21st century.

Followed by Mr. George W. Bush's, former President of the U.S, commitment early on in his tenure to "get the big relationship right and counted India among them." The decisions taken by both former U.S. President Mr. Bill Clinton and Mr. George W. Bush were due to the advantage that would accrue from transforming the bilateral relations. The transforming relations between India and the United States would help advance the interests of both countries with respect to defeating terrorism, preventing the proliferation of weapons of mass destruction, security and stability of the world. Thus, the transforming relationships were given shape by former U.S. President George W. Bush and Indian Prime Minister Mr. A.B. Vajpayee.[46]

And last but not the least, the contribution of the people-to-people ties has also been very significant. The number of Indians living in America and vice versa has increased a lot. The figure has increased from one million in 2000 to one and half million in 2007. It has the potential to bridge the gap and brings the two countries close together. The number of Indians residing in America has reached a particular level that it would be able to influence the political decisions of the United States better than the past.[47] Thus, the ongoing strategic relationship is in the process of transforming. In the long run, it would require both sides to be serious about not allowing any issue to become a hindrance to it. The more the relationship transform, the better will be for both the countries.

1.5 Significance of India-U.S. Strategic Relations

From the Indian and American point of view, the relationship between them has a global significance. The real significance of India-U.S. relations lies in the significant role that both countries can play in the twenty-first century. This partnership will enable both countries to harness the vast potential of bilateral relations, drawing upon complementarities and each other's intrinsic strengths, and work together to address regional and global challenges. India and the United States represent a fifth of the world population and account for more than a quarter of the world's economy have a lot to do for peace, prosperity, democracy and freedom in the world. The global significance of the expanding India-U.S. relations lies in playing a key role to ensuring peace, security and stability in the world. It also lays in convergence of interests that India and United States share. This convergence would insist both countries to work together for achieving the above objectives.[48]

The relationship between India and the United States is not just for the benefit of the two countries but also for the good of the international community. Over the last few years, India's importance as a strategic partner has increased a lot. The United States are well aware of the fact that it is not possible to maintain strategic stability and economic prosperity of the South Asian region without India's participation and assistance. The location of India also makes the relationship very vital. Geographically, India occupies an important place in the Indian Ocean region that stretches from Persian Gulf in the west to the Malacca strait in the east, making it an important player in ensuring security in the region. This has no doubt attracted the attention of the U.S. towards India in this changing scenario.

Keeping this in mind, it was former U.S. Secretary of State, Mr. Colin Powell in his Senate confirmation hearings in March

2001, and Ms. Condoleezza Rice in early 2005 have proposed the possibility of Delhi and Washington working closely together in the region.[49] This is further supported by the statement of former Indian Prime Minister Mr. Atal Bihari Vajpayee during the Combined Commanders' Conference in November 2003 that, "...the strategic frontiers of today's India, grown in international stature, have expanded well beyond confines of South Asia...Our security environment ranges from Persian Gulf to straits of Malacca across the Indian Ocean, including Central Asia and Afghanistan, China...and South-east Asia. Our strategic thinking has also extended to these horizons."[50] This statement reflects the responsibility of India in ensuring security in this region.

No other two countries better understand the danger poised by the activities of terrorism than India and the United States is to. As part of its efforts to bring about a peaceful world, India and the United States will bolster joint efforts to counter terrorism and meet other challenges to Peace. In addition, the two countries are also prepared to work together to prevent the proliferations of nuclear weapons and their means of delivery. To meet these increasing challenges, both India and the United States have to play a vital role. And the expanding security cooperation between India and the United States is good for understanding the challenges facing the world.[51]

1.6 India-U.S. Strategic Relationship: Convergences and Divergences

The expanding India-U.S. relations are witnessing a convergence and divergence of interests on range of issues. The convergence offer the opportunity for working together and keeping them engaged and the divergence has the potential to restrict it from expanding. The Defence framework agreement signed on June 2005 spelt out the areas where India-U.S. interests converge. They are combating terrorism, preventing the proliferation of weapons of mass destruction, security of the Sea-Lanes of Communication (SLOCs), ensuring regional and global stability, ensuring peace, security and stability in the Indian Ocean region, preserving energy security and last but not the least promotion of democracy.[52]

Combating Terrorism: Why cannot there be convergence of India-U.S. interest on fighting terrorism when they remain the two countries that have suffered grievously to terrorism. India in particular, has been facing this problem for the last many decades and has lost thousand of innocent lives fighting the menace. Eradicating the menace of terrorism poses a serious challenge to international community in general and in particular to both India and the United States. Both countries have every reason to come closer and be strongly committed to fighting terrorism.

Despite continuous commitment to tackle the menace of terrorism, India and United States adopt diverse method, making it difficult for both the countries to achieve the objective. When it comes to terrorism, India's main concern is terrorism supported by Pakistan, in which U.S. is not ready to accept. The U.S self interest stand and the inability to understand India's problem might delay the two countries from achieving the objective of eradicating the menace of terrorism. The U.S. selective approach to combat terrorism is in consonance with the interest of Pakistan and not for India, which calls for indiscriminate treatment. No doubt, the 11 September events provided the two countries with a common security cause in the fight against terrorism.[53] It is a great time now that India and the United States build a consensus and work together to counter all forms of terrorism. Otherwise, time will run out of their hand.

Securing Sea-Lanes of Communication: Given their dependence on sea for their trade, both countries have the same stake in ensuring security and stability of Sea lanes of communication. Nearly ninety seven per cent of India's trade with other countries including the import and export of Oil and Gas depend on sea. With expanding trade relations with other countries, the volume of shipping will also increase. Increasing energy demands due to the increase in population also calls for security of the SLOCs. Therefore, uninterrupted flow of the passage of goods through SLOCs is vital for India's economy.[54] The U.S. has a huge interest in economic resources of Persian Gulf and in the uninterrupted supply of oil from the Persian Gulf, protection of SLOCs from all kinds of harassment and interdiction becomes very important.

Since the end of cold war, both India and the United States have carried out a number of Joint exercises in the Indian Ocean region. These exercises could lead to SLOCs patrols to help ensure the free flow of traffic through SLOCs. Indian navy in cooperation with the U.S. navy and the navy from other countries could play a vital role in protecting sea lanes against piracy, drug-smuggling and arms-trafficking, etc.[55]

Promotion of Democracy: Promotion of democracy is also one of those areas where India-U.S. interests coincide. India and United States have a vital role to play in convincing and helping others to become a democratic country. While engaging the longest ever strategic dialogue between India and the U.S. after Pokhran II tests, Washington sought the support of India in an initiative to promote democracy worldwide. It was during his visit to India in 2000, Clinton made a proposal for setting up a Center for Asian Democracy. India became the founding members of the Com-munity of Democracies initiative in 1999.[56]

In a joint statement released on 18 July 2005, the leaders of the two countries resolve to create an environment conducive to promotion of democratic values, and to strengthen democratic practices in societies which wish to become more open and pluralistic. Both sides consider the effective democratic governance as central to healthy economic development and prosperity and also to building peaceful societies.[57]

However, after the U.S. illegal unilateral intervention in Iraq, a number of questions have been raised by many countries over the promotion of democracy worldwide. How can a nation preach other nations to become a democracy when he is involved in abuses of the rule of law in the fight against terrorism? India has to be very cautious before any step is taken, so as to avoid itself from getting trapped into an unnecessary burden. With this, the American objective of achieving democracy promotion world-wide is in disarray.[58]

Central Asia: Central Asia emerge as an area of huge stake to both India and the United States after the disintegration of Soviet Union owing to two reasons- one is the presence of rich oil and gas resources in the region, while the other one is the challenges of terrorism and its related activities such as smuggling of arms and narco-trafficking, facing the countries in the region.

The very geo-strategic and geo-economic importance of Central Asia had attracted the attention of other countries such as Russia, China, Iran and Pakistan. They are also keeping an eye on region and even trying to keep the region under its influence. Cooperation between India and the United States is crucial to meeting their increasing energy needs. Both sides can play a crucial role in ensuring stable security in the region because any insecurity in the region will have its implications to both countries and India in particular due to its close proximity. For India and the United States to achieve its objective, the first thing to do is to ensure political stability in the region.[59]

CARs became an area of utmost importance after the September 11 incidents because of the possibility of the region becoming a breeding ground of terrorism. Among the Central Asian Republics, Turkmenistan, Uzbekistan and Tajikistan share a border with the terrorist affected area of Afghanistan and Tajikistan in particular is very close to Pakistan occupied Kashmir (POK). The location of Tajikistan makes it highly vulnerable to terrorist activities and therefore it is a case of concern for both India and the United States.[60] Any instability in Afghanistan would have serious implications not only to India and United States but also for Central Asian Republics. At this end, both India and United States should consider working together for a stable and friendly government in Afghanistan, which also holds the key to security and stability in CARs. Therefore, stable and secure Afghanistan is in the interest of India, the United States and Central Asian Republics.

Given the common stake in Central Asia, both countries must ensure that the region does not become hostage to violent activities such as terrorism, smuggling of arms and weapons, drug smuggling, etc. India and the United States together should offer assistance to Central Asian Republics in tackling these challenges.

1.6.1 India-U.S. Divergences

Areas where India-U.S. interests diverge are nuclear proliferation, transfer of technology, Pakistan issue, human rights violation and trade related issues. These factors have the ability to slow down or impede comprehensive cooperation.

Nuclear proliferation: Nuclear issue remains the main irritants to India-U.S. relations. India has from the very beginning been consistently opposed to the U.S. position on proliferation of nuclear and its related weapons. So far, it has been successful to avoiding U.S. pressure to signing nuclear non-proliferation treaty (NPT) and Comprehensive test ban treaty (CTBT). India opposed such treaties owing to its discriminatory nature and lack of comprehensiveness respectively. It divides the world into two group-have and have not, thereby allowing the nuclear weapons power to carry on nuclear weapons programme, while not allowing the same to others who seeks to acquire it for the security purposes.[61]

While India and the United States share the same objective of preventing the proliferation of nuclear and its related weapons but the difference lies in their perception and their approach to achieving it. India calls for universal nuclear disarmament while the U.S. calls for achieving the objective of non-proliferation regionally.[62]

Technology Transfer Issue: Denial of technology to India is one issue of divergences between India and the United States. Indian official consider the U.S. as a country not to be relied upon for the transfer of technology, while the U.S. on the other hand, consider transfer of technology with India a difficult task at the ignorance of India's track record of not exporting any technology to any other suspected countries.

Unlike India, China despite of more restrictive the U.S. trade regulations, enjoy a robust high technology trade with the United States.[63] After the Next Step in Strategic Partnership, very little have been achieved so far in the areas of dual use technology but transfer of critical technologies to India remain nonstarter. The U.S. was ready to transfer those items of technology that comes under the IAEA inspection such as turbines, etc. The main impediment that stood on the way to a fruitful technological cooperation is the U.S. unwillingness to recognise India as a nuclear power.[64] India and United States has made an attempt for easy transfer of technology but the latter's inability to understand India's threat perception has also been the roadblock. The U.S. even adopted the policy of denial of dual use technology to curb the proliferation of nuclear and missile technology to the non-adherents of the control regime like India. On the other hand, the U.S. is not concerned about the proliferation of such technology by the nuclear power to non-nuclear power. If the U.S. is so serious about stopping the proliferation of Weapons of mass destruction then why only India, Why not targeted other countries.[65]

Pakistan Issue: The issue of Pakistan remains to be one of the main areas of divergences between India and the United States. During the cold war period, the issue of Pakistan looms large on India-U.S. relations. Even after the end of cold war, Pakistan factor would play a very crucial role in India-U.S. relations. India is against the U.S. policy of treating both the Asian powers equally (more details on this issue will come in chapter 4).

Intellectual Property Rights: The issues of intellectual property rights stand on the way of increased trade relationship between India and the United States. On April 1993, United States designated India as a priority country for immediate punitive action under the special 301 provision of the U.S. Trade Act 1974 unless the latter improved its enforcement of intellectual property rights. [66]

After having identified the areas of convergence and the areas of divergence in the post cold war era, the next step what India and the United States should take is to explore the ways and means of resolving these issues. This will no doubt strengthen and broaden the evolving strategic relationship.

1.7 Objectives of the Study

The study has the following objectives-

a. To study the defence and military relations between India and the United States.

b. To study the economic and trade relations between India and the United States.
c. To analyse the implications of India-U.S. relations to major powers of the world including China, Russia, Japan and Indian Sub-continent.
d. To study the opportunities and challenges of the India-U.S. civil nuclear deal.
e. To examine the past and explore the futuristic prospects of India-U.S. Strategic Relations.

1.8 Hypothesis of the Study

Following hypothesis has been formulated keeping in mind the research problem.

a. The more the interests of India and U.S. converge, the deeper, the stronger and healthier would become the relationship.
b. The nuclear issue will remain the sticking point in India's strategic relations with U.S.
c. Increased economic cooperation rather than the defence cooperation would remain the hallmark of India-U.S. strategic relations.
d. The military-to-military interactions, holding of joint military exercises and a regular dialogue by the defence policy group involving the officials of both countries on strategic issues at the second track will help in mutual understanding between India and the United States.
e. Cooperation in non-military nuclear activities such as science and technology, space cooperation, energy and medical sciences will provide a major boost to India's relations with the U.S.

1.9 Review of Literature

Plentiful literature is available on this topic in the form of books, government documents, articles in magazines and journals, and the Internet. While several books written on the subject provide the background and detailed analysis, the recent articles bring the discussion up to date. Besides, the author has also relied on the Internet and electronic media for the latest inputs. Effort has also been made to make use of works of both Indian and American writers.

Chintamani Mahapatra works on *Indo-US Relations in the 21st Century* focus on growing relationship that started after the erstwhile Soviet disintegration. It gives an understanding of the major factors that really helped the transform the relationship in a multi-faceted aspects encompassing political, economic and defence and military-to-military relations.[67] This book is followed by another very good book edited by Kanti Bajpai and Amitabh Mattoo just before the turn of the 21st Century named, *Engaged Democracies: India-U.S. Relations in the 21st Century*[68] It explores the multi-dimensional relationship between India and the U.S. and charts a course for the future. It also spelt out areas where the two countries need to focus on.

Ashok Kapur and others edited book entitled, *India and the United States in a Changing World*[69] covers various aspects of India-U.S. bilateral relations such as military-to-military relations, economic and trade relations, nuclear issue and also Kashmir dispute. It analysed how all of these issues affect the bilateral relations and offers pragmatic policy recommendations. This is followed by another timely book edited by Sumit Ganguly and others on the topic, *US-Indian Strategic cooperation into the 21st century: More than words.*[70] The importance of this book lies in the fact that it strictly focuses strategic aspects of bilateral India-U.S. relations. It examines the existing areas of cooperation and discord and offer suggestions for expanding the growing strategic relationship between India and the

United States.

Gary K. Bertsch and others on *Engaging India: Strategic Relations with the World's largest Democracies*[71] that addressed multilateral aspects on India-U.S. relations including Pakistan factor, China factor, nuclear issue and other areas of future cooperation. It spelt out the policy recommendations of what India and United States must do to sustain the relationship. This is followed by another book on *Indo-US Relatons: Divergence to Convergence* written by Vivek Chadha.[72] It gives clear understanding of how the relationship started shifting from divergence to convergence during the last almost two decades since the cold war end. Besides analyzing the trade and economic relations, it also discussed how the interests of both India and the United States diverge on other region such as South-East Asia, Russia, Central Asia and West Asia.

Stephan J. Blank traced the rising power and capabilities of India and its influence on the region in his book, *Natural Allies: Regional Security in Asia and Prospects for Indo American Strategic Cooperation*.[73] He highlighted the bilateral defense agenda and rationale for Indo-US strategic partnership. *India in the World Order: Searching for a Major Power Status* published in 2003, by two highly regarded scholars of Baldev Raj Nayar and TV Paul of the McGill University, Montreal, examined "the prospects and implications of India's integration into the major power system in the twenty first century.[74]

Mr. Amit Gupta's works on *The US-India Relationship: Strategic Partnership or complementary Interests* gives an insight into whether the two nations are really in for a great partnership or is this only a momentary shift in policy? In the introduction, the author wrote that the envisaged partnership between India and the US was not possible. The book analysed and illustrated how, despite convergent national and strategic interests, the two nations may never be able to engage into a meaningful strategic partnership unless some major shifts in the policies take place.[75]

Testimony by Walter K. Andersen on *"India and the United States: A Different Kind of Relationship"*, before House Committee on Foreign Affairs: Subcommittee on the Middle East and South Asia United States House of Representatives, highlighted the importance of the growing relationship. He also made a point that the growing relationship should not mean India has subjugated its national interests to the U.S. interests. The two countries will work together in areas where they will gain mutual benefit.[76]

"US-India Strategic Partnership: Implications for China", an article written by Zhang Guihong gives a Chinese perspective on the growing relationship between India and U.S. and how it would have its implications for China. It spelt out the areas of convergences and divergences between China, the U.S. and India. On the basis of which, he made an argument that India and the U.S. cannot go for containment strategy against China.[77]

For understanding on whether India-U.S. is really aimed at the containment of China, an article by V R Raghavan titled *"Indo-US Strategic Partnership: China as a Factor"*, was really helpful. It highlighted the reasons as to why containment cannot be in the interests of both India and the U.S. It also mentioned the Chinese response to the growing relationship between India and the United States.[78]

Ashley J. Tellis, *"The Merits of Dehyphenation: Explaining U.S. Success in Engaging India and Pakistan"*, published in Washington Quarterly gives an input into the paradigm shift in the U.S. approach toward India and Pakistan since the turn of the twenty-first century. It also highlighted how the United States is going to benefit by adopting the different strategy toward India and United States and not allow Pakistan factor to pose a roadblock to the growing relationship.[79] A research report by Zafar Nawaz Jaspal on *"The Indo-US Strategic Relationship and Pakistan's Security"*, really gives an insight into how Pakistan perceives the growing relationship between India and United States. This response is in the light of the civilian nuclear cooperation signed between India and the United States.[80]

Ashley J. Tellis Testimony before the Senate Foreign Relations Committee on, *"U.S.-India Atomic Energy Cooperation: Strategic and Nonproliferation Implications"*, makes a point that the agreement is not aimed at undermining the nuclear non proliferation. It highlighted how India can play a crucial role in terms of preventing the proliferation of nuclear weapons. India, despite not being a member of NPT has not proliferated any forms of nuclear technology and its related materials to other countries.[81] Besides these, I have also relied on the Internet and electronic media for the latest inputs on the changing dimension of India-U.S. relations.

1.10 Methodology

The study is carried out by adopting the historical-analytical approach. A historical approach has been followed for the study of about what had happened in the past. In analyzing the post cold war strategic relations between India and United States that witnessed significant transformation, the methodology adopted is analytical. It is a method in which the researcher has attempted to analyze and interpret both the primary and secondary sources available at various University libraries and Research Institutes. These documents were used to study the post cold war India-U.S. strategic relations. The primary source used during my study includes Speeches and Remarks given by the Indian and American Officials, Government documents, memoirs and collected papers. The secondary sources used are books, articles in journals and periodicals, reports, newspaper and various websites dealing with the topic.

1.11 Significance of the Study

The study of the relationship between India and United States after the end of the cold war period is strategically important in the context of transforming India-U.S. relations that holds the key to peace, security and stability in the international system. The post cold-war period that started after the Soviet disintegration has seen the relations between the two countries shifting from estrangement to engagement. The study is significant in terms of understanding the policy changes occurred during this period. The study would give an insight into the direction where the relationships between the two countries are heading. The study would be of interdisciplinary in nature. It would be of great interest to the policy makers, strategic analysts of both countries and also those interested in the study of the relationship between the two world's largest democracies.

1.12 Outline of the Study

The topic for my study is entitled **"India and United States of America's Strategic Relationship in the Post Cold-War Period."** The people of India and the United States was not expecting the relationship to improve after the end of the cold war, due in part to the kind of relations that India and the United States enjoy during the last almost five decades, before the erstwhile Soviet disintegration However, the relationship started improving once both sides enter the last decades of the twentieth century. Since then, both sides have made significant adjustments to ensure that the relationship keeps on improving. The growing relationship would no doubt benefit both countries. What is most important today is that both sides understand the importance of improving the relationship given the common values and interests shared by them. The study would give an understanding of how the relationship is going to benefit both sides and also the international community. What steps needs to be taken to further improve the relationship.

The study has been divided into seven chapters. The first chapter is the introduction of the topic. In this chapter, I have discussed how the relationship started improving after the end of cold war. Then the concept of Strategic relationship is also defined. Moreover, areas of convergences and divergences between the two countries are also examined. The Objectives of the study, hypothesis, methodology of the study and its significance are also mentioned. The second chapter is all about the defence and security relations between India and United States. This chapter would find focusing on every aspect of defence and military relations such as military-to-military exercises, defence supply relationship, technology transfer and its impediments. In this section, the opportunities and challenges of the recent defence agreement signed between the two countries are also analysed.

Trade and economic relations have occupied the third chapter. In this chapter, the researcher has attempted to analyse the significance of the economic relations. Trade and investment relations that have witnessed significant improvement in the last one decade are also discussed. Major areas of irritants are also examined. Moreover, the prospects of economic and trade relations has been highlighted in the last section of this chapter. In the fourth chapter, researcher has made an attempt to discuss on how Pakistan as a factor is going to impact on the growing relationship between India and the United States. This chapter also focused on the paradigm shift in the U.S. approach toward India and Pakistan that has enabled U.S. to successfully engage both South Asian rivals. This is followed by the response of Pakistan to India-U.S. relationship. The Kashmir issue between India and Pakistan has also been discussed. Lastly, the recent developments such as Mumbai terror attack and the U.S. Af-Pak strategy is also analysed.

The fifth chapter in on India-United States Relations: China and Great powers as a Factor. This chapter is based on the argument that India's relationship with other major powers of the world including China, Russia and Japan will be decided based on India's interest rather than dictated by the U.S. interest because India's interests is not subjugated to the U.S. interests. The first section of this chapter has been devoted to the post cold-war U.S.-China relations and Sino-Indian relations. It also analysed the response of China to India-U.S. relationship. This is followed by analysing the possible implications of India-U.S. relations to Russia and Japan. The chapter then suggests that the these countries instead of getting involved in a containment strategy against each other, they should look forward to finding out areas of strategic cooperation that would will have a crucial bearing on Asian and Global security.

The next chapter has been devoted to the landmark civilian nuclear cooperation agreement signed between India and United States. It seeks to study the rationale behind this agreement and what would both countries gain out of this significant agreement. It also analyse the paradigm shift in the U.S. nuclear policy toward India that had enabled this agreement to happen. It also discusses the obstacles to the landmark agreement, both domestic and international. Lastly, the chapter examines the regional and global implications of the agreement.

The concluding chapter gives an overview of the above chapters and then observes the areas of future cooperation. The two countries have made mutual commitment to further strengthening the bilateral relationship in a way that is mutually beneficial to both countries. Given the huge scope for improvement, the two countries have a huge task ahead in the coming decades before it gets maturity. An area that holds the key to future prospects includes security cooperation, military-to-military ties, economic and trade relations, energy cooperation, science and technology cooperation, etc. Finally, the suggestions of what need to be done to further strengthen the relationship much better than the past achievements have been made.

Endnotes

[1] Sumit Ganguly, "The Start of a Beautiful Friendship?", World Policy Journal (New York), vol. XX(1), Spring 2003, pp. 25-26.

[2] P.K.Das, New Heights in Indo-U.S. Relations (Jaipur: Raj Publishing House, 2005), p. 117.

[3] Gautam Adhikari, "U.S.-India Relations: Reports on AEI's Roundtable Discussions", American Enterprise Institute for Public Policy Research (AEI) Working Paper #112, 22 June 2005, pp. 3-5, available at <http://www.aei.org/docLib/20050622_Indiareport.6.22.05.pdf>.

[4] Sumit Ganguly, "America and India at a Turning Point", Current History (Philadelphia), vol. 104(680), March 2005, p. 120.

[5] Remarks by Karl F. Inderfurth, Assistant Secretary of State for South Asian Affairs at the Confederation of Indian Industry, 3 September 1997, Strategic Digest (New Delhi), vol. 27(7), October 1997, p. 1580 and also refer to Stephen P. Cohen, India: Emerging Power (New Delhi: Oxford University Press, 2002), p. 312.

[6] Robert D. Blackwill, "The United States, India and Asian Security", in K. Santhanam and Srikanth Kondapalli (eds.), Asian Security and China 2000-2010 (New Delhi: Shipra Publications, 2004), p. 36.

[7] People, Progress, Partnership: The Transformation of U.S-India Relations (New Delhi: Public Affairs Section, Embassy of the United States of America, n.d.), p. 10.

[8] Christopher S. Raj in K.P. Vijayalakshmi, et. al., (eds.), Report on National Workshop on the Changing Contours of Indo-US Relations (Bangalore: International Strategic and Security Studies Programme and National Institute of Advanced Studies, 2006), p. 121.

[9] Bhabani Mishra, "India-US Relations: A Paradigm Shift", Strategic Analysis (New Delhi), vol. 29(1), January-March 2005, p. 80.

[10] C. Raja Mohan, "Fostering Strategic Stability and Promoting Regional Cooperation", in Garry K. Bertsch, et. al., (eds.), Engaging India: US Strategic Relations with the World's Largest Democracy (New York: Routledge, 1999), pp. 27-28.

[11] Ravi Tomar, "Indo-US Relations in a Changing Strategic Environment", Research Paper No. 20, Department of Parliamentary Library, Australian Parliament, 25 June 2002, pp. 8, 12, available at <http://www.aph.gov.au/library/pubs/rp/2001-02/02rp20.pdf>.

[12] Anil Kumar Singh, India's Security Concerns in the Indian Ocean Region (New Delhi: Har-Anand Publications Pvt. Ltd., 2003), p. 130.

[13] People, Progress, Partnership: The Transformation of U.S-India Relations, n. 7, p. 11.

[14] Krishnaswamy in K.P.Vijayalakshmi, et. al., (eds.), Report on National Workshop on the Changing Contours of Indo-US Relations (Bangalore: International Strategic and Security Studies Programme and National Institute of Advanced Studies, 2006), p. 142.

[15] Devin T. Hagerty, "Are We Present at the Creation? Alliance Theory and the Indo-US Strategic Convergence", in Sumit Ganguly, Brian Shoup, et. al., (eds.), U.S- Indian Strategic Cooperation Into the 21st Century- More Than Words (London and New York: Routledge, 2006), p. 21.

[16] T. V. Paul and Mahesh Shankar, "Why the US-India Nuclear Accord is a Good Deal", Survival (United Kingdom), vol. 49(4), Winter 2007-08, p. 111.

[17] Chintamani Mahapatra, "The US and Major Asian Powers", in Jasjit Singh (ed.), Asian Strategic Review (1993-94) (New Delhi: Institute for Defence Studies and Analyses, 1994), pp. 93-94.

[18] S. D. Muni and C. Raja Mohan, "India's Options in Changing Asia", in R. R. Sharma (ed.), India and Emerging Asia (New Delhi: Thousand Oaks: London: Sage Publications, 2005), p. 59.

[19] W. Lawrence S. Prabhakar, "Strategic Dimensions of India-United States Relations in Post Cold War Era", in N. K. Jha (ed.), India's Foreign Policy in a Changing World (New Delhi: South Asian Publishers, 2000), p. 74.

[20] Stephen P. Cohen, n. 5, pp. 285-86.

[21] Brian Shoup and Sumit Ganguly, "Introduction", in Sumit Ganguly, et. al., (eds.), "US-Indian Strategic Cooperation Into the 21st Century: More Than Words (London and New York: Routledge, 2006), p. 3.

[22] Harry Harding, "The Evolution of Strategic Triangle: China, India and the United States", in Francine Frankel R. (ed.), The India-China Relationship: Rivalry and Engagement (New Delhi: Oxford University Press, 1995), p. 321.

[23] Surjit Mansingh, "Improving Relations with the United States", in a Seminar Proceedings on Perspective on National Security, National Defence College, New Delhi, 23-26 November 1998, p. 84.

[24] Surjit Mansingh, "Indo-US Relations: a Closer Relationship?", Economic and Political Weekly (Mumbai), 18 May-4 June 2005, p. 2221.

[25] Surjit Mansingh, n. 23, p. 84.

[26] See Abhay R Karve, Indo-US Strategic Relations: Moving from Estrangement to Engagement, Paper submitted to the National War College, National Defense University, p. 4.

[27] Lalit Mansingh, "Indo-US Strategic Partnership: Are We There Yet?", Institute of Peace and Conflict Studies, Issue Brief No. 39, October 2006.

[28] Surjit Mansingh, n. 24, p. 2221.

[29] Abhay R. Karve, n. 26, p. 4.

[30] Refer to Rudra Chaudhuri, "Strategic Partnerships", Seminar Magazine (New Delhi), July 2009, available at <http://www.india-seminar.com/semsearch.htm> and Shrikant Paranjpe, "India and Russia: The Litmus Test of Strategic Partnership", in P.L. Dash (ed.), India-Russia Relations: The Post Cold War Era (Mumbai: Nehru Centre, 2011), pp. 59-60.

[31] Harold A. Gould, "U.S.-Indian Relations: The Early Phase", in Harold A. Gould and Sumit Ganguly (ed.), The Hope and the Reality: U.S.-Indian Relations from Roosevelt to Reagan (New Delhi: Oxford and IBH Publishing Co. Pvt. Ltd., 1993), pp. 17-36.

[32] Aftab Alam, US Policy Towards South Asia: Special Reference to Indo-Pak Relations (Delhi: Raj Publications, 1998), pp. 113-116.

[33] Madan Lal Goel, "Indo-American Relations in a New Light", in Nalini Kant Jha (ed.), India's Foreign Policy in a Changing World (New Delhi: South Asian Publishers, 2000), p. 61.

[34] Norman D. Palmer, The United States and India: The Dimensions of Influence (New York: Praeger Publishers, 1984), p. 21.

[35] Ibid., pp. 24-30.

[36] Ibid., p. 47.

[37] Ibid., pp. 53-55.

[38] Dennix Kux, Estranged Democracies: India and the United States (New Delhi: Sage Publication, 1993), pp. 314-15.

[39] M.R. Srinivasan, "Challenges and Opportunity", Economic and Political Weekly, 27 August 2005, p. 3806.

[40] Chintamani Mahapatra, n. 17, p. 92.

[41] Cherian Samuel, "Indo-US Defence Cooperation and the Emerging Strategic Relationship", Strategic Analysis, vol. 31(2), March 2007, pp. 214-15.

[42] Virgina Foran, "The Case for Indo-US High-Technology Cooperation", Survival, vol. 40(2), Summer 1998, p. 76.

[43] David J. Louscher, Alethia H. Cook and Victoria D. Barto, "Military Relations between US and India: Assessment and Prospects", in Ashok Kapur and Y.K. Malik, et. al., (eds.), India and United States in a Changing World (New Delhi: Sage Publications, 2002), p. 309.

[44] Devin T. Hagerty, n. 15, p. 20 and also refer to Robert D. Blackwill, "A Friend Indeed", National Interest (Washington, DC), May/June 2007, p. 16.

[45] Sekhar Ghosh, "Indo-US Relations: The New Vistas", India Quarterly (New Delhi), vol. LVIII(1), January-March 2002, p. 67.

[46] People, Progress, Partnership: The Transformation of U.S-India Relations, n. 7, pp. 10-11.

[47] Madan Lal Goel, n. 33, p. 63.

[48] Anil Chait, From Estrangement to Engagement: Threats and Opportunities in Indo-U.S. Relations and the Roles of their Armed Forces (Carlisle, PA, February 2006), p. 1.

[49] Bhabani Mishra, n. 9, p. 85.

[50] G.S. Khurana, "Maritime Security in the Indian Ocean: Convergence plus Cooperation Equals Resonance", Strategic Analysis, vol. 28(3), July-September 2004, p. 417.

[51] William Clinton and Atal Bihari Vajpayee, India-U.S. Relations: A Vision for the 21st Century, New Delhi, 21 March 2000.

[52] See, New Framework for the U.S.-India Defense Relationship, Washington, DC, 28 June 2005, available at <http://

www.indianembassy.org/press_release/2005/June/31.htm>.and also refer to Cherian Samuel, n. 41, pp. 218, 229.

[53] Sekhar Ghosh, n. 45, pp. 65-66.

[54] Jasjit Singh, "India's Strategic and Security Interests", in Jasjit Singh (ed.), Indo-US Relations in a Changing World: Proceedings of the Indo-US Strategic Symposium (New Delhi: Institute for Defence Studies and Analyses, 1992), pp. 95-96.

[55] Anil Kumar Singh, n. 12, pp. 50, 52.

[56] C. Raja Mohan, "Balancing Interests and Values: India's Struggle with Democracy Promotion", Washington Quarterly, vol. 30(3), Summer 2007, pp. 100, 104-06.

[57] See, "India-United States Joint Statement", Washington, DC, 18 July 2005, Strategic Digest (New Delhi), vol. 35(8), August 2005, p. 989.

[58] Thomas Carothers, "Repairing Democracy Promotion", available at <http://www.carnegieendowment.org/publications/index.cfm?fa=view&id=19576&prog=zgp&proj=zdrl>.

[59] P. Stobdan, "Changing Strategic Landscape in Central Asia: Implications for India's Security", in V. Nagendra Rao and Mohammad Monir Alam, Central Asia: Present Challenges and Future Prospects (New Delhi: Knowledge World, 2005), p. 233.

[60] Meena Singh Roy, "Major Powers in Central Asia: Implications for India", in S.D. Muni (ed.), Asian Strategic Review 2007 (New Delhi: Academic Foundation, 2008), p. 301.

[61] Dinesh Kumar, "Defence in Indo-US Relations", Occasional Paper, Institute for Defence Studies and Analyses, August 1997, pp. 48-51 and Rajpal Budania, "The United States and South Asia: Strategic Concerns and Interactions Patterns", in B.M. Jain (ed.), International System and Great Power Relationship (Jaipur: INA Shree Publishers, 2008), p. 59.

[62] Lawrence Prabhakar, n. 19, p. 75.

[63] Narottam Gaan, India and United States: From Estrangement to Engagement (New Delhi: Kalpaz Publications, 2007), pp. 211-213.

[64] Harinder Sekhon and Cherian Samuel, "Bush II Presidency: Implications for Indo-US Relations", Observer Research Foundation Policy Brief, 04 February 2005.

[65] Lawrence Prabhakar, n. 19, pp. 71-72.

[66] See, "Keesings Records of World Events", vol. 39(5), May 1993, p. 39467.

[67] Chintamani Mahapatra, Indo-US Relations in the 21st Century (New Delhi: Knowledge World in Association with the Institute for Defence Studies and Analysis, 1998).

[68] Kanti Bajpai and Amitabh Mattoo, Engaged Democracies: India-U.S. Relations in the 21st Century (New Delhi: Har-Anand Publications Pvt. Ltd., 2000).

[69] Ashok Kapur, et. al. (eds.), India and the United States in a Changing World (New Delhi: Sage Publication, 2002).

[70] Sumit Ganguly, et. al., (eds.), US-India Strategic Cooperation Into the 21st Century (London: Routledge, 2006).

[71] Gary K. Bertsch, et. al. (eds.), Engaging India: Strategic Relations with the World's Largest Democracies (New York: Routledge, 1999).

[72] Vivek Chadha, Indo-US Relations: Divergence to Convergence (New Delhi: Macmillan India Ltd., 2008).

[73] Stephen, J. Blank, Natural allies? Regional Security in Asia and Prospects for Indo American Strategic Cooperation (Carlisle, PA, September 2005).

[74] Baldev Raj Nayar and T. V. Paul, India in the World Order: Searching for Major-Power Status (New Delhi: Cambridge University Press, 2004).

[75] Amit Gupta, The US-India Relationship: Strategic Partnership or Complementary Interests? (Carlisle, PA, February 2005).

[76] Walter K. Andersen, "India and the United States: A Different Kind of Relationship", Testimony before House Committee on Foreign Affairs: Subcommittee on the Middle East and South

Asia United States House of Representatives, Washington, DC, 25 June 2008.

[77] Zhang Guihong, "US-India Strategic Partnership: Implications for China", International Studies (New Delhi), vol. 42(3&4), July-December 2005

[78] V R Raghavan, "Indo-US Strategic Partnership: China as a Factor", U.S.I. Journal (New Delhi), vol. CXXXVII(570), October-December 2007.

[79] Ashley J. Tellis, "The Merits of Dehyphenation: Explaining U.S. Success in Engaging India and Pakistan", Washington Quarterly (Washington, DC), vol. 31(4), Autumn 2008.

[80] Zafar Nawaz Jaspal, "The Indo-US Strategic Relationship and Pakistan's Security", South Asian Strategic Studies Institute Research Report 9, December 2007.

[81] Tellis, Ashley J., "U.S.-India Atomic Energy Cooperation: Strategic and Nonproliferation Implications

", Testimony before the Senate Foreign Relations Committee on, 26 April 2006.

INDIA-UNITED STATES DEFENCE AND SECURITY RELATIONS

2.1 Introduction

The defence and security relationship between India and the United States during the cold war era has been rightly described by Selig Harrison, the U.S. specialist on South Asian affairs, as "dialogue between the deaf." Although India and United States are not engaged in any form of conflict like India had with two of its neighboring countries such as China and Pakistan, but the two largest democracies did not enjoy a constructive defence relations in the past. Divergent security perceptions and the lack of political understanding are the main reasons behind the lack of a meaningful defence and security cooperation. One cannot expect a better defence and security cooperation when the two countries have different opinions on key international issues.[1] Today, understanding between the two countries on key international issues seems to be improving, but that does not mean understanding on all key international issues. The main argument of this chapter is that the relationship has a global significance and both countries have a lot to gain out of this cooperation. India must look forward to strengthening the defence and security cooperation with the U.S. and pursue its respective interests.

Ever since the cold war end, defence and security cooperation between India and the United States have started burgeoning. Expanding defence cooperation between India and the United States signifies mutual desire to meet the twenty-first century challenges. The objective of the expanding defence and security cooperation is to achieve inter-operability. It is aimed at developing capabilities and confidence, jointly confront multilateral security issues such as protection of the sea lanes of communication, ensure free and uninterrupted passage of energy supplies and conduct joint peacekeeping operations, combating terrorism and preventing the proliferation of weapons of mass destruction (WMDs). The evolving defence ties are for the mutual benefit of the two countries and not directed at any third party. Both sides have a lot gain from this expanding defence relationship.[2]

Since then, defence and security relations between India and the United States have been the subject of debates and discussion in both countries due to the cold war mindset. Lots of questions had been raised from within the country as to why India want to have a relationship with a country which is not a reliable one and that it has supported India's adversary Pakistan through out cold war period. Why to have a relation with that country which has not supported India in time of needs?

Several developments that emerged before and after the cold war end has contributed to start a closer defence and security cooperation between the world's largest and powerful democracies, India and the United States, respectively. The end of cold war and the collapse of erstwhile Soviet Union was the key to closer India-U.S. defence and security cooperation. With the end of cold war India had lost a close and a reliable strategic partner in the form of Soviet Union that had in the past provided India with defence and security needs. Russia, the successor state of erstwhile Soviet Union was facing the economic crisis was neither in a position to provide security guarantee for India nor was reluctant to continue supply of military equipment on the same terms and conditions that India used to enjoy with erstwhile Soviet Union. This had left no option for India but to engage with the United States that emerge the sole super power in the new world order after the collapse of Soviet Union.

Secondly, India even before the end of cold war was very much eager to diversify its sources of supply for advance weapons and equipment. Such India's intention coincided with the U.S. looking for a partner, also played a part in bringing the two countries closer.[3] The third factor is that of loosing relevance of Pakistan to the United States strategic goals after the erstwhile Soviet disintegration.[4] And last but not the least, the ability of both countries to identify common strategic challenges was also equally significant. All of these factors created an ample opportunity for the start of robust military cooperation.[5]

The evolving defence and security cooperation is not without any reasons or consequences. Defence and security cooperation is evolving in response to changing role of India as a regional and major power that has a significant role to play in the twenty-first century world via-a-vis fighting terrorism, ensuring regional and global security and stability, preventing the proliferation of weapons of mass destructions (WMDs), etc. America today perceives India as a growing world power with which we share common interests. For the U.S to achieve its global and regional interests, require a stable and a reliable partner, India can be one of them. This should remain the foundation for a stronger defence and security cooperation.[6]

The post cold war period had seen a significant change in the strategic thinking of both countries. Both the sides responded positively to the changing international strategic environment. Initially, the defence and security cooperation between India and United States was limited to holding seminars, exchange of visits. Later, it was expanded to include exchange of military doctrines, military training and even arms supplies and purchases. However, by the turn of the twenty-first century, owing to the number of significant measures taken by the administration of the two countries, defence and security cooperation reached a new level where the two countries witnessed increasing number of military-to-military exercises of multi-dimensional activities. Since the September 11 incident, both security understanding and military-to-military exercises involving all the branches of the armed forces have improved significantly. Increasing number of exercises should not be misconstrue in a way that India has entered into an alliance with U.S. targeted at third country, because this is one of the many defence relations that U.S. has developed with other friendly countries.[7]

With gaining understanding, we can see increasing number of high-level official visits. After two years of no such defence and security relations brought about by the Indian nuclear tests, the relationship started improving after the visit by Jaswant Singh who was the in charge of both External Affairs and Defence Minister of India to U.S. in April 2001. The visit was an important one in terms of bringing back the military-to-military relations on the track and also decision has been taken to renew the military ties that was suspended after Pokhran II tests. For the first time, Chairman of the US Joint Chiefs of Staff General Henry Shelton visited India in July 2001. This was followed by the visit of U.S. Defence Secretary Donald Rumsfeld to New Delhi in 5 November 2001, where he meet Indian Defence Minister Mr. George Fernandes and discuss on how to strengthen the level of military and defence ties between the two countries. Given the significant improvement that emerge after the turn of the twenty-first century, U.S. Ambassador to India Robert D. Blackwill make a statement before the press conference that both countries were, "set to embark on a new phase of defence relationships."[8]

The September 11 incidents and India's unconditional support to U.S. in the fight against terrorism was also a turning point in India-U.S. defence and security cooperation. United States had lifted sanctions that were imposed after the Pokhran II tests, resulting in an increase of dual use exports to India. The current approval rate of license applications has moved above 90 per cent. Moreover, the commercial military sales grew from a meager $5.6 million in 2003 to $64 million in 2005.[9]

It was after years of long negotiation, both India and United States came forward to announcing the "Next Step in Strategic Partnership." The signing of the high-technology transfer agreement would definitely open the way for the transfer of advanced technology to India. One of the senior Indian Official confirmed that the agreement will "create a more comfortable and friendlier regime", even while not entirely ending the U.S. restriction on high-tech exports to India. India on its part must have to ensure that such technologies are not transferred to any third party or that it is not used in its missile and nuclear programs.[10]

Overall, defence cooperation between India and United States has so far witnessed significant improvement in every aspect such as the quantity and quality of training exercises, seminars, exchange of military personnel, high-level visits unit/ship visits, subject matter expert exchanges, technology cooperation and defence sales.[11] This chapter seeks to examine the post cold-war India-U.S. defence and military relations. Within this the study would try to answer for the following questions. What are the changes that have occurred during the last almost two decades? What would India gain out of this relationship? What are the main area of irritants to defence and security cooperation? Where the defence relationship is heading forward.

2.2 Start of an Unexpected Military Relationship

The long overdue military relationship between India and United States started during the tenure of Late Indian Prime Minister P. V. Narasimha Rao. Both India and United States was determined to start a constructive military relationship that would be beneficial to both the countries. The initiative has been taken by Lt. Gen. Claude M. Kickleighter, former commander of the Army in Pacific, who went for a landmark visit to India when there was a sea change in the international security environment. During his visit, he made significant number of proposals to intensify the level of defence and military cooperation. It calls for reciprocal visits of Chief of Army Staff, conducting strategic symposium annually that will be participated by Indian and U.S. armies, establish executive steering committee to review, refine and redefine the agreed upon goals and objectives, exchange of staff, staff information exchanges for the reciprocal flow of information, training to be provided to commandoes and mutual participation in regional conferences in order to improve the ability to work together.[12]

After the successful visit of Claude Kickleighter, there was a flooding in high-level official visits from India to U.S. and vice-versa. From the Indian side, the first one to visit United States was former Army Chief General S.F. Rodrigues along with some others in August 1991. In reply, Admiral Charles Larson, Commander in Chief of the US Pacific Command visited India in October 1991. Indian Defence Minister Mr. Sharad Power also visited U.S. where he held detailed discussion with U.S. Vice-President Dan Quayle and Defence Secretary Richard Cheney. Indian Defence Minister Mr. Sharad Power after coming back from U.S. had announced that 'the direction in India-U.S. relations had totally changed' that the two countries would be conducting joint naval exercises later in the summer. It was the Ministry of State for External Affairs, Eduardo Faleiro who made the announcement in the Lok Sabha on 17 March 1992.[13] The entire visit was instrumental in inculcating security understanding between the two countries.

In response to the Claude Kickleighter proposal, both countries set up an Army Executive Steering Group (ESG) in January 1992, followed by the Navy and Air Force in March 1992 and August 1993, respectively. The Army Executive Steering Group is co-chaired by the Indian Vice Chief Army Staff and the C-in-C of the U.S. Army Pacific (USARPAC), the Navy ESG by the Indian Deputy Chief of Naval Staff and the Commander of the U.S. Seventh Fleet and the Air Force ESG by the Indian Vice Chief of Air Staff and the C-in-C of the U.S. Pacific Air Force. The Executive Steering Groups of the three services meet regularly.

This has given way to the first ever joint training exercise named Teak Iroquois. It was conducted in February 1992, in which the army and air force paratroopers of the two countries participated. The second such exercise was held in October 1993. Between May 1992 and mid 1997, the navies of the two countries had witnessed three rounds of naval exercises- Malabar I, II and III. More details about these exercises will come in the later part of this chapter.[14]

Taking note of the development in the first two years after the end of cold war, Lawrence Eagle-Burger, U.S. Secretary of State had told the Indian Foreign Secretary J.N. Dixit in March 1992 that, "putting aside nuances and semantics about issues on which India and U.S. disagree, it is time now to adopt a practical approach. Our joint effort should be to adopt a problem-solving orientation in policies toward each other. Scoring point and old attitudes of irrelevant confrontation should be abandoned. Both sides predicate developing bilateral relations on positive lines while clearly acknowledging that there are some on which there are fundamental differences which will remain constant between the U.S. and India." In reply, Dixit said, "...as far as the U.S. did not over interpret or misinterpret India's differences of opinion with that country (USA) on basic issues such as nuclear non-proliferation, transfer of technology and intellectual property rights and as far as U.S. policies did not negatively affect India's **national** security in all its dimensions, India would be willing to adopt the practical approach..." Moreover, Chairman of the House Affairs committee, Lee Hamilton had said in April 1994 that, "India in recent years has proved to be a reliable American partner." These statements gives a very clear evidence that both the countries was ready not to let down defence cooperation for any reasons and instead focus on enhancing the level of military cooperation.

At the same time, the two countries was engaged in a series of dialogue at the official level to help remove misperceptions and improve more understanding on various issues such as nuclear proliferation, technology transfer, etc., that has the capability to circumscribe the evolving relationship. In addition to this, the annual Indo-American bilateral strategic dialogue organized jointly by the Indian Institute of Defence and strategic analysis (IDSA) and INSS of Washington based National Defence University also serves to remove mutual misperceptions and enhance understanding.[15]

2.3 Strategic Breakthrough in India-U.S Defence and Military Cooperation

The first strategic breakthrough in India-United States relations was provided by the visit of U.S. Defence Secretary William Perry to India in January 1995 and the signing of the landmark agreement named "Agreed Minutes on Defence Relations." The agreement created a roadmap for defence and security cooperation between India and United States in the post cold war period. During his visit, William Perry has said,

"The end of the cold war opened a new era in United States-India security relations. Old barriers to our cooperation have been replaced by new opportunities. We, in the United States, are excited by these opportunities and want to increase the security links between our two democratic nations. Doing so will allow us to better pursue our common security interests and provide a base understanding for working out differences."[16]

The second strategic breakthrough was provided by the successful completion of the Next Steps in Strategic partnership (NSSP). The NSSP between India and United States was announced in January 2004. It calls for cooperation in quartet of areas such as civilian nuclear activities, civilian space programs, High-technology trade and missile defence. Cooperation in these areas was almost limited or non-existent in the past. But now, it paves the way for greater cooperation on strategic, energy security and economic matters.[17]

The third strategic breakthrough was provided when Indian Defence Minister Pranab Mukherjee and U.S. Defence Secretary Donald Rumsfeld signed a ten year Defence framework agreement in June 2005. The framework agreement is the first such formal defence pact between the two states since 1995. The agreement would allow cooperation in weapons production, technology transfer, naval patrols and missile defence but excluded nuclear technology.[18]

2.3.1 Agreed Minutes on Defence Relations and its Significance

The U.S. Secretary of Defence, William Perry made a historic visit to India on January 1995. Agreed Minutes on Defence relations was the first such post cold war defence agreement signed between India and United States. India and United States together recognize the importance of expanding the defence and security relationship as an important part of the overall burgeoning strategic relations between the two countries.

The Agreed Minutes agreement set out the roadmap for military cooperation between India and United States. The agreement serves three significant purposes:

One that both sides agreed for civilian-to-civilian cooperation to supplement the evolving military-to-military ties, envisaging a periodic consultation between the senior civilian officers in the Department of Defence and the Indian Ministry of Defence (MOD). Secondly, both sides agreed to work together in the fields of Defence research and production, which would find its scope and consultation with the Joint Technical group (JTG), and thirdly, they have also agreed to increase the service-to-service cooperation. This would facilitate the professional contacts and exchanges, observation of each other's military exercises, professional training and joint exercises.[19]

In his statement before the USIS in New Delhi on January 1995, Defence Secretary Perry highlighted the necessity and benefit of expanding the defence cooperation between the two countries. This was followed by his statement at the Foreign Policy Association on his trip to India and Pakistan on 31st January 1995 that military-to-military ties are an important component of any healthy strategic relationship.[20]

The significance of the Agreed Minutes on defence relations was the creation of the three separate groups such as Defence Policy Group (DPG), the Joint Technical Group (JTG) and the Joint Steering Committee (JSC). These groups would ensure more interaction and facilitate discussions between the two countries. Its significance also lies in building trust between the two countries, which would remain the foundation of any meaningful defence relations. Building a trust require helping both sides understand each other's defence policies and strategic intentions. The major task ahead after signing the first ever defence accord is to identify the specific areas of cooperation.

The results after the Agreed Minutes were quite handy because the defence cooperation between the two countries improves significantly.[21] On May-June 1995, military units from both the countries conducted joint exercises on land and at sea. In additionm, U.S. Special Forces and Indian Para-commandos held high altitude exercises in the Nahan hills about 150 miles north of Delhi.[22] However, it would have been more effective had there been no issues of Nuclear non-proliferation treaty (NPT) and Comprehensive test ban treaty (CTBT). U.S. position on both of these issues hindered the fruitful progress of the defence and security relationship between the two countries. Agreed minutes on defence relations gained momentum when both the issues diminishes after the end of the Clinton Administration and the beginning of George Bush Junior period as the President of U.S.[23]

2.4 India-U.S. Defence and Security Mechanism

Defence Policy Group (DPG) remains the primary mechanism guiding the defence cooperation between India and United States. It is led by Defence Secretary on the Indian side, while the U.S. side is headed by Under Secretary of Defence for Policy. It has four sub-groups Military Cooperation Group (MCG), the Joint Technology Group (JTG), the Senior Technology Security Group and Defence Production and Procurement Group (DPPG).[24] It gives policy level direction to defence cooperation, reviews all matters and resolves broader defence cooperation policy issues.

Military Cooperation Group (MCG): It reviews Services related cooperation matters and inter-service coordination.

Joint Technology Group (JTG): It looks after the potential for cooperation in defence research and development.

Senior Technology Security Group (STSG): It deals with undertaking review of technology security issues and also increases mutual understanding of each other's policies and systems in respect of technology security for defence-related equipment.

Defence Procurement and Production Group (DPPG): This would review opportunities for cooperation in defence acquisition, transfer of technology, collaboration and defence related industries.

Defence Joint Working Group (DJWG): It would undertake mid-review of progress made in the fulfillment of decisions taken by the DPG. It also reviews matters, which need to be taken up by the DPG.

Service-to-Service Executive Steering Groups (ESGs): It review service-to-service cooperation and report it to the Military Cooperation Group.[25]

The first meeting of the DPG and JTG was held after seven months of signing the first ever defence agreement, in September 1995. The main focus of meeting was on the transfer of technology, testing of defence equipment, simulations of war scenarios and management of defence activities. The second meeting was held in October 1996 with a limited agenda focusing on defence evaluation. This was followed by the third meeting held in January 1998 where the two countries discussed very closely the kinds of defence items that India needed and also about the establishment of a test-and-evaluation directorate in the Defence Research and Development Organisation (DRDO). This was the last meeting between the two countries before India conducted the nuclear that brought the meeting between the two countries defunct. The nuclear tests brought a temporary setback to the India-U.S. defence and security relations.[26]

However by the turn of the twenty-first century, when the relationship started regaining to its previous position due in part to the strategic shifts in U.S. perception about India. This has given way to the fourth meeting of the India-U.S. Defence

Policy Group that took place in New Delhi in 3-4 December 2001. At this meeting, delegations of both countries reviewed the ongoing defence cooperation. Both sides agreed to increase the pace of the high-level policy dialogue, military-to-military exchanges and other joint activities. Moreover, India and United States agreed to oversee implementations of the visits, exercises and training programs:

1. Training for combined humanitarian airlift.
2. Combined special operations training.
3. Small unit ground/air exercises.
4. Naval joint personnel exchanges and familiarization.
5. Combined training exercises between U.S. Marines and corresponding Indian forces. [27]

This step is aimed at strengthening the level of military-to-military relations between the two countries.

In the last thirteen years, seven rounds of meeting for DPG was convened, the last meeting took place in Washington, D.C. on 21-23 November 2005, where the two sides engaged in an intensive discussions on international strategic and security situation and also about on how to enhance the present level of India-U.S. defence cooperation according to what has been enshrined in the defence framework agreed on June 2005 during the Indian External affairs Minister Mr. Pranab Mukherjee visit to United States.[28]

The eighth Army executive steering group meeting between the two countries was convened in Pune on 9-10 December 2003, under the command of Lt. Gen. James Campbell of the U.S. Army pacific and Lt. Gen. B.S. Takher, director general of military operations. At this meeting, three important decisions were taken which will be operationalised during 2004. One is the exchange of observers during various training programmes then reciprocal exercises and at last subject matter expert exchange (SMEE).

The Army-to-Army cooperation between India and United States has the following mutually agreed aims:

1. promote mutual understanding through doctrinal exchanges, visits, courses and seminars.
2. advance cooperation in areas of mutual interest through SMEEs and
3. increase interoperability through exercises and joint combined training programmes.[29]

2.5 New Phase in India-U.S. Defence and Security Cooperation

The defence and security cooperation entered a new phase by the turn of the twenty-first century. The groundwork has been laid during the visit of Mr. Bill Clinton, former President of U.S. to India in 2000. It has given way to setting up of the joint working group on counterterrorism and international peacekeeping.

The first half decades after the dawn of twenty-first century was a productive one for both the countries. Both sides have taken some of the important steps to take the relationship to a much better level. Unlike Mr. Bill Clinton, Mr. George W. Bush after taking charge as the next president of U.S. have taken the case seriously to accommodate India and expand the evolving defence and security relations to meet the twenty-first century international security challenges. This became evident when he without any hesitation lifted the sanctions imposed after the Pokhran II tests. Such a quick decision was important to jumpstart the much needed defence ànd military cooperation between the two countries. India on its, part extended unconditional support to United States in the fight against terrorism when it's World Trade Center and Pentagon came under sever attack from terrorist, losing thousand of innocent lives.

With this, security understanding between the two countries has improved a lot. This has also given way for revival of the Defence policy group meeting, military-to-military exercises that came to a standstill after the tests.

The decision of the Indian Government to provide naval escorts to American military assets passing through the Malacca Straits during the Operation Enduring Freedom in June and July 2002 was not less insignificant. This was very important in terms of sending a message to United States that India can be an important partner in the years to come to meet the challenges ahead. With this, there emerged the convergence of interests between India and United States in the stability and security of Indian Ocean. United States on the other hand realised the potential role that India can play in ensuring stability to the Indian Ocean. This is evident from the fact that after just two months gap both sides convened the largest ever Malabar exercises in September 2002. This was followed by Aircraft exercises named Cope-India 2002 in Agra. Since then, joint military exercises became a routine work. Decisions have also been taken by the U.S. Government to approve more than 700 licenses for direct commercial defence sales to India.[30]

The Defence Policy Group meeting held in December 2001 outlined the emerging defence cooperation in this way:

'The two delegations underscored the importance of a stable, long-term defence supply relationship as part of the overall strategic cooperation between India and United States. Since the waiver of sanctions, a number of applications for export licenses have been approved by the US Departments of State and Defence and are in the process of notification to Congress. These include licenses related to weapon locating radars. The United States also agreed to expeditious review of India's acquisition priorities, including engine and systems for Light Combat Aircraft, radars, multi-mission maritime aircraft, components for jet trainer and high performance jet engines. To assist this licensing and sales process in the future, the two sides have resolved to establish a separate Security Cooperation Group to manage the defense supply relationship between India and the United Sates.'[31]

Both sides underlined the importance of a stable, long-term defence supply relationship as part of the overall strategic relationship between India and United States. In an effort to strengthen the regained military and defence relationship, former Indian Defence Minister George Fernandes visited the United States in January 2002. The visit was a significant one for India because it was during this visit India was able to obtain assurances from Washington that it would not interfere with the sale of Phalcon airborne warning and control radar systems from Israel, enhance military cooperation, supply P-3Orion maritime Patrol aircraft, Harpoon anti-ship missiles and Sea Hawk helicopters. Moreover, U.S. has approved for the sale of 21 military systems to India, ranging from targeting radar to aircraft engines to submarine rescue facilities.

It was during this very visit that both countries signed a U.S.-India bilateral General Security on Military Information Agreement. This would pave the way for a greater exchange of classified technical defence related information between the two countries.[32] The high-level visits from both sides have also improved. Indian defence Minister visit was followed by General Richard B. Myers, Chairman of the U.S. Joint Chief of Staff visit to India on 17-18 February 2002. So, during the last eight months two Chairman of the U.S. Joint Chief of Staff had visited India. U.S. Ambassador to India, Robert D. Blackwill in his speech delivered on 26 February 2002 came out with some of the useful figure on India-U.S. relations that since December 2001 when the relations between the two countries revived, the number of U.S. general officer visits to India has witnessed the largest ever.

And in the last fifteen months, the U.S. Navy conducted five port calls and a search and rescue exercises. Both sides have agreed to expand the counter terrorism cooperation and training and to extend participation at the national, bilateral and multinational exercises. It was also unanimously decided after the March 2002 India-U.S. Joint Technical Group (JTG) to explore the opportunities for joint research, development and production of military systems.

In the same month, the Security Cooperation Group (SCG) met in Washington to address future military sales and other licensing procedures and acquisition so as to enhance India-U.S. military interoperability. Since then, both sides have taken the case of transfer of weapons and equipment seriously that for the first time in the month of May 2002, Indian industry delegation visited the U.S. to explore means and opportunities for joint ventures and technology cooperation.[33] More details on the defence supply relationship and the expanding military exercises are coming in the later part of this chapter.

It must be noted that when the understanding improves, it would pave the way for lot many areas of cooperation. That is what had happened in India-U.S relationship. Besides defence, both sides have also agreed to cooperate in areas such as law enforcement, fighting terrorism, proliferation of weapons of mass destruction and missile defence. It was during former National Security Advisor Brajesh Mishra visit to United States in December 2002, both sides discussed on cooperation in areas which are of keen interest to India such as civil nuclear energy, commercial space applications and high-technology trade and he was able to obtained political commitment from the Bush administration in the aforementioned areas.

It becomes a reality in January 2004 when both the countries signed the "Next Step in Strategic Partnership". The agreement opens the door for greater bilateral cooperation in the areas of dual-use high technology goods, civilian space cooperation and civilian nuclear cooperation plus missile defence.[34]

2.5.1 Training Programme between India and United States

Another area which also witnessed improvement is the international military education and training programme. The IMET programme is an exchange programme which facilitates professional contacts and specialised training between the armed forces of the two countries. Such programmes are intended for mutual benefit of the two countries.[35] Even during the cold war period, India has been offered to be part of this programmes but denied due to cold war politics and the fear of India's military being influenced by American military. However, with the security understanding between the two countries improved by the turn of the twenty-first century, military officer's exchanges also gained momentum. In the year 2002, 37 Indian officers went to United States to attend the training courses and the budget allocation for the same year to India was $1 million. This was followed by 34, 48 and 41 Indian officers attended the military training courses for the year 2003, 2004 and 2005 respectively (See table 2.1). The budget allocation for the year 2004 and 2005 was $1.5 million respectively.

Table 2.1: Indian Military Personnel Training Under IMET Programme.

Department	2003	2004	2005
Army	17	19	7
Navy	8	8	9
Air Force	4	17	21
Coast Guard	5	4	4
Total	34	48	41

Former Chief of Army Staff General V.P. Malik has expressed the need for "substantial increase in IMET programmes and regular exchanges of information between military schools in both countries on military doctrines, operating procedure and rules of engagement" as a means of intensifying defence cooperation.

Table 2.2: U.S. Officers Training in India Under ITEC.

Name of the college	2000-01	2003-04	2004-05
Defence Services Staff College	2	1	2
National Defence College	1		1

Source for Table 2.1 and 2.2: Cherian Samuel, "Indo-US Defence Cooperation and the Emerging Strategic Relationship", Strategic Analysis (New Delhi), vol. 31(2), March 2007, p. 221.

Similarly U.S. military officers underwent training programme in India on a reciprocal basis under the Indian Technical and Economic cooperation (ITEC) programme. Under this programme, the American military officers were given training on security and strategic studies, defence management, artillery, electronics, mechanical engineering, marine and aeronautical engineering, anti-marine warfare, logistics and management and qualitative assurance services. In the year 2000-01, 2003-04 and 2004-05, the number of American officers underwent training were 3, 1 and 3 respectively (See table 2.2).[36]

2.5.2 Expanding Scope of Military-to-Military Relationship

The never expected military-to-military relations that gained momentum after 9/11 events is not at the cost of any of the two countries. Ever since U.S. President George W. Bush replaced former President Bill Clinton as the new President of U.S., military-to-military relations started burgeoning. However one thing that we should not forget is that the foundation has been led by Mr. Bill Clinton during his last tenure when he visited India after a gap of twenty-two years. Former U.S. President Mr. George W. Bush was committed to strengthen the military relationship with India. Despite India not sending its troops to Iraq at the request of U.S., military-to-military relations went on improving, reflecting U.S. desire to strengthen the relations. Another point which we can note from the Iraq war is that India will not participate in any operations undertaken by U.S. if it is not in the interest of the India.

The main objective of this military-to-military tie is achieving interoperability. The stronger the military-to-military ties between the India and United States, the better will be for both the countries to better understand each other's systems and doctrines. And the more the exercises between the armed forces of the two countries, the greater will be the rationale for providing India with advanced technologies of the twenty-first century.[37]

India's defence and military cooperation with the United States seeks to create a stable, peaceful and a secure environment in the region and the world through conflict prevention and resolution. It would enhance the defence capability of both countries in the areas of defence equipment and human resource potential through exchanges and technology transfer, joint research and development and joint production. It would also promote defence and military interoperability. Moreover, military-to-military cooperation would promote military interoperability for eventualities of joint deployment in case of disaster relief and humanitarian assistance.[38]

Many critics have raised concerns about the expanding military relations with U.S., but one thing which we have to remember is the fact that United States is not the only country with whom India had engaged in a closer military relations. India has engaged in a military cooperation with a variety of nations. India had a formal defence agreement with nine different countries, security dialogue with six countries, formal defence cooperation agreement with thirty three different countries, out of which seven is in the form of draft and one in the form of letter of intent. We have military courses with forty six different countries, assistance programme with nineteen countries, defence equipment cooperation with twenty seven countries and exchange of visits with fifty countries. The purpose of telling this is to relax those who are against the ongoing defence and military relations between India and United States.[39]

While maintaining a close military-to-military relations with the world's most powerful democracy, United States, India must be very careful and must ensure that:

- the relationship is not against the interest of our country.
- ensure that it does not become a subsidiary partner in any form of relationship.
- ensure that it does not pose any threat to India's relationship with other major powers with which India has shared a close relationship in the past and at present. As far as this is concerned Indian Prime Minister Manmohan Singh has made it very clear when he said, 'I don't think our relationship with the US is at the cost of our relationship with China, Russia, for that matter, the EU'.[40]
- it will not participate in any form of operations if it is not in the interest of India.

  any form of military engagement must be based on reciprocity and equality.[41]

As the years move ahead there are a huge scope for improving military-to-military relationship between India and United States. Former Indian Army General V. P. Malik has expressed the possibility of increasing the present joint exercises up to a brigade equivalent level in the next five years or so. He further added that to achieve the objective of interoperability, the joint training between the two countries should start focusing on areas such as communications, concepts and doctrines including peace-enforcement and peace-keeping, command and control structure, logistics and transportation capability including integration of airlift capability and intelligence sharing.[42]

2.5.3 India as Potential Partner for U.S.

Today, India stands at the threshold of becoming a potential partner for U.S. India, with 1.1 million active personnel excluding those in reserve, is the second largest army in the world. Indian army are well trained, highly motivated and a professional one that has the operational flexibility and warfare capabilities.

India's expertise in successfully conducting desert and jungle terrains, tackling rural and urban insurgencies, urban and jungle counterinsurgencies and its long standing experience in peacekeeping operations would be very hard for the U.S. to ignore. Moreover, India has a high-altitude warfare capability. During the Kargil conflict with Pakistan, India had shown its capability by successfully engaging with the Pakistan soldiers from the Northern light infantry at altitudes of 14,000 to 17,000 feet. According to one U.S. Army foreign area officer, some of the future scenarios that the U.S. military is likely to encounter (especially military operations other than war) would be informed by Indian approaches to counter-insurgency which may be more suitable than the current U.S. practices.

Apart from these, another area where India could be a partner for U.S. is in training of armed forces. India has many training institute for various dimensions such as college of combat, the infantry school, the Defence Services Staff College, the National Defence College, the High-altitude warfare school and the counter insurgency and jungle warfare school. Since the establishment of the Centre for United Nations peacekeeping (CUNPK) in New Delhi in 2000, it has been providing training to personnel from various parts of the world such as Asia, Africa, Europe, UK and U.S. During the period between 2003 and 2004, India has provided training to more than 3,200 army personnel.[43] Besides these, the Indians have a very good experience in the non-combat operations like giving aid to civil authorities for maintenance of law and order, disaster relief and humanitarian assistance and last but not the least maintenance of essential services. All of these are necessary aspects in the changing nature of conflict and it turns out to be handy in the case of conflict resolution.[44]

2.6 Joint Military-to-Military Exercises by the Turn of the Twenty-First Century.

Initially, military-to-military exercises between India and United was limited in scope. But today, with every passing year, military-to-military exercises are gaining its momentum and expanded its scope. Since the dawn of the twenty-first century in general and 9/11 events in particular, military exercises and operations are increasing in size, intensity and complexity. The increasing number of military-to-military exercises involving all the three branches is also a result of the gaining security understanding between the two countries. In 2006, India and U.S. conducted the largest bilateral air exercises. From the Indian side, SU-30 MKI aircraft was deployed, while America deployed F-16 jets.[45]

Over the last seven years since the turn of twenty first century, both the countries have conducted a staggering fifty combat exercises. In January 2009, U.S. soldiers will be visiting Belgaum Commando School for "Exercise Shatrujeet". This will be followed by an advanced transport and helicopter fleet exercise between IAF and USAF in Agra and Chandigarh. This exercise will include operations by Special Forces after paradropping from transport aircraft like the Indian IL-76s and AN-325 and the American C-130J Super Hercules. Besides, USAF will also be deploying its multi-mission Chinese Helicopters during the exercise.[46]

2.6.1 Bilateral India-U.S. Naval Exercises

Since the end of cold war, the navies of the two countries have conducted eleven rounds of Malabar exercises reflecting the growing importance the U.S. gives to military cooperation with India. It is codenamed as the Malabar Exercise because it is held off India's southwestern Malabar Coast. The purpose of such exercise basically is designed to increase interoperability between the two navies while cementing the cooperative military relations between the two countries. The ongoing military exercise is in response to the growing strategic relationship between the two countries. After the 9/11 events, United States in particular had declared India as a natural partner in the fight against terrorism.[47]

The first ever joint bilateral naval exercises named Malabar-I held in May 1992 was limited in scope, preliminary and exploratory in nature. While the second and third rounds of the Malabar exercises were three dimensional in nature comprising of maritime reconnaissance aircraft, surface ships and submarine. During this exercises, the U.S. navy used nuclear powered submarine and the P-3C Orion maritime patrol and attack aircraft.[48] The Malabar 1996 exercise encompasses anti-submarine warfare (ASW) tactics and mock destruction of submarines. At the naval executive steering group meeting held in Singapore from 12-14 November 1996, both sides had agreed for conducting the fourth joint naval exercises in early 1997 at a much better scope and more sophisticated than the previous exercises. Unfortunately, the exercise could not take place as decided owing to the possibility of nuclear tests. After which, the bilateral Malabar exercises between the navies of the two countries lapsed owing to a series of India's nuclear tests in May 1998.[49]

However, due to timely and longest ever strategic dialogue between the two countries, the military relations between the two started improving by the dawn of twenty-first century. Both sides had agreed to return to the joint Malabar exercises from 2002 onwards, indicating their eagerness to strengthen the military relationship. In September-October, 2002, the fourth in a series of Malabar exercises took place in the Arabian Sea where USS Chancellorsville and the USS Paul F. Foster participated and the Indian navy ships involved were the INS Delhi and INS Gomati. It comprises of the surface, sub-surface and air warfare over the Arabian Sea. Since then, there has been a continuous Malabar exercises without even a year break.[50] In the 2003 Malabar exercises around 1,500 Indian and American naval personnel took part in a three day naval exercises. The 2003 exercise centered on anti-submarine warfare tactics. Besides this, it would also focus on VBSS (visit, board search and seizure operations). At a joint press conference, captains of the four Indian and American warships said the exercise would greatly enhance mutual understanding of the two navies.[51]

Before the start of the Malabar 2004 exercises, Indian Navy spokesman Commander Vinay Garg had said that, "In order to streamline interoperability and derive maximum training value for such exercise, the two navies have also evolved standard operating procedures (SOPs), which would be tested during the exercise." He further added that the thrust of the exercise would be on anti-submarine warfare, sea control missions, fleet air defence, surface firing, maritime interdiction operations and VBSS operations, nighttime underway replenishments and a "war at sea."[52] With every passing year the military exercises gained sophisticated and becoming more complex. The Malabar 2005 exercise was the largest naval exercise India had with any other country. It was for the first time that India had introduced its aircraft carrier INS Viraat, while U.S. introduced its aircraft carrier Nimitz. The exercises reflected the increasing security understanding between the two countries. The thrust of the Malabar 2005 exercise was on aviation inter-operability, advanced anti-submarine warfare, sea control missions, fleet air defence, surface firings, maritime interdiction and VBSS operations towards anti-piracy and counter terrorism actions at sea. SOPs evolved will be tested and updated during this exercises. The highlights of this exercise were the 24-hour-long naval mock war.[53] The same year India and United States was also engaged in joint naval salvage exercise named 'SALVEX CY-05' off Kochi from 12-23 September 2005. This exercise involves joint diving, salvage operations and underwater demolition.[54]

The Malabar-2006 exercise was the eighth of the series of bilateral India-U.S. naval exercises. This time also the navies of the two countries were engaged in anti-submarine operations, maritime interdictions, weapon firings, Visit Board Search and Seizure operations, Dissimilar Air Combat (DACT), cross deck flying and a simulated 'war at sea'.[55] For the first time Malabar exercise was carried out two times in a year-one in Okinawa (bilateral), while the other one in Bay of Bengal (multilateral). Every time they came up with new ideas that would add to the scope and depth of the exercise.

2.6.2 Multinational Naval Exercises Involving India

U.S. is not the only country with whom India has engaged in close military exercises. India enjoys military exercises with Russia, France, China, Britain, Japan, Singapore, etc. After a gap of almost 36 years, the U.S. 7th fleet was back in the Bay of Bengal in September 2007. Unlike the previous one, this time U.S. came with a second aircraft carrier, a nuclear submarine and scores of fighter jets. It is meant for ensuring peace and security in the region. For the first time bilateral Malabar exercise was expanded to include three other countries-Australia, Singapore and Japan. India was engaged in joint war games with United States and three other friendly countries. This is the biggest and the largest ever joint naval peacetime exercises between India and United States in which about 25 ships, 150 aircraft and 20,000 personnel took part.[56]

With increasing military-to-military exercises involving India, many held the view that India has given away its independent foreign policy. In response to this wrong speculation India's Defence Minister, Mr. A.K. Antony had said, "The propaganda that conduct of joint military exercises will amount to surrendering India's independent policy had no basis as such exercises had taken place under all government since 1992." This is quite right because whatever development that have taken place so far is the continuation of what have been done before. He further added that, "Joint exercises are some (of the) measures for maintaining good order at sea in the (Indian Ocean) region. India also holds interactions and joint exercises with some other countries including USA. In such interactions, issues of mutual interest including providing security to sea-lanes in IOR (Indian Ocean region), are also discussed."

The significance of the 2007 exercise was highlighted in what Indian Navy Vice-Admiral Suthan said, "got an opportunity to see how the 'art' of launching jets with catapults was being sustained as his force has 'lost the art' after the retirement of its INS Vikrant aircraft carrier years ago. Besides this, the Indian navy was exposed to NATO procedures. These procedures as such were evolved by the U.S. These procedures are new to India. In these NATO procedures, U.S. Navy F/A-18 super Hornets operating from the carriers Nimitz and Kitty Hawk flew upwards of 20 "buddy" re-fuelling sorties with the Indian

Navy's Sea Harriers flying from INS Viraat. Later, it was extended to other sector of the exercise as well in areas like anti-submarine warfare drills and aerial offensive and defensive manoeuvers.[57]

All together twenty seven vessels, eight from the Indian navy, fourteen from the U.S. Navy, two each from the Japan Maritime Self Defence Force (JMSDF), Royal Australian Navy (RAN) and one from the Republic of Singapore Navy (RSN).

2.6.3 India-U.S. Army-to-Army Exercises

The army-to-army exercises between India and United States can be categorized into two types- one is the Special Forces exercises called the Vajra Prahar while the second one is the regular army exercise called Yudh Abhyas. The first Special Forces exercises were conducted in Agra in 2002, while the first army exercise was held in Mizoram in March 2004. Description of these two exercises and other such exercises are given below.[58]

Given the increasing challenges posed by the insurgency and terrorism to both India and United States, joint special operations are very important. Joint special operations will benefit both the countries in meeting the serious challenges posed by the terrorist and insurgent activities. Since 9/11, joint special operations between the Armed Forces of the two countries have become a routine work. United States believe that the Indian special operations forces have a significant role to play in the fight against terrorism and in operations other than war.

For the first time, after a gap of 39 years, Indian armed forces were engaged in a Joint Combined Exchange Training (JCET) exercise with the U.S. Special operations Command in May 2002 in Agra. This JCET is part of India-U.S. engagement named "Balance Iroquois", which India refers to this as "Vajra Prahar".

In this exercise, 90 troops from SOCOM and PACOM and 150 Special Forces from the Indian Army were involved (Air Forces from both the countries also took part for lift).[59]

The exercise was aimed at weapons familiarization, battle drills and airborne operations. In this exercise, the special forces of the two countries tested each other's equipment and jumped from each other's planes. Indian commandos jumped from a U.S. Air Force MC-130 Hercules transport aircraft using U.S. parachutes, while U.S. Special Forces wearing Indian parachutes jumped from Indian AN-32 and IL-76 transport aircraft. It was a learning experience for both the countries and was conducted successfully. Lt. Col. G.S. Buterbaught, Commander of the 353 Special Operations Wing after the conclusion of the exercise was quoted as saying, "I have trained with several foreign air forces and the Indian Air Force is certainly among the most professional forces I have known."[60]

This was followed by a combined exercise between the special forces of the two countries in April 2003 in the jungle terrain in Mizoram, located in the Northeastern part of India. This exercise was aimed at providing training on how to deal with the terrorist hideout in the jungle terrain of Mizoram. In this exercise, members of the Indian Army 21st Parachute (Special Forces) Battalion and U.S. Army Special Forces lived and trained together at India's Counter-insurgency Jungle Warfare School at Vairengte in Mizoram. Moreover, Indian and American forces were engaged in "Vector Iroquois" in Guam in May and June 2003. Within few months i.e. on September 2003, India and U.S. forces were also engaged in Balance Iroquois exercises in the Tibetan plateau in Leh.[61] Both sides learn on how to employ combat teams in the jungle terrain more effectively. The main objective of such exercise was to develop effective tactics for tracking, patrolling, reconnaissance, surveillance and ambushes of terrorist operating in the dense jungle terrain.[62]

The latest Yudh Abhyas was carried out for a three week long at Babina in Uttar Pradesh in 2009 under the tutelage of the army's Southern Command. It is aimed at counter insurgency and counterterrorism operations in a semi-urban setting using tactical armoured vehicles. It was during this exercise, United States for the first time introduced Stryker infantry armoured vehicles outside of its operational area to a foreign land.[63] Indian side was represented by Mechanised Infantry Battalion comprising of about 50 infantry combat vehicles while the American forces comprises of 17 Strykers of the IInd Squadron of 14 Cavalry of 25 Stryker Brigade Combat Team with 325 personnel.[64]

From the above discussion it becomes very clear that the focus of Joint Special Forces operations is on airborne operations, counter-terrorism training, jungle warfare, etc., to meet the twenty-first century challenges.

2.6.4 India-U.S. Air Force to Air Force Exercises

The air forces of the two countries carried out Cope-India and Cope Thunder series of exercises in India and the U.S. respectively. So far six rounds of such exercises have been completed. Such forms of exercises are also meant for achieving interoperability. In the first ever air transport exercise named Cope India-02, the air force and army personnel of the two countries observed each other's procedures such as loading and unloading procedures, expeditionary airfield operation and Para-dropping of personnel and cargo from the aircraft.

For the first time, the IAF participated in a multilateral exercise named Cooperative Cope-Thunder-03, where 31 Indian observers got the opportunity to interact with observers from other countries. Followed by IAF participation in a Cope-Thunder 2004 exercise where countries like Malaysia, Japan, Mongolia, Canada, Italy and United Kingdom also took part.[65]

In the Cope-India series of exercises, the air forces of the two countries engage in fighter tactics, fly against each other on a one-on-one combat basis, as well as simulated combat scenarios. The Cope India 2004 air exercise was the first such air combat exercise where the IAF personnel displayed its skills effectively. Because of which they were highly acknowledged by the American counterpart. According to Colonel Mike Snodgrass, Commander of the 3rd Wing at Elemendorf USARB (United States Air Force Base), the training standard and some of the equipment of the IAF was decidedly better than what they had anticipated.

The simulated combat operations which is part of this exercise comprises of offensive and defensive counter air scenarios. In the offensive counter air scenarios attempt has been made to intercept an enemy strike aircraft by making use of American F-15Cs aircraft before reaching the target that was guarded by a large number of Indian fighters, while in the defensive counter air F-15Cs would attempt to defend a target against Indian fighters. Overall, the IAF outplayed USAF in this form of exercise.[66]

When the air forces of the two countries came forward for the third cope India exercise in 2005, the aim was to enhance mutual operational understanding and to refine procedures for future joint exercises between the IAF and the USAF. Both the sides set forth four objectives to be achieved during the exercise:

1. learn about each other's operational concepts through closer interaction.
2. familiarise fighter controllers with each other's procedures and terminologies and train together with AWACS.
3. familiarise ground crew with each others maintenance practices and,

4. to identify the areas of commonality in terms of operations and administration for the future exercises.

According to Col Rusty Cabot, director of the USAF for the exercise, "during the exercise all the objectives were achieved by both the air forces where the pilots from both the sides performed brilliantly." The Cope India 2005 exercise was significant one for Indian Air Force because it gave the opportunity to exercise in AWACS environment over the Indian skies. One Indian pilot at the base said, "these are the kind of manoeuvres which will benefit us immensely when we get our own AWACS." The exercise was divided into three phases: The first phase was about the flying of basic missions, the second one was a complex one with both sides flying mixed packages pitted against each other and in the last phase the pilots flew a missions where the AWACS platform escorted by two F-16s and Su-30 MKIs each was attacked by a mix of USAF and IAF.

According to Air Marshal F H Major, Air Office Commanding-in-chief of the IAF's Eastern Air Command "though the exercise were conducted simulating a 'hot war scenario', they were not against any third country and were meant to enhance peace and stability in the region."[67] Lt. Gen. David A Deptula, Vice Commander of the USAF's Pacific Air Forces who was present at the closing ceremony of this exercise was quite happy with the performance of the Indian Air Force. He said at the end of the exercise that "though the exercise had gained the trust of each other's air forces so that in the future- for any possible contingency that pops up-we'll be able to hit the ground running and work together. What ultimately does is improve peace and stability in the region."[68] (For more details see Table 2.5)

2.6.5 Advantages of Military-to-Military Exercises

Military-to-military exercises between India and United States occupy an important place in the rapidly growing U.S.-

India strategic relationship. The more the exercise they conduct on a variety of activities, the more they will learn from each other. U.S. can learn from India's expertise and vice-versa. India's experience in jungle warfare in the northeastern states is somewhat that U.S. have to think of. Such exercises no doubt build understanding and confidence between the forces of the two countries.[69]

India has enough experience to offer to the U.S. when it comes to counter-insurgency operations. In conversation with Times of India, Shekatkar, former General Officer Commanding of the Indian army's 4th corps at Tezpur, Assam, said, "We have a tremendous expertise in handling terror-induced situations, besides executing surgical strikes with the least possible collateral damage." He further added that, "on a long-term basis, joint exercise will serve to the benefit of both countries.[70] During the Cope India-02, an air mobility exercise between the two countries, the Indian Air Force and Army learned to conduct airdrop operations from C-130J Hercules tactical airlift aircraft. Moreover, the more the two countries exercise together, the greater the rationale to provide India with compatible equipment, communications and technologies.[71]

The naval exercise would bring a close understanding among the naval forces of the two countries and in the long run would pave the way for close cooperation in the non-military operations such as anti-piracy which posed a serious challenges to the security of the sea, safety of the sea-lanes, drug-trafficking and its related activities such as smuggling of arms patrols and other issues relating to maritime order at sea. It is a platform where the forces of the two countries were given the opportunity to understand each other's rules of engagement, operating procedures and communications plans and aircraft operations.[72]

According to Cmdr. Thomas Kearney, who led USS Alexandria during the Malabar 04 exercise, "I learned more about diesel submarine operations working with the Indian submarine INS Shankul than I would at home, because we don't have diesel submarine in the U.S. navy. And John Sorce, Commanding officer of Cowpens is of the view that, "sure, we were learning about each other....it's all about building allies and friendships so if called upon in later days, it makes it easier for us all to work together and perform together."[73] From the above discussion, it becomes very clear that by engaging more and more military exercises with U.S., India would gain the following:

1. get exposure and access to American military technology.
2. it would opens the way for access to high end technology military equipment.
3. enhance our military capability through professional military exchanges, advancing military skills, war-fighting skills at the tactical and strategic levels.

The more the military exercises between India and United States, the rationale for a more efficient provision of military capability through sharing of logistics capabilities. This would also create a stable, secure and peaceful environment in the region and world.[74]

2.7 Technology Transfer Remains Non Starter

If there is one area which did not receive enough attention even after the end of cold war, it is none other than transfer of technology. Technology transfer has been the problems to India-U.S. relations right from the very beginning. Technology transfer does not figure in the immediate areas of cooperation that has been decided in the Agreed minutes on defence relations accord. The main reason behind this is the lack of mutual trust and the U.S. linking of technology transfers to nonproliferation objectives. Secondly, the United States approach to maintain balance between India and Pakistan. Initially, American considers arms transfer would destabilize the South Asian region. Such a U.S. position became very clear when the U.S. Under Secretary of Defence Mr. Walter Slocombe made a statement before the Asia society on 8 June 1995 that "any deepened security relationship between U.S. and India would not affect the traditional close cooperation between U.S. and Pakistan." The United States wants to improve the defence and security ties with India step by step, without losing its long time partner Pakistan.[75]

Indian nuclear test of 1974 has given birth to a number of stringent nuclear export control regime such as Missile Technology Control regime (MTCR), Nuclear Supplier Groups (NSGs), London's club that prohibited India from sharing nuclear related technology with other countries. These regimes aimed at preventing the proliferation of both India's missile and nuclear programs. Therefore, India has been a victim of the U.S. sponsored technological control regimes for more than four decades since the implementation of NPT.[76] In 1992, when India and Russia had entered into an agreement for the transfer of cryogenic rocket engines for India's Geo-synchronous satellite launch vehicle (GSLV), United States objected the agreement on the ground that it violated the MTCR. As a result of which, technology transfer to India could not take place. Later, United States imposed a two year ban on transfer of technology and trade with both Indian Space research organization (ISRO) and Glavkosmos of Russia. So for the fruitful technology transfer, such mutual misunderstanding has to be cleared first.[77]

Technology transfer has been the main hindrance to achieving the robust military-to-military relationship. With the increase in military-to-military exercises involving all the three branches, India want to have a better transfer of technology with United States. That is why it is being said that technology transfer the litmus test on the part of the United States. If the United States is expecting India to play a key role in this emerging world order, then there must be a transfer of technology to the latter. Technology transfer should find a place in this burgeoning strategic relationship between the two world's largest and powerful democracies. What India needs today is advanced state-of-the-art technology. India is not happy with the pace of the technology transfer between the two countries. It must be noted by the U.S. that technology transfer is the key to the U.S. commitment to help India emerge a major power.[78]

2.7.1 India-U.S. Defence Supply Relationship

Defence supply relationship between India and the United States during the first decade after the end of cold war was almost negligible as part of the overall India-U.S strategic relationship. This aroused question regarding as to why the U.S. is hesitant to supply defence equipment to India. The arms transfer from the U.S. was not moving in line according to what the States Department Spokesman of the U.S., John Hughes had said before the end of the cold war and at the time when the relationship started improving between the two countries, "we want to help India to meet its legitimate security needs and believe military sales would make a positive contribution."[79] Even the first defence accord signed between the two countries named "Agreed minutes on defence relations" in 1995 was not able to provide the strategic breakthrough on defence supply relationship.

The transfer of defence technology to India got a major jolt when the U.S. imposed a two year ban on sensitive technology export to both India and Russia owing to signing of an agreement between the two for collaboration on India's Agni missile development programme to develop ballistic and rocket technologies.[80] This was followed by the ban on transfer of technologies to India by the U.S. after India exposed its nuclear capability in May 1998.[81] However, by the turn of the twenty-first century, the U.S. seems to take the defence supply relationship seriously, resulting to a gaining momentum of the same. The decision of the former U.S. President George W. Bush to lift the sanctions was a turning point in the defence supply relationship. Since then, the U.S. Government has received as many as 81 applications for approvals by Congress. Out of which, 20 have already been approved by the interagency process and are in various stages of notifications to Congress. Applications received by the U.S. for Congressional approval is for Agni Satellite launch, helicopter spare parts, micro denoators, specialized electric motors and AN/TPQ-37 artillery locating radars. In addition to these, other large number of high priority items including aircraft engines, undersea remotely operating vehicles, submarine combat systems, multi-mission maritime patrol aircraft, satellite launch vehicle technical data and equipment for combating terrorism are in the various stages of Congressional clearance.

It was during the Defence policy group meeting at New Delhi on December 2001, both sides have resolved to establish a separate Security Cooperation Group to look after the defence supply relationship. On 17April 2002, India and the United States entered into a first major defence deal for the purchase of eight advanced radars worth approximately $146 million. Under this agreement, India will receive eight AN/TPQ-37 Fire Finder radars, which are ground based designed to detect and locate the precise site of an enemy's artillery and rocket systems. This is not the first one India has signed a defence deal with the United States. Before this private U.S. companies had delivered the former military related equipment and dual-use goods to India in 1994 worth more than $97 million.[82]

With increasing Special Forces operations, there should also be an increase in the exchange of special equipment. India in particular is very much keen on procuring Special Forces equipment such as night vision goggles, special rifles, assault vehicles, kayaks, masks, protective gear for nuclear, biological and chemical environments. Besides, to meet its security concerns along the international border and line of control in Kashmir, India also felt the need of self-propelled and air defense artillery guns, attack helicopters, early-warning devices and electronic warfare systems, unmanned aerial vehicles, thermal, infrared, acoustic and image intensification devices. The army in particular seeks to acquire ground sensors and long-range artillery, light-weight rocket launchers, specialized grenades, armor-protected light vehicles, modern binoculars, compass, sniper rifles etc. India requires such equipment to deal with the highly armed and well trained militant. Such equipment would enhance the capabilities of India's Special Forces commandos. India has acquired eight Raytheon AN/TPQ-37 Fire Finding long-range weapon locating radar from the United States in July 2003.[83]

In July 2004, approval has been given to India for the sale of self-protection systems for the aircraft carrying Indian head of State.[84] Since the dawn of twenty-first century, arms sales are in rise. With the increase in dual use materials export to India, the commercial military sales grew from a mere $5.6 million in 2003 to a $64 million in 2005. The increase in dual use export to India can also be attributed to the landmark "Next Step in Strategic Partnership" agreement signed in January 2004. United States in March 2005 made an announcement that it would offer India co-production rights for both the F-16 and F-18E/F. While on the other side, the United States had offered Pakistan to purchase F-16s.

The signing of the landmark agreement on "New Framework for the U.S.-India Defense Relationship" in June 2005, without any doubt further strengthened the pace of defence cooperation between the two countries. India ink the arms deal with the U.S. worth $1.059 billion for the purchase of six Lockheed Martin C-130J "Super Hercules" transport aircraft in May 2007. Before this, India had finalised with the U.S. for the purchase of 12 Thales-Raytheon Systems AN/TPQ-37 Firefinder artillery locating radar, 40 General Electric F 404-GE-F2J3 engines for its Light Combat Aircraft (LCA), deep submersible rescue vessel systems and spares for Sea King helicopters. In view of the improving defence sales from the United States to India, the then the U.S. State Department official Nicholas Burns had said in November 2007 that, "A significant Indian defence purchase from the United States... would be a great leap forward and signal a real commitment to long-term military partnership."[85] Really, given the significant improvement that both the countries have reached so far, smooth and unhindered defence supply would have been an added advantage to the evolving relations. More details on Actual and Proposed US–India Arms Transfers can be seen in table 2.6.

2.7.2 Impediments to India-U.S. Defence Supply Relationship

Defence supply relationship since the end of the cold war has not been easy for both the counties due to certain factors. One reason for the lack of defence supply has been the difference in perception on defence sales. Indian view technology transfers as a crucial component of U.S.-Indian defence and security relationship, whereas American does not perceive the defence sales as important. So it is very important that both sides have a close understanding on it. Mr. Gautam Adhikari, visiting fellow at the American Enterprise Institute in Washington, is of the opinion that, "in the area of defence sales, there are differences in the perception and purpose apart from the problems of India's armed services being loaded mostly outdated Soviet-designed equipment." He further added that, "The Indians wants U.S. investment in the Indian defence sector and view technology transfer as a crucial component of a closer U.S.-Indian military relationship. The Americans are less willing to see why technology transfer should play key role in the military, which they see as part of a larger strategic objective in Asia, and view Indian intentions with a degree of suspicion."

Reliability has been another problem to transfer of defence equipment between India and United States. United States is not willing to provide India with state-of-the-art advanced technologies that would give the latter strategic edge over its long time close ally Pakistan. While at the same time, America has even charged India for reluctancy to acquire defence equipment and for acquiring such equipment from other countries.[8686] India Report by John E. Carbaugh, Jr. on, "US-India Defense Ties Stymied By Continuous Difference Over military Sales", available at

<http://www.usindiafriendship.net/archives/viewpoints/carbaugh-102003.htm>.

The U.S. non-proliferation policy was also another major impediment to sharing of equipment. The United States had continuously linked the arms transfer to the non-proliferation in the past. For instance, the decision of the U.S. Government to not supply future engines for India's Light Combat aircraft came when they had already supplied eight engines in 1998.[87] Both sides have to be blame for the unsuccessful defence trade relationship. Both sides have to take certain steps before the smooth and unhindered defence supply relationship. Although India and United States have a perennial and continuous dialogue and a number of agreements have been signed, defence supply has not been able to fructify as agreed owing to bureaucratic procedures.[88]

For fear of losing its strategic autonomy, India have so far not agreed to signing defence cooperation agreements with the U.S. over Basic Exchange and Cooperation Agreement for geo-spatial cooperation (BECA), Logistics Support Agreement (LSA), Communication Interoperability and Security Memorandum of Agreement (CISMOA) and End User Monitoring Agreement (EUMA), Proliferation Security Initiative (PSI) and the Container Security Initiative (CSI). The BECA calls for the exchange of geospatial information between two governments, mutual technical assistance and cooperative production programmes. The CISMOA lays down protocols for interoperability and assures the security of communication between the armed forces of the two countries. The LSA allows the armed forces of the two countries to procure fuel and supplies from each other's facilities. The PSI aims at preventing proliferation of nuclear material through interdiction of ships in international waters. India has refused to sign the PSI despite being one of the first countries to stop, board and confiscate the cargo of missile components" from a North Korean ship en route to Pakistan during the 1990s.[89] In this regard India's national security advisor, Shivshankar Menon has critically said that, "A country that doesn't develop and produce its own major weapon platforms has a major strategic weakness, and cannot claim true strategic autonomy. This is a real challenge for us all."[90] Besides, lack of fast decision-making, transparency and accountability and India's policy of self-reliance is another problem.

2.7.3 Prospects for Defence Supply Relationship

There are huge prospects for defence supply relationship. India and the United States have come from a no military relationship to a much better military-to-military relationship today. Seemingly, defence supply relationship has moved from almost nothing to some achievement in recent years. It is also good to learn that both countries are disappointed with the pace and direction of defence sales. Both sides in recent years have made a commitment to strengthen the defence supply relationship.

Since 2001, the U.S. has delivered Firefinder weapon-locating radar to India. It is also considering providing India more counter-terrorism equipment that can be used for its special operations forces and even materials to support India's peace-keeping training capabilities. The U.S. has taken the initiative for easy transfer of equipment to India. For instance, today India does not require Congressional notice for those major defence items on India's wish-list costing over $14 million. Such offer has been provided only to its close allies such as South Korea and Japan.[91]

By the turn of the twenty-first century, the United States under the leadership of President George W. Bush was very much committed to open a new chapter in the field of advance defence technology transfer to India which was very limited in the past. Accordingly, he has taken a decision to provide India with advanced sophisticated sensors, command and control, early warning and missile defence and would also consider co-production of items such as P-3 Orion antisubmarine warfare aircraft, attack helicopters, jet engines, amphibious ships, etc. that are of great interest in India.[92]

With the expanding defence supply relationship, for the first time largest American firms such as Lockheed Martin and Boeing Co. is seriously considering the golden opportunity of competing with the firms of Russian and European rivals to capture the attractive Indian markets for the supply of 126 multi-role fighters to India. India made an announcement for this biggest deal worth in the range between $10 and $12 billion in August 2007. Besides, Lockheed Martin and Boeing, others American military contactors are also keen to capture this opportunity of supplying the number of multi-role fighters that India required.[93] Also the 126 multi-role fighter aircraft, other lists of weapons and equipment that American companies want to sell to India include a fleet of maritime reconnaissance aircraft (MRA) for the Indian navy, sophisticated air defence and air traffic control systems, short-haul cargo planes and upgraded patriot missiles. Therefore, as the defence and security relationship between the two world's largest democracies improved, we can expect a more conducive environment for the defence transfer to move forward.

It was during his visit to India in June 2012, the U.S. Secretary of Defense Leon Panetta's has said that, "The United States is firmly committed to providing the best defense technology possible to India. We are both leaders in technology development and we can do incredible work together." He further added that there is a need that both sides move beyond a focus on individual arms sales to regular cooperation that increases the quantity and quality of our defense trade. In this regard, Washington was moving to reform export controls that have limited weapons transfers to India.[94]

2.7.4 India Offers a Huge Defence Market to U.S.

According to Congressional research service report published in 2005, among the developing countries, India account for $7.9 billion worth of conventional arms transfer internationally during the period between 2001 and 2004. India ranked second only to China with $ 10.4 billion. With the increasing rise of the defence budget over the last few years, India is in a good mood to acquire more sophisticated arms and equipment to meet the increasing security challenges. Ever since India started diversifying its sources of supply, Israel has really benefited from the India's arms procurement. In the year 2003 alone India brought $2.76 billion worth of weapons and ammunitions encompassing Barak anti-ship missile interceptors, surveillance systems and unmanned aerial surveillance crafts.[95] The Indian navy, for its innermost layer surveillance purpose is going for Israel's two Heron UAVs (unmanned aerial vehicles), with three ground control stations and two ship control stations for Rs 386 crores. Moreover, we also have Rs 1,163 crores projects for developing rotary-wing UAVs for use from warships.

Presently, Indian navy is also in hunt for six advanced medium range maritime reconnaissance planes, for Rs 1,600 crores to boost up its snooping capabilities. Given India's increasing defence arms and equipment requirement to meet its challenges, it is up to the U.S. how far they are able to catch up this opportunity.[96]

2.7.5 Limitations of Military and Defence Relationships

The expanding military-to-military relations also have its limitation. It encompasses:

- India's obsession with strategic autonomy. In his testimony before House Armed Services Committee, the US Pacific Command Commander, Admiral Robert Willard has commented that "India's historic leadership of the non-alignment movement and desire to maintain strategic autonomy somewhat constrain cooperation at a level USPACOM (US Pacific Command) desires."[97]
- lack of responsive decisions making on the part of Indian.
- too much civilian control of India's military has restricted the scope of further progress of the military-to-military relationships.
- in the Indian system, centralisation of decisions making is given to the higher level bureaucracy, while in the American system, decision making is decentralised and the responsibility is given to the lower levels of bureaucracy.

- transparency has been another limitation to the expanding military relationship between India and the United States. The American has charged the Indian system for the lack of transparency.[98]
- American defence bureaucracy in the Pentagon must respond with greater speed to Indian requests and the same is to India.

2.8 Next Steps in Strategic Partnership (NSSP)

Discussion on the trinity issues such as high-technology goods, civilian space and civilian nuclear cooperation started much before 2004. Taking the opportunity of the changing scenario by the turn of the twenty-first century, it was India who pressurise United States to reduce restriction on the export of dual-use high-technology goods and increase cooperation in civilian nuclear and space programme. Top Indian officials were serious about including these issues to the transforming strategic relationship between India and the United States. In October 2003, the U.S. Secretary of State Colin Powell asserted that progress is being made on the "glide path" towards agreement on the "trinity" issues. As against the statement of the Secretary of State, some members of the U.S. Congress have expressed concern that dual-use technology trade with India might allow the country to advance its military nuclear projects. However, the U.S. Commerce Department has stated that future civil nuclear and civil space cooperation with India will take place only within the limitations of our commitments under multilateral nonproliferation regimes.[99]

After a series of discussions, both the countries made an announcement for the formation of High Technology cooperation Group in November 2002. There after within the gap of just three months, both the countries signed the statement of principles for High Technology Commerce in February 2003.

Since then, there has been continuous and regular number of meetings at both the official and non-official level. The formation of the HTCG was meant to instill confidence in both countries that would result in a better high-technology trade. What is more important is that all of these developments came in the face of domestic laws and international obligations to both India and the United States.[100]

The formation of the HTCG was instrumental in compelling India and the United States to move a step forward for a 'Next Step in Strategic Partnership' in January 2004. On 17 September 2004, India and the United States signed a document on end use verification arrangement. Under the agreement, India had agreed to take reciprocal steps on export controls so as to bring it in line with the international norms without becoming full member of international export control regimes such as missile technology control regime (MTCR). Before three days of the announcement of 18 July 2005 joint statement, Indian department of commerce notified its revised export control law and regulations named Special chemicals, organisms, materials, equipment and technologies (SCOMET). Then on 18 July 2005, the landmark joint statement announced the completion of "Next Step in Strategic Partnership".[101]

This is a huge step toward acknowledging India as part of the solution to the nuclear proliferation rather than problem to it. With this, India can expect to receive controlled technologies without surrendering its nuclear weapons program. What the Bush administration wants in return was that India imposes a strict, comprehensive export controls that conformed to the international standards and also to ensure that such technologies are not used to advance its own strategic programs.[102] Under the NSSP, India would be able to acquire a variety of dual-use technologies for its space program. Both India and the United States will jointly develop, produce, operate and even launch satellite's containing the U.S. components.[103]

The India-U.S. joint statement on 17 September 2004 announced the significant progress made toward the implementation of the NSSP initiative. It talks of the economic and strategic benefits that would accrue from the implementation of the NSSP. It further added that the implementation of the NSSP would not pose any threat to regional and global security.

Following are the significant improvement that have witnessed following the successful completion of the NSSP. They include,

- extension of ISRO Headquarters from the Department of Commerce Entity list.[104]
- only one per cent of the U.S. exports to India require a license and over 90 per cent of license applications were approved in FY 2005.
- processing time for dual use application has dropped by 25 per cent to 34 days on average.
- since the implementation of the NSSP, more than half the value of controlled dual use trade to India no longer requires a license.[105]

2.9 Defence Framework Agreement: Challenges and Opportunities

The evolving and the expanding defence and security cooperation between India and United States got a major boost when India and the United States came forward to signing the landmark Defence framework agreement. The agreement was signed between Defence Minister of India, Mr. Pranab Mukherjee and the Secretary of Defence of the United States Mr. Donald Rumsfeld in Washington, DC on 28 June 2005. This is the second such defence accord signed between India and the United States that came after ten years of signing the Agreed Minutes. The framework agreement would uplift the level of ongoing defence cooperation between the two countries.

The framework agreement is a reflection of the commitment and understanding on the part of the two countries. This framework agreement is broader than the previous one signed in 1995 titled Agreed minutes on defence relations. It lays out the road-map for future India-U.S. defence relations. The framework agreement is in response to the developments that have taken place in the last five years since the dawn of twenty-first century in general and the revival of the defence relations by the end of 2001 in particular. Since then there has been an increase in military contacts and exercises, civilian defence personnel and most importantly security understanding between the two countries has improved. By signing the defence framework agreement, India has done nothing wrong and neither should it be construed as entering into an alliance with the United States.[106]

2.9.1 Mixed Response to Framework Agreement in India

In India, the defence framework agreement received mixed response from different quarters. Many experts look at it through the prism of transforming India-U.S. relations in general and defence and military relations in particular. They see the defence framework agreement as an important step in strengthening the transforming defence relations, which is key to the strategic relationship between India and the United States. One eminent strategic thinker is in favor of the agreement when he say that, "the U.S. will need more to sustain its pre-eminence than India would need the U.S. to keep its ranking in international hierarchy" (thereby positing that India will have equal leverage within the relationship), and that "most countries, which rose to be world powers, did so only by depending initially on another."

While some strategic community questions regarding India's strategic autonomy and national interests.[107] Besides, the framework agreement has also been criticised by the opposition parties. Nothing objectionable point has been mentioned in the framework agreement which would result in India becoming a client state or it would struck into the American dictatism. It has clearly spelt out that India would participate in multinationals operations when it is in their interests. Despite of this, left parties and CPI (M) general secretary, Prakash Karat went on to criticising the framework agreement when they say that 'let it (agreement) remain a framework, do not add flesh to it and put it in the dustbin'. Even retired Air Marshall R.S. Bedi questions the ability of India to 'protect its sovereignty and maintain strategic autonomy in this overwhelming one-sided relationship'. He further says that, 'if India will 'be able to resist being relegated to the subsidiary relationship.' But one thing the critics should not forget is that the relationship is for the mutual benefit of the two countries. If India had entered into a framework agreement, it is in keeping with the futuristic situation and gains than what it would loose.[108]

Confusions relating to the framework agreement can be cleared by what the Indian Defence Minister and now the External Affairs Minister, Mr. Pranab Mukherjee had said after signing the framework agreement that, "it was only an expression of intention- the Framework contains only enabling provisions. It is an enabling document that provides a framework within which specific cooperation can take place…the presumption that shared interests involving the U.S. must necessarily mean primacy of the U.S. interests, reflects a lack of self confidence in ourselves…we will be able to recognize and resist anything that is not in our national interest, not confuse the U.S. interests with ours, or subordinate our interests to the U.S. interests." Implementation of the framework agreement would require political will and foresightedness of the strategic gains that would accrue from this defence agreement with the United States.[109]

2.9.2 What the Framework Agreement is all about or what it Seeks?

The framework agreement stipulates both a vision for future India-U.S. defence cooperation and the ways by which both sides can achieve the common objective. The increasing commonalities of interest have also compelled both the countries to signing this framework agreement. The commonalities that both the countries share are maintaining security and stability, defeating terrorism and religious extremism, preventing the proliferations of weapons of mass destruction (WMDs), protecting the free flow of commerce via land, air and sea. To achieve the above objective, both sides have agreed to conduct joint bilateral and multinational exercises, strengthen the militaries capabilities, and expand two-way defence trade and many others.[110] (For more details go to appendix II).

The defence framework agreement offers both challenges and opportunities to India. The challenges lie in identifying the rationale behind the U.S. approach and in ensuring that India has its own defence priorities and objectives rather than dancing to the tune of the U.S. strategic objectives. It must have to be very cautious before taking any steps rather than learning after committing the mistakes. The opportunities will be to opening the new vistas for closer defence and security cooperation.

Overall, India-U.S. Defence framework agreement focus on three aspects, defence trade and even co production, research and development; security and stability; increase joint and combined exercises between the armed forces. The significance of this agreement has been highlighted by Ashley J. Tellis as, "A formal agreement has the advantage of engendering stable cooperation, defining formally understood obligations, and leading to increase in mutual confidence that could pave the way for more ambitious combined operations."[111]

Within the defence and security cooperation, the framework agreement gives an opportunity for the Indian defence industry to place itself better in a world where defence industries of the advanced countries are globalizing. It also gives India the bargaining power in the field of technology transfer and co-production from the three main sources of armaments in the world-the U.S., Europe and Russia.[112]

2.9.3 India and United States Inks Largest Ever Defence Deal

The advantage of signing the framework agreement was seen recently when India and the United States signed the largest ever defence deal for the purchase of eight long range maritime reconnaissance (LRMR) aircraft from aerospace major Boeing. This is aimed at strengthening the Navy's intelligence gathering capabilities. The deal worth $2.1 billion was concluded between Defence Ministry's Joint Secretary and acquisitions manager (maritime systems) Preeti Sudan and Boeing's integrated defence systems vice-president and country head Vivek Lall here on 1 January 2009.

The Indian Government had approved the deal in its last Cabinet Committee on Security meeting in 2008 after protracted talks. With this, the Indian navy will get its first aircraft under the deal by the end of 2012 and early 2013 and the rest aircraft would be delivered in phases by 2015-16. The P-8I is highly sophisticated aircraft armed with torpedoes, depth bombs and harpoon anti-ships missiles and is capable of anti-submarine warfare and anti-surface warfare. It has an operating range of over 600 nautical miles, with 5.5 hours on station. The P-8I would replace India's eight ageing and fuel-guzzling Russian Tupolev-142M turboprops currently being operated by Navy. The contract also reserves the option for India to order four to eight more such planes.

According to the sources, the P-8I contract was "a direct commercial agreement with Boeing", with "some issues of end-use verification yet to be fully sorted out" with the US government. According to the Boeing official, the purchase of such aircraft would greatly help inter-operability and supportability objective of both the India and the U.S.[113]

Besides, Indian Government has already announced the approval of various other weapons systems purchases from the U.S, including the C-17 Cargo aircraft in June 2011 and additional orders of the C-130J. There are other lists of weapons and equipment that American companies want to sell to India, which includes a fleet of maritime reconnaissance aircraft (MRA) for the Indian Navy, sophisticated air defence and air traffic control systems, short-haul Cargo planes and upgraded patriot missiles.[114] Much of the progress in this area has been made after the New Framework for the U.S.-India Defense Relationship was concluded.

2.10 Other Areas of Strategic Cooperation

Besides the above mentioned areas of cooperation, there are also other areas of strategic cooperation between India and the United States. These are the areas which presents a huge scope for cooperation between the two countries in the coming years. They are missile defence system cooperation, Peacekeeping operations, cyber-security, and law enforcement cooperation.

Missile Defence System: As far as missile defence cooperation between India and the United States is concerned, there is lack of unanimity among the task force member. Some members favored missile defence cooperation between the two countries. They are of the view that such cooperation is in consistent with the new cooperative security relationship that India and the United States has entered. While the other members of the task force are not in favor of it because of the view that it would result to aggravating regional security and stability and increase the risk of nuclear escalations and also upset the global nuclear non-proliferation norms.[115]

Peacekeeping Operations: Peacekeeping is one of the many areas of cooperation where India's experience matters. This is one area where India and the United States can look forward to cooperation. India has made significant contribution to peacekeeping under the mandate of UN during the last fifty years.

India has established a centre for UN peacekeeping in New Delhi in 2000. In response, the U.S. has allocated a grant of $ 800,000 for the purchase of equipment and for training purposes in 2005. Since 2003, the armies of the two countries have been co-hosting the South Asia peacekeeping operations and command post exercise every two years. In February 2003, a joint U.S.-Indian Army peacekeeping exercise named "Shantipath" was held at the United Service Institution in New Delhi. The exercise was driven by latest computer war-gaming simulation and attended by 150 participants from eleven different countries excluding India and United States. It was designed to familiarize participants with techniques for conducting peacekeeping operations in a multilateral environment.[116] This was followed by Command Post exercise co-hosted by Indian and the U.S. army, held in Hawaii from 14-23 July 2005, attended by the officers from Bangladesh, Nepal and Srilanka.[117] India and the United States together can assist in building world wide capacity to conduct successful peacekeeping operations and enabling other countries to field trained capable forces for peacekeeping operations.

Cyber-Security Cooperation: It can be another area of cooperation between India and the United States. The events of 9/11 brought in serious thinking about cyber security cooperation. In November 2001, former Indian and the U.S. President, Atal Bihari Vajpayee and George W. Bush respectively, jointly announce that India and U.S. would cooperate in cyber-terrorism.

However, it was the initiative of former U.S. Ambassador to India, Robert D. Blackwill, who brought the two countries closer to jointly cooperate in the cyber-security cooperation. Cyber-security cooperation encompasses protection of critical infrastructure, safeguarding national communication systems, defence information assurances.

The first and second plenary meeting of the cyber-security forum took place in April 2002 and 2004 respectively. According to the leader of Indian delegation, the focus of the meeting was on developing the expertise and technology required for India to master the threats posed to the cyber-security across a range of domains. In the year 2004, India-U.S. information security summit was held. With increasing economic interaction between the two countries, protection of the state-of-art data also becomes imperative.

The significance of cooperating on cyber-security was highlighted by the U.S. Under Secretary of Commerce, Kenneth I. Juster, when he told at the summit meeting between Indian and U.S. on information security as, "Information security- also known as cyber-security is one of the keys to unlocking the full potential of the trade and technology relationship between U.S. and India. All levels of society today from individuals, to companies, to governments- rely on information technology and information network in their daily lives- to communicate, to manage activities to transact business, and to provide essential services to the public. As commerce between the United States and India continue to expand, consumer and corporations will seek to ensure that their personal information and business proprietary data are secure, and that information services are reliable and protected. Without adequate levels of security, we run the risk of backlash among consumers and loss of confidences among business people, which could severely limit progress in our trade and technology relationships."[118]

Cyber-terrorism cooperation assumes great significance in the context of increasing challenges posed by the activities terrorism. As far as India is concerned, its information warfare capability is relatively small in programmatic terms and of uncertain quality. Besides these, both sides should look forward to cooperating in computer forensics, network surveillance and protection of supervisory control and data acquisition systems to defeat terrorism.[119]

Law Enforcement Cooperation: Law enforcement cooperation between India and United States is not a new one. Cooperation between the two countries in this area started way back in 1972, when the U.S. Drug enforcement Administration set up its office in New Delhi. However, seriousness about the need to expand the scope and depth of law enforcement cooperation emerged only after the terrorist attack on the U.S. Homeland in September 2001.This was followed by the terrorist strike in the Indian Parliament house on 13 December 2001. These are the two major events that brought the two countries closer to law enforcement cooperation.

With the increase in terrorist incidents in every part of the world and the growing linkage among the terrorist groups, there is a need for cooperation among the like minded states to tackle the issue seriously. Given their challenges faced and the destructiveness brought to them, cooperation between India and the United States on law enforcement becomes very important.

Initiatives have been taken by both the countries in the field of law enforcement. India has allowed the United States to set up a Federal Bureau of Investigation office in his country, while Central Bureau of Investigation has made a presence in the U.S. Besides, other American law enforcement agencies such as Drug Enforcement Administration (DEA) and the U.S. Department of Homeland Security, Immigration and Customs Enforcement (ICE), also have a bureaus in India.[120]

2.11 Conclusion

It seems that both countries are fully committed to transforming the defence relations without any concerned about the past incidents. This is reflected in the developments that have taken place since 1991. The relationship has traveled a long way to reach at this stage and a long way to move forward. In between these, they have resolved some of the key problems and still there are some issues which need to be resolved. India-U.S. defence and security cooperation in the post cold war period had seen a significant improvement in every aspects including, high-level military exchanges, joint and combined military-to-military exercises, military training and last but not the least defence sales. As such India-U.S. defence and security cooperation is a relationship for the mutual benefit of the two countries based on the converging strategic interests. This convergence has the possibility to cement the strategic relationship. Both sides have a huge task ahead before the emerging military and security relations reached a level of satisfaction.

The hard fought developments in recent years are a reflection of a healthy, maturing and evolving relationship. The ongoing defence and military relationship needs constant nurture so that it does not fell to a meager issue. They must have to ensure that the bilateral issues don't become a hurdle to the ongoing relationship.[121] The sustainment and further enhancement of the ongoing defence and military relations would rely on the reciprocity of benefits and sacrifices. Given the kind of interests that both countries share ranging from fighting terrorism and preventing the proliferation of weapons of mass destruction and ensuring stability in the south Asian region in general and international community in particular, one can expect a long-term and a lasting defence and security cooperation between India and the United States.

General Kickleighter initiative provided the initial breakthrough in defence and security cooperation and is strengthened by the subsequent agreement on the ways to further strengthen the defence and military cooperation between India and United States. The only area where there is some hesitation is the dual-use technology transfer. It is due to the difference in perception. The U.S. is not fully convinced to it due to the fears of loosing stability in the Asian subcontinent.

Given the increasing challenges posed by the threats of terrorism and other issues, cooperation between India and the United States in the field of intelligence sharing and on joint training of counter-terrorism is necessary. The significance of the joint military-to-military exercises lies in enhancing the confidence between the two countries thereby resulting in the removal of misunderstanding. It would no doubt enhance the skills of each other's armies.

Whatever developments that have taken place in the field of military and defence relations between India and the United States was made possible due to the reduction of the differences in nuclear issue. Today nuclear issues is of little problem for both the countries, resulting in a concentration on improving the ongoing military relationship between the countries. Otherwise there is no way where we can see such a significant improvement.

It is more likely that the military to military relations between India and the United States will continue to improve even when President Barack Obama replaces former U.S. President George W. Bush. According to senior U.S. official, "Barack Obama is particularly keen on Indian and American military working closely together in combating terrorism in South Asia."[122] Defence and security relations in the coming decades will in no way break down.

Table 2.3: Indo-U.S. Joint Malabar Exercises.

Name	Year/ Place	Equipments deployed	
		India	United States
Malabar-I	29 May 1992/ Goa	Two warships.	Two warships.
Malabar-II	10-15 May 1995/ Cochin Coast in Indian Ocean.	Submarine, two destroyers, Sea King ASW helicopter and Tu-142 maritime reconnaissance aircraft.	Nuclear powered submarine, two frigates and P-3 antisubmarine helicopter.
Malabar-III	May 1996 / Cochin Coast in Indian Ocean.		
Malabar-02	Sep-Oct 2002/ Arabian Sea.	Delhi Class destroyer comprising INS Delhi, Godavari-class frigate INS Gomati and Shishumar-class submarine INS Shankul and tanker Aditya. Indian maritime reconnaissance aircraft.	USS Chancellorsville, a Ticonderoga class guided missile cruiser and USS Paul F Foster, Spruance-class destroyer. US maritime reconnaissance aircraft.
Malabar-03	5-7 October 2003 / Arabian Sea off Kochi.	Indian Navy deployed two guided missile frigates--INS Brahmaputra and INS Ganga--along with the submarine INS Shalki and several other aircrafts.	U.S. deployed two highly sophisticated warships--USS Fitzgerald and USS Chosin and nuclear submarine USS Pasadena supported by tanker and maritime patrol aircraft.
Malabar-04	1-10 October 2004/ Konkan coast.	Delhi Class destroyer a Brahmaputra-class guided missile frigate, a HDW Submarine, INS Mysore, the tanker INS Aditya, a replacement tanker, TU-142 long range patrol aircraft and ship based helicopter.	USS Alexandria, a Los-Angles-class nuclear-powered submarine armed with Tomahawk cruise missiles, the frigate USS Gary, guided missile cruiser USS Cowpens, Ticonderoga missile cruiser and Oliver Hazard Perry class guided missile frigate, P-3C maritime patrol and reconnaissance aircraft, TU 142 M Maritime Reconnaissance Anti-Submarine Warfare aircraft (MRASW) and Donier maritime Patrol aircraft (MPA).
Malabar 2005	25 September to 5 October 2005/ Arabian Sea.	INS Viraat, aircraft carrier (with Sea Harrier fighters and Sea King helicopters), Delhi Class guided missile destroyer, Godavari class guided missile	USS Nimitz, aircraft carrier (with FA-18 Super Homet fighter and E2C Hawkee Air Early Warning aircraft), two Aegis class destroyers, one Los Angles class SSN and P3C Orion aircraft.

Name	Year/ Place	Equipments deployed	
		India	United States
		destroyer, Godavari class guided missile frigate, shishumar class submarine, underway replineshment tanker, TU 142M Long range Maritime patrol and Anti-submarine aircraft, Dornier 228 Maritime patrol aircraft and other multi-role helicopters.	USS Nimitz, aircraft carrier (with FA-18 Super Hornet fighter and E2C Hawkee Air Early Warning aircraft), two Aegis class destroyers, one Los Angles class SSN and P3C Orion aircraft
Malabar 2006	24 October to 5 November 2006/ Goa Coast.	Mysore (Delhi class destroyer), guided missile frigates Beas and Ganga, underway replineshment tanker-Shakti, a large landing Ship (Tank) Gharial, the Sub-surface killer Submarine INS Shankul, Coast Guard Ship Samar and reconnaissance aircraft and Sea Harrier fighters operating from shore.	USS Boxer (landing platform-helicopter and dock), the cruiser USS Bunker Hill, destroyers Benfold and Howard, the US Coast Guard Cutter Midgett, the Canadian frigate Ottawa, the nuclear powered submarine USS providence and a P3C Orion (operating from Goa).
Malabar 07-1	6-11 April 2007/ Okinawa Coast	Indian Navy ships such as Mysore, Rana, Ranjit, Jyoti and Kuthar	U.S Navy fielded six destroyers, one nuclear submarine, shore based fighters (F 16), P3C Orion
Malabar 2008	17-24 October 2008/ Arabian Sea.	INS Mumbai, an indigenous Delhi Class guided missile destroyer, INS Rana, a Rajput Class guided missile destroyer and four guided missile frigates, namely, INS Talwar, Godavari, Brahmaputra and Betwa. In addition, INS Aditya which is an underway replenishment tanker and one Shishumar class submarine, Sea Harrier fighters, fixed and rotary wing aircrafts.	USS Ronald Reagan, a nuclear powered aircraft carrier, USS Chancellorsville, USS Gridley, USS Decatur, USS Thach and USS Bridge, an underway replenishment tanker. In addition, one submarine, USS Springfield and one P3C Orion aircraft will also participate in the exercise.

Name	Year/ Place	Equipments deployed	
		India	United States
Malabar 2010	23 April 2010/ Goa Coast.	Indian navy was represented by INS Mysore (D 60), Delhi-class guided destroyer, Frigates comprising of INS Godavari (F 20), INS Brahmaputra (F 31) and INS Tabar (F 44) and INS Shishumar submarine.	U.S. forces participated with the Ticonderoga-class guided-missile cruiser USS Shiloh (CG 67), Arleigh Burke-class guided-missile destroyers USS Lassen (DDG 82) and USS Chafee (DDG 90), Oliver Hazard Perry-class guided-missile frigate USS Curts (FFG 38), Los Angeles-class fast-attack submarine USS Annapolis (SSN760), P-3 Orion aircraft, SH-60 helicopters and a Sea, Air and Land (SEAL) special forces detachment.
Malabar 2011	April 2011 Okinawa.	The Indian navy was represented by IN ships Delhi, Ranvir, Ranvijay and Jyoti .	The US Navy units USS Sterett, Stethem and Preble, Ronald Reagan, Chancellorsville, Santa Fe, Blue Ridge, Carl Brashear participated in the exercise.
Malabar 2012	April 2012/ Bay of Bengal.	The Indian Navy was represented by Guided missile frigate INS Satpur, Guided missile destroyers INS Ranvijay and INS Ranvir, Missile corvette INS Kulish, Fleet tanker INS Shakti, Maritime patrol aircraft Tu-142M and other rotary wing aircraft.	The US Navy was represented by Aircraft carrier USS Carl Vinson (CVN 70), Guided-missile cruiser USS Bunker Hill (CG 52), Guided-missile destroyer USS Halsey (DDG 97), Logistics ship UNNS Bridge, Los Angeles-class submarine USS Louisville, P-3C Orion aircraft.

Source:

1. Annual Report 1992-93, Ministry of External Affairs, Government of India, p. 78.
2. Anil Kumar, India's Security Concerns in the Indian Ocean Region (New Delhi: Har-Anand Publications, 2003), p. 128.
3. Rashmi Jain (ed.), The United States and India, 1947-2006: A Documentary Study (Delhi: Radiant Publishers, 2007), p. 320.
4. "People, Progress and Partnership: The Transformation of U.S-India Relations" in Public Affairs Section, Embassy of the United States of America, New Delhi, pp. 42-43.
5. "Indo-U.S. Naval Exercise Begins Today", available at <http://www.hindu.com/2003/10/06/stories/2003100602700500.htm>.
6. "US to Send Nuke Submarine for Naval Exercise with India", Aerospace and Marine *International* (Mumbai), vol. 1(19), October 3, 2004, p. 8.
7. Rick Chernitzer, "Malabar 04 Exercises Conclude Successfully off Indian Coast", available at <http://www.globalsecurity.org/military/library/news/2004/10/mil-041014-nns02.htm>.
8. Annual Report 2004-05, Ministry of Defence, Government of India, pp. 49-50.
9. "Malaber 2005: Indo-US Naval Exercise in the Arabian Sea", Defence Digest (New Delhi), September-October 2005, p. 14.
10. "Malabar 2006", Indian Defence Review, vol. 22(1), January-March 2007, p. 74.
11. Annual Report 2007-08, Ministry of Defence, Government of India, p. 32.
12. See, "Indo-US Bilateral Naval Exercise – MALABAR 08", available at <http://vayu-sena.tripod.com/exercise-cope-india-vayu.html>.
13. See, "Malabar 2010: Indo – U.S. Joint Naval Exercise Concludes", available at < http://www.marinebuzz.com/2010/05/04/malabar-2010-indo-u-s-joint-naval-exercise-concludes/>.
14. Annual Report 2011-2012, Ministry of Defence, Government of India, p. 37.

Table 2.4: Joint Multinational Malabar Exercise Involving India and U.S.

Name	Year/Place	Equipments Deployed		
		India	U.S	Other countries
Malabar 2007	4-9 September 2007/ Bay of Bengal.	Seven Warships, including the aircraft carrier INS Viraat, Viraat Sea Harrier jets, Sea King helicopters and Air Force's Jaguar deep-penetration strike aircraft.	13 Warships, including the Nimitz, USS Kitty Hawk, the nuclear submarine USS Chicago, two guided-missile cruisers, and six guided-missile destroyers.	Australia was represented by frigate and tanker, Japan sent two destroyers and Singapore sent a frigate for the drill.
Malabar 2009	26 April - 3 May 2009/ Okinawa Coast.	India was represented by two guided missile destroyer- INS Mumbai (D62) and INS Ranvir (D54); guided missile Corvette INS Khanjar (P47) and a replenishment tanker INS Jyoti (A58).	United States participated with USS Blue Ridge (LCC 19), USS Fitzgerald (DDG 62) and USS Chafee (DDG 90), fast attack submarine USS Seawolf (SSN 21) and various P-3C Orion and Sh-60 Seahawk aircraft.	Japan participated for the second time with one guided missile destroyer JDS Kurama (DDH 144) and one guided missile frigate JDS Asayuki (DD 132).

Source: 1. Mahendra Ved, "Indian Navy's Malabar and other Exercises", India Strategic, vol. 2(9), September 2007, p. 13.2. See, "Malabar 2009", available at < http://www.bharat- rakshak.com/NAVY/Galleries/Bridges/2009/Malabar/>.

Name of Exercises	Year/Place	Equipments deployed	
		India	U.S.
Cope India-02	21-26 October 2002/ Agra.	IL-76, eight AN-32	Five C-130 aircraft,
Cooperative Cope Thunder-03	5-20 June 2003/ Alaska.	One IL-76	
Cope India-04	15-27 February 2004/ Gwalior.	Mirage 2000s, MiG-21Bisons, MiG-27s and the formidable Sukhoi-30MK/Ks.	F-15C 'Eagle' aircraft equipped with the newest long-range, high-definition radars possibly AESA
Cooperative Cope Thunder-04-1	15-30 July 2004/ Alaska. .	Six Jaguars, two IL-78, two IL-76	
Cope India-05	7-19 November 2005/ Kalaikunda, Bengal	Four Su-30Ks, two Su-MKIs, four MiG-27Ms, six Mirage 2000H/THs, six upgraded MiG-21 Bisons, one An-32B tactical transport and a P-37ground-control intercept (GCI) radar based at Salua Air Station. Composite Battery of S-125 M1 Pechora and 9M33 ZRK-Romb OSA-AKM surface-to-air missile systems and related P-15M target acquisition and RSN-125 fire-control radars.	12 Lockheed Martin F-16CJs (armed with wingtip-mounted Raytheon-built AIM-120C-7 AMRAAM air combat missile simulators, cubic corp-built airborne, pod-contained instrumentation to collect and process GPS-based flightpath monitoring data for post-mission debrief, plus Raytheon AN/ASQ-213 pod-mounted anti-radiation missile targeting systems. One Boeing E-3C Sentry AWACS airborne early warning control (AEW & C) aircraft.
Cooperative Cope Thunder-05.			

Source: 1. V.P. Malik, "Indo-US Defense and Military Relations: From 'Estrangement' to 'Strategic Partnership", in Sumit Ganguly, et. al., (eds.), US-Indian Strategic Cooperation into the 21st Century: More Than Words (London and New York: Routledge, 2006), pp. 104, 07.

2. Cope India 2004- An analysis (With inputs by Sayan Majumdar), available at <http://www.indiadefence.com/COPE.htm>.

3. S. Prasun K. Sengupta, "In tandem: Indian Lessons for American Pilots at Cope India '06", *Force* (New Delhi), vol. 3(4), December 2005, pp. 19-20.

Endnotes

[1] Chintamani Mahapatra, Indo-US Relations Into the 21st Century (New Delhi: Knowledge World in Association with the Institute for Defence Studies and Analysis, 1998), pp. 92, 98.

[2] People, Progress, Partnership: The Transformation of U.S.-Indian Relations (New Delhi: Public Affairs Section, Embassy of the United States of America, n.d.), p. 38.

[3] David J. Louscher, Alethia H. Cook and Victoria D. Barta, "Military Relations between the US and India: Assessment and Prospects", in Ashok Kapur, et. al., (eds.), India and United States

in a Changing World (New Delhi: Sage Publication, 2002), pp. 298-301.

[4] Ibid., pp. 310-11.

[5] Ibid., pp. 319-20.

[6] V. P. Malik, "Indo-US Military Ties are Inevitable", available at <http://in.rediff.com/news/2007/sep/18malik.htm>.

[7] Chintamani Mahapatra, "The United States and Asian Powers", in R.R. Sharma (ed.), India and the Emerging Asia (New Delhi: Thousand Oaks: London: Sage Publications, 2005), pp. 173-75.

[8] Prakash Karat, "Vajpayee Government: Covertly Forging Military Ties with US", People's Democracy (New Delhi), vol. XXV(48), 2 December 2001, p. 7.

[9] Saileja, "Indo-US Defence Cooperation", World Focus (New Delhi), vol. XXIX(7), July 2008, pp. 258-59.

[10] N.S. Gehlot and Anu Satsangi, Indo-Pak Relations: Twists and Turns from Partition to Agra Summit and Beyond (New Delhi: Deep and Deep Publications, 2004), p. 273.

[11] Steven Sboto, "Indo-US Military Cooperation- Taking Stock", available at <http://www.faoa.org/journal/sboto1203.html>.

[12] Jyotika Saksena and Suzette Grillot, "The Emergence of Indo-US Defence Cooperation", in Garry K. Bertsch, et. al., (eds.), Engaging India: US Strategic Relations with the World's Largest Democracies (New York: Routledge, 1999), pp. 157-58.

[13] Ramesh Thakur, The Politics and Economics of India's Foreign Policy (New Delhi: Oxford University Press, 1995), pp. 164-65.

[14] Dinesh Kumar, "Defence in Indo-US Relations", Occasional Paper, Institute for Defence Studies and Analyses, August 1997, pp. 44-45.

[15] Chintamani Mahapatra, n. 1, pp. 103-08.

[16] Anil Kumar Singh, India's Security Concerns in the Indian Ocean Region (New Delhi: Har-Anand Publications Pvt. Ltd., 2003), pp. 127-28.

[17] V.P. Malik, "Indo-US Defense and Military Relations: From "Estrangement" to "Strategic Partnership", in Sumit Ganguly, et. al., (eds.), US-Indian Strategic Cooperation into the 21st Century: More Than Words (London and New York: Routledge, 2006), pp. 91-92.

[18] See, New Framework for the U.S.-India Defense Relationship, Washington, DC, 28 June 2005, available at <http://www.indianembassy.org/press_release/2005/June/31.htm>.

[19] W. Lawrence S. Prabhakar, "Strategic Dimensions of India-United States Relations in the Post Cold War Era", in N.K. Jha (ed.), India's Foreign Policy in a Changing World (New Delhi: South Asian Publishers, 2000), p. 74.

[20] Rashmi Jain (ed.), The United States and India, 1947-2006: A Documentary Study (New Delhi: Radiant Publishers, 2007), pp. 317-18.

[21] Jyotika Saksena and Suzette Grillot, n. 12, pp. 158-59.

[22] Ramesh Thakur, n. 13, p. 580.

[23] Christopher Sam Raj in K.P. Vijayalakshmi, et. al., (eds.), Report on the National Workshop on Changing Contours of Indo-US Relations (Bangalore: International Strategic and Security Studies Programme and National Institute of Advanced Studies, 2006), p. 121.

[24] Rashmi Jain, n. 20, p. 346.

[25] See, "India-US Defence Cooperation", available at <http://www.indianembassy.org/newsite/indodefence.asp>.

[26] Jyotika Saksena and Suzette Grillot, n. 12, p. 159.

[27] Rashmi Jain, n. 20, p. 328.

[28] Ashok Sharma, "Indo-U.S. Strategic Convergence: An Overview of Defence and Military Cooperation", Claws Paper no.2, New Delhi, 2008, p. 13.

[29] See, "A Fresh Start: New Moves to Improve Indo-US Army Cooperation", Force (Noida), vol. 1(3), January 2004, p. 52.

[30] Saileja, n. 9, pp. 258-59.

[31] C. Raja Mohan, Crossing the Rubicon: The Shaping of India's New Foreign Policy (New Delhi: Viking, 2003), pp. 113-14.

[32] Vijay Sakhuja, "From Malabar to Malacca: Post Cold War Indo-US Naval Relations", Indian Defence Review (New Delhi), vol. 17(2), April-June 2002, pp. 26-27

[33] Ravi Tomar, "India-US Relations in a Changing Strategic Environment", Research Paper no. 20, June 25, 2002, available at <http://www.aph.gov.au/library/Pubs/rp/2001-02/02rp20.htm>.

[34] C. Raja Mohan, n. 31, p. 114.

[35] Rashmi Jain, n. 20, p. 314.

[36] Cherian Samuel, "Indo-US Defence Cooperation and the Emerging Strategic Relationship", Strategic Analysis, vol. 31(2), March 2007, pp. 220-21.

[37] C. Christine Fair, "US–Indian Army-to-Army Relations: Prospects for Future Coalition Operations", Asian Security, vol. 1(2), April 2005, pp. 158, 165.

[38] K A Muthanna, Enabling Military-to-Military Cooperation as a Foreign Policy Tool: Options for India (New Delhi: Knowledge World, 2006), pp. 205-06.

[39] Ibid., pp. 195-200.

[40] Vivek Chadha, Indo-US Relations: Divergence to Convergence (New Delhi: Macmillan India Ltd., 2008), p. 160.

[41] Ibid., pp. 152-153.

[42] V. P. Malik, n. 6, available at <http://in.rediff.com/news/2007/sep/18malik.htm>.

[43] C. Christine Fair, n. 37, pp. 158-160, 162.

[44] V. P. Malik, n. 6.

[45] Pramit Mitra and John Ryan, "Gathering Stream: India and the United States Extend Military Ties", in South Asia Monitor, Centre for Strategic and International Studies, Washington, DC, No. 99, 2 October 2006, available at <http://www.csis.org/media/csis/pubs/sam99.pdf>.

[46] See, "Indo-US Defence Ties will only Get Better", Times of India (Pune), 13 December 2008.

[47] See, "Naval-Gazing Off the Malabar Coast", 07 October 2004, available at <http://www.rediff.com/news/2004/oct/07spec.htm>.

[48] Dinesh Kumar, n. 14, pp. 44-45.

[49] Anil Kumar Singh, n. 16, pp. 128-129.

[50] People, Progress and Partnership: The Transformation of U.S-India Relations, n. 2, pp. 42-43.

[51] See, "Indo-U.S. Naval Exercise Begins Today", available at <http://www.hindu.com/2003/10/06/stories/2003100602700500.htm>.

[52] See, "US to Send Nuke Submarine for Naval Exercise with India", Aerospace and Marine International (Mumbai), vol. 1(19), 3 October 2004, p. 8.

[53] See, "Malaber 2005: Indo-US Naval Exercise in the Arabian Sea", Defence Digest (New Delhi), September-October 2005, pp. 14-16.

[54] Annual Report 2005-06, Ministry of Defence, Government of India, pp. 37-38.

[55] See, "Malabar 2006", Indian Defence Review, vol. 22(1), January-March 2007, p. 74.

[56] For more details see table 2.3 & 2.4. Also refer to Annual Report 2007-08, Ministry of Defence, Government of India, pp. 32-33.

[57] Mahendra Ved, "Indian Navy's Malabar and Other Exercises", India Strategic (New Delhi), vol. 2(9), September 2007, pp. 10-13.

[58] Cherian Samuel, n. 36, p. 219.

[59] C. Christine Fair, n. 37, p. 164.

[60] See, "2002: Balance Iroquois- Renewing India-U.S. Defence Cooperation", Prepared by Asia-Pacific Defence Forum Staff, available at <http://forum.apan-info.net/Fall02/19_21/

20.html and http://forum.apan-info.net/Fall02/19_21/21.html>.

[61] C. Christine Fair, n. 37, p. 164.

[62] Robert D. Blackwill, "U.S.-India Defence Cooperation", available at <http://www.hvk.org/articles/0503/157.html>.

[63] See, "India, US Armies Fight Urban Terror", available at< http://news.rediff.com/slide-show/2009/oct/15/slide-show-1-yudh-abhyas-2009-images.htm>.

[64] See, "India, US Armies Fight Urban Terror", available at <http://news.rediff.com/slide-show/2009/oct/15/slide-show-1-yudh-abhyas-2009-images.htm#contentTop>.

[65] V.P. Malik, n. 17, p. 104.

[66] See, "COPE INDIA 2004- AN ANALYSIS (With inputs by Sayan Majumdar)", available at <http://www.indiadefence.com/COPE.htm>.

[67] Ajit K. Dubey, "Progressing Partnership: India Exercises Once Again with the US During COPEINDIA 05", Force (New Delhi), vol. 3(4), December 2005, p. 18.

[68] S. Prasun K. Sengupta, "In Tandem: Indian Lessons for American Pilots at Cope India '06", Force, vol. 3(4), December 2005, p. 19.

[69] Pramit Mitra and John Ryan, n. 45, available at <http://www.csis.org/media/csis/pubs/sam99.pdf>.

[70] See, "Joint Exercises Offer Better Understanding Among Nations", Times of India (Pune), 12 December 2008.

[71] People, Progress and Partnership: The Transformation of U.S-India Relations, n. 2, pp. 42-45.

[72] Vijay Sakhuja, n. 32, pp. 25-26.

[73] Rick Chernitzer, "Malabar 04 Exercises Conclude Successfully Off Indian Coast" available at <http://www.globalsecurity.org/military/library/news/2004/10/mil-041014-nns02.htm>.

[74] K A Muthanna, n. 38, pp. 19-20.

[75] Rashmi Jain, n. 20, p. 319.

[76] Baldev Raj Nayar and T.V. Paul, India in the World Order: Searching for Major-Power Status (New- Delhi: Cambridge University Press, 2004), pp. 13-15.

[77] Annual Report 1992-93, Ministry of External Affairs, Government of India, p. 77.

[78] C. Christine Fair, n. 37, pp. 163, 169.

[79] Dinesh Kumar, n. 14, p. 37.

[80] David J. Louscher and others, n. 3, pp. 311-12.

[81] Ibid., pp. 315.

[82] Rashmi Jain, n. 20, pp. 328-31.

[83] C. Christine Fair, n. 37, p. 167.

[84] V.K. Kapoor and Vinod Anand, "India-US Relationship on an Ascending Trajectory", U.S.I. Journal (New Delhi), vol. CXXXVI(565), July-September 2006, p. 3.

[85] Saileja, n. 9, pp. 257-59. <http://www.usindiafriendship.net/archives/viewpoints/carbaugh-102003.htm>.

[87] Dinshaw Mistry, "Ideas, Technology Policy, India's Helicopter, Combat Aircraft and Lunar Orbiter Programs", in Swarna Rajagopalan (ed.), Security in South Asia: Ideas, Institutions and Initiatives (London: New York and New Delhi, 2006), p. 141.

[88] K A Muthanna, n. 38, p. 142.

[89] Deva R Mohanty and Uma Purushothaman, "India-U.S. Defence Relations: In Search of a Direction", Observer Research Foundation Occasional Paper 23, August 2011, pp. 16-17.

[90] Refer to "India Can't Claim Strategic Autonomy Without Own Weapons: NSA", available at <http://www.dnaindia.com/india/report_india-can-t-claim-strategic-autonomy-without-own-weapons-nsa_1575014>.

[91] John E. Carbaugh, Jr., n. 86.

[92] Ashley J. Tellis, India as a New Global Power: An Action Agenda for the United States (New Delhi: India Research Press, 2005), p. 68.

[93] Saileja, n. 9, pp. 257-59.

[94] Quoted from Alexander David, "Panetta Calls for Deep U.S-India Defense Ties, More Arms Trade", available at <http://www.reuters.com/article/2012/06/06/us-usa-india-defence-idUSBRE8550MO20120606>.

[95] Pramit Mitra and John Ryan, n. 45.

[96] See, "India Quietly Inks Defence Deal with US", Times of India (Pune) 5 January 2009.

[97] Statement of Admiral Robert F. Willard, U.S. Navy Commander, U.S. Pacific Command Before the House Armed Services Committee on "U.S. Pacific Command Posture", 6 April 2011, p. 18.

[98] K A Muthanna, n. 38, pp. 154-55.

[99] See, "Fresh Impetus to Indo-U.S. Military Relations: An Overview of Indo-U.S. Bilateral Security Relations", in R.K. Jasbir Singh, Indian Defence Yearbook 2004 (New Delhi: Natraj Publications, 2004), pp. 430-31.

[100] G Balachandran, "Indo-US Relations: Perception and Reality", Strategic Analysis, vol. 29(2), April-June 2005, p. 205.

[101] V. Siddhartha in K. P. Vijayalakshmi, et. al., (eds.), Report on the National Workshop on Changing Contours of Indo-US Relations (Bangalore: International Strategic and Security Studies Programme and National Institute of Advanced Studies, 2006), pp. 231, 233.

[102] Ashley J. Tellis, n. 92, p. 5.

[103] Ibid., pp. 75-76.

[104] Ashok Sharma, n. 28, pp. 20-21.

[105] See, "Joint Statement: US-India on High Technology Commerce", Strategic Digest (New Delhi), vol. 35(12), December 2005, pp. 1619-1620.

[106] See, "Military Bonds: Indo-US Military Cooperation is Increasing by the Day", Force, vol. 3(8), April 2006, p. 39.

[107] Verghese Koithara, "India-US Defence Cooperation: Expectations and Prospects", Economic and Political Weekly (Mumbai), vol. XL(32), 6-12 August 2005, p. 3586.

[108] Vivek Chadha, n. 40, pp. 154-55.

[109] V.K. Kapoor and Vinod Anand, n. 84, p. 3.

[110] For more details See, New Framework for the U.S.-India Defense Relationship, Washington, DC, 28 June 2005, available at <http://www.indianembassy.org/press_release/2005/June/31.htm>.

[111] See, "Promising Journey: Cooperation with the US Military will Benefit India", Force, vol. 3(8), April 2006, p. 37.

[112] Ashok Sharma, n. 28, p. 24.

[113] See, "India Signs Deal with US for Long-Range Maritime Aircraft", Sakaal Times (Pune), 6 January 2009 and "India Quietly Inks Defence Deal with US", Times of India (Pune), 5 January 2009.

[114] Anit Mukherjee and Manohar Thyagaraj, "Competing Exceptionalisms: US-India Defence Relationship", Journal of Defence Studies, vol. 6, No. 2, 2012, pp. 16-19.

[115] Frank G. Wisner, et. al., New Priorities in South Asia: US Policy Toward India, Pakistan and Afghanistan (New York: Council on Foreign Relations, 2003), p. 28.

[116] People, Progress, Partnership: The Transformation of U.S.-Indian Relations", n. 2, pp. 46-47.

[117] Annual Report 2005-06, Ministry of Defence, Government of India, p. 29.

[118] Ashley J. Tellis, n. 92, pp. 82-88.

[119] Naroottam Gaan, India and the United States: From Estrangement to Engagement (New-Delhi: Kalpaz Publications, 2007), p. 197.

[120] People, Progress, Partnership: The Transformation of U.S.-Indian Relations, n. 2, pp. 49, 51.

[121] Dipankar Banerjee in K. P. Vijayalakshmi, et. al., (eds.), Report on the National Workshop on Changing Contours of Indo-US Relations (Bangalore: International Strategic and Security Studies Programme and National Institute of Advanced Studies, 2006), p. 137.

[122] See, "Indo-US Defence Ties will only Get Better", Times of India (Pune), 13 December 2008.

INDIA-U.S. TRADE AND ECONOMIC RELATIONS

3.1 Introduction

Trade and Economic relations between India and the United States are an important dimension of the transforming strategic relations between the two countries. Economic and trade relations provided the much-needed sound foundation for enlarging the strategic relations between the two economically powerful partners. After the disintegration of the erstwhile Soviet Union, India-U.S. trade and economic relations have undergone remarkable developments, with both sides very much eager to broader the existing pattern of trade and economic relations. Economic relations have played no less significant role than defence relations in bringing the relations between the two world's largest democracies closer. It comes into play when all forms of cooperation between the two world's largest democracies came to a standstill. This chapter argues that there are huge scope for improvement in trade and economic relations given the fact that both sides work hard to remove the existing barriers.

With gaining political understanding, economic cooperation between the two sides has also made significant progress during the last two decades. The implementation of the economic reforms was the most important decision taken by India that has no doubt opened the way for easy passage of American goods, capital, services and technology. That today, the United States have become India's largest trading partner, major collaborator in joint ventures and the largest investment partner.[1] What makes India an indispensable partner for the U.S. is that the former holds the environment needed for the latter's higher level of economic success. The economic complementarities between India and the United States in the areas of trade and investment has been the binding factors bringing the two countries closer than never before in the past. The Indian need for capital and the American need for market can be fulfilled by working closely together.[2]

To free from the economic crisis and the need to integrate its economy to the international economy, India in 1991 brought certain economic policy changes. India has introduced changes in industrial and trade policies to improve its efficiency, productivity and competitiveness of its economy. Besides, it also brought changes in industrial licensing, foreign collaborations, investment by NRIs, portfolio investment by foreign institutional investment, reduction in tariff rate and simplification of export-import procedures, opening of the IT-sector, reducing public expenditure investment norms to attract inflow of capital from both the domestic and foreign enterprises in sectors like banking, insurance, retailing etc. All of these changes were the engine of growth for Indian economy.[3]

Today, there are very good reasons why the United States would like to engage in a closer economic and trade relations with India. India's economic performance speaks for itself. Since the liberalisation of its economy, India was able to maintain an annual average growth rate between five to seven per cent. Given the current growth rate, it is projected that by the end of the second decades of the twenty first century, India would become the third largest economic power behind the United

States and China. India, with the second largest population in the world, the eight largest industrial economy, ranked second to the U.S. in terms of world's largest pool of scientist and engineers and last but not the least its middle class size is double that of Japan. India had replaced Germany to become the fourth largest economy in terms of purchasing power parity in the year 2000. Given India's significant achievement in the last almost one and half decades, Western Scholars was compelled to make certain statements that are in favor of India. Their statement calls for closer cooperation between India and other powerful countries. Mr. Henry Kissinger predicts that in the twenty-first century, the international system will be dominated by six major powers: the U.S., Europe, China, Japan, Russia and probably India. This is followed by the predicament of Mr. Samuel Huntington that during the coming decades, "India could move into rapid economic development and emerge as a major contender for influence in world affairs."[4] India's Gross National Product (GNP) of $2.14 trillion in Purchasing power parity (PPP) terms is larger than that of three P-5 countries such as Russia, France and Germany. This way, in PPP terms, India's economy is more than twice that of Russia.[5]

The expanding trade relation reflects the close interests of the two countries. The two-way trade between India and the United States had witnessed a significant jump from meager $5.6 billions in 1990 to $43.38 billion in 2008 representing an impressive 675 per-cent growth in a span of 18 years. What is significant is the fact that throughout these periods, India enjoys a favorable balance of trade with the United States at an increasing pace.[6]

Apart from Trade, Foreign Direct Investment (FDI) also increases from 1991 onwards. The FDI inflows to India grew from US $11.3 million in 1991 to US $4132.8 million as on August 2004, reflecting an increase of 36473.45 per cent. The U.S.

account for 11 per cent of the total actual FDI inflow to India. Given the kind of figure that both the countries enjoy, one can say that there is a huge scope for investment. This is further supported by the fact that there is a wide gap between the approvals and the actual inflow. The present inflow is just one-fourth of the approvals. Since 1996, the United States has emerged as the attractive destination for Indian investment. Out of the total $11083.11 million approved for direct foreign investment by India during the period between 1996 and 2004, the U.S. share $2080.367, constituting 18.77 per cent of the total approval. Despite of not reaching a satisfactory level, the U.S. is India's leading trade and investment partner.[7] The reason why the trade and economic relations is not able to reach its satisfactory level is the presence of unsolved issues between the two countries. To reach at a satisfactory stage, both sides must have to develop a consensus on underlying trade and investment related issues and concerns. This chapter seeks to critically analyse the post-cold war trade and investment relations between the two countries. It also discusses the significance of the economic and trade relations. It also explores economic and trade issues that have circumscribed the prospering relations. Later, it explores the implications of the recent financial crisis to trade relations and to Indian economy. Lastly, it focuses on areas of future prospects.

3.1.1 Factors influencing India-United States Bilateral Economic Relations

India-United States economic relations is most likely to be influence by a number of factors. This includes the following points:-

a. India's long-term GDP growth in a liberal and free market society and the advantage that would accrue from trade and investment with India to the United States are likely to influence bilateral trade and economic relations.

b. For the U.S. to be in competition with other emerging economic power needs a country which can satisfy American interests to remain a pre-dominant economic power, India is one of them. India in the coming decades has a significant role to play.

c. India and the United States in the coming decades would depend on the supply of energy from other countries to meet its increasing energy needs. This may compelled both countries to work together for nuclear power generation.

d. American needs for manpower in the working age group and the presence of large quantity and quality of manpower in the working age group in India is also another factor to be considered. India has a high skilled and highly qualified workforce well versed with English and able to adjust in any condition is what America need.[8]

In a year, India produces 2.5 million graduates, of which 250,000 are engineers. India has 28 per cent of the global available workforce in comparison to China with just 11 per cent. Shanghai, which is the main economic centre in China, has a 20 per cent population that is above 59 years of age and it is projected that by 2020, it would rise to one third. On the contrary, the figure of workforce in India will be increasing. Therefore, the presence of a large number of manpower equipped with necessary requirement that can satisfy the needs of other countries will be the driving force for India-U.S. relations.[9]

3.1.2 Significance of India-U.S. Trade and Economic Relations

India and the United States are the two largest democracies in the world, representing a fifth of the world population and account for more than a quarter of the world's economy has a lot to contribute in bringing economic stability in Asia and the world at large. The significance of India-U.S. trade and economic relations can be traced from the following points:

a. The U.S. constitutes about 30 per cent of the world exports, while China constitutes only just 5 per cent of the world exports.
b. Since the liberalisation of the economic reforms in India in 1991, the United States have emerged as the single largest trading partner of India that accounts for 18 per cent of India's exports. This is followed by UK, China / Hong Kong.
c. The bilateral trade volume between India and the United States is about 21-22 billion dollars, followed by 13 billion dollars or so between India and China.
d. The United States is the single largest foreign investor in India that account for about 20 per cent of FDI in India.[10]

3.2 India's Economy after the End of Cold War

The post cold war witnessed a major economic crisis in India that was a result of the oil price shocks due to the Gulf war of 1990, disintegration of long time strategic and economic partner Soviet Union and a sharp depletion of its foreign exchange reserves. India took the bold steps of implementing economic reforms that bring an end to the license raj and opening up of private sectors. The reforms process include reducing tariff and non-tariff barriers, relaxation of FDI rules, exchange rate and banking reforms, was instrumental for the robust and prosperous growth of the Indian economy. The decision to open up its economy and integrate it to the international economy would always remain the basis of the successful Indian economy.

With this, trade and investment relations with other countries and foreign investment inflows started improving in a way that had never experienced before. FDI inflow to India in 1990 was just $100 million, but within six years, it jumped to $2.4 billion. The ratio of FDI inflows to GDP has also improved. However, the 1997 Asian financial crisis and the Indian decision to carry out nuclear tests in May 1998 brought a temporary setback to the prospering Indian economy. The average GDP growth rate in the first decade after the liberalization of Indian economy hovers abound 5.6 per cent.

By the turn of the twenty-first century, there is no way of backtracking India's economic growth that had started improving.[11] The Indian economic growth rate of 8.5 per cent each in 2004 and 2005 was quite impressive, followed by a much better growth rate of 9.4 per cent in 2006. Because of which, India has emerged as the twelfth-largest global economy when measured by the size of its GDP in market rate and the fifth-largest global economy in terms of purchasing power parity.[12] However, today, Indian economy is the fourth largest in the world behind the U.S., China and Japan. India is most likely to replace Japan in the coming few years. This is justified by the fact that the size of India's economy was 73 per cent that of Japan. However, in 2006, the figure has risen to 99 per cent.[13] India's economic performance would have been much better had there been continuous step-by-step reforms. It has been the continuous trade and investment reforms that resulted to better GDP, trade and investment growth in China. That is one point of difference between India and China.[14]

3.3 Start of a Better Economic Relationship

India took the initiative role by introducing economic reforms process. Economic reforms programme and the resulting economic developments in India are the main driving factor behind the closer economic partnership. It seems that the report prepared by Carnegie Endowment and Asia Society

Study Mission after the end of cold war on how the India-U.S. relations should look like, where they have made certain recommendation to the U.S. government, was instrumental in bringing State Department officials closer to strengthening economic and trade relationships with India.

The U.S. eagerness for a better economic partnership was very much clear when the U.S. Commerce Department counted India among the ten Big Emerging Markets in the world along with China, South Korea, Indonesia, Turkey, South Africa and others. This is further strengthened by the frequency of official visits from the U.S. to India and vice-versa. The U.S. Deputy Secretary of State, Strobe Talbott and Assistant Secretary of State for South Asian Affairs Robin Raphel visited India in 1994 to remove the political misunderstanding that exists even after the cold war end to facilitate better environment for trade and investment. Followed by the visit of Indian Prime Minister P.V. Narasimha Rao in May 1994, where he expresses India's desire to strengthen economic and trade cooperation with the United States. The main agenda of his visit was on trade, investment and transfer of technology.

In his address to the joint meeting of the U.S. Congress, late Prime Minister Narasimha Rao had said,

"Perhaps the most impressive aspect of India's ambitious economic reform programme is the smoothness with which the transition from a close, protected economy to an open, export-oriented economy has occurred...India's vast domestic market, huge educated, semi-skilled work force, sound financial institutions, and time-tested and democratic system offer tremendous investment opportunities for forward-thinking companies."

Indian Prime Minister Rao visit was important in terms of clearing the misunderstanding that circumscribes the relationship.[15] This was followed by the U.S. energy Secretary Hazel

O' Leary who along with a business delegation visited India in July 1994 to conclude 11 private sector agreements in power and energy. Then comes the turn of the U.S. Secretary of Commerce Ron Brown who visited India along with 26 CEOs in 1995 where they concluded commitments on projects worth $7 billion. It was during Secretary Brown's Presidential mission to India, both sides created an India-U.S. commercial alliance-a super forum for bilateral consultations that would facilitate closer business-to-business links between the two countries. The commercial alliance focus on four major sectors such as power, Information Technology, transportation infrastructure and food packaging. These are the main foundations for the further progress of the India-U.S. economic relations.[16]

Both India and the United States have blamed each other for the unsatisfactory trade relations. Initially, it was the U.S. trade protectionism and stringent health and sanitary regulations that have restricted faster growth of Indian exports to U.S.[17] At the ignorance of these, the U.S. have cited India's laws on intellectual property rights, such as patents, copyrights and trademarks as inadequate and pose a serious strain on the U.S. Commerce. The United States Trade Representative initiated an investigation on India's policies and practices concerning the protection and enforcement of Intellectual property rights, finally decided to identify India as a priority foreign country under the special 301 provisions of the trade Act. India continued to remain under the priority watch list in the year 1994 and 1995.[18]

Despite of the economic reforms by India, American exports to India was hindered by market access barriers, high import tariffs, lack of adequate infrastructure owing to bureaucratic delays[19] import licensing, customs procedures, procurement practices and procedures are neither transparent nor standardized and lastly discrimination against foreign suppliers.

For more trade turnover the U.S. wants India to reduce its tariff rates on American exports to India. However, with gaining understanding of the need to expand the relations, India on its side have taken steps to bring down its tariff rates from a peak of 300 per cent in 1991 to just 52 per cent in 1996/97 budget and a commitment for further progress. Such a move has no doubt helped in expanding the trade relations. However, the U.S. is still not fully satisfied with the present level of tariff rate and additional duties imposed on the U.S. exports to India.[20]

3.4 India-U.S. Trade and Economic Relations by the Turn of the Twenty-First Century

Economic factor has played a key role in bringing the two countries closer and in transforming the relations. Since the initiation of the economic reforms, Indian economy has witnessed a dramatic improvement and no way of stopping. Such an improvement has attracted the attention of the American Businesses that there has been an increase in the number of American firms presence in India. American firms are well aware of the presence of a large pool of skilled brains power and the advantage that it could gain out of it. The liberalization process has opened the excellent opportunity for the American firms to access Indian market and changed its mindset about the Indian economy from a poor, underdeveloped economy to an emerging market.

Today the U.S. has emerged as the single largest trading partner and the largest investor to India. This is viewed in terms of the significant improvement in India's exports to the U.S. and the improving investment towards India. However if we look at the total trade turnover, it is far below the potential due in part to insufficient the U.S. exports to India. Nevertheless, the good news is that the balance of trade is in favor of India.

So far, the U.S. investment and exports to India has remained flat. American Officials has charged India for its firmness to undergo more reforms that would provide more market opportunities for American goods and services. They are not satisfied with the level of market access that has been provided to them. They wanted more reforms and more market access. They are of the view that the U.S. market remains much more open to India firms and their products than the Indian market is to the U.S. trade and investment.[21] Today, American firms are increasingly making its presence felt in India. Mc Donald was first opened in New Delhi on 13 October 1996. Since then it has made significant strides that within six years the company has expanded to 40 Soutlets in India. Besides, other food chains and consumer goods firms like Dominos, Pizza Hut, Pepsi, Coca-Cola, Reebok, Nike and Avon has made its presence in India. Moreover, India also provides huge markets for consumer products like Computer, telecom equipment, mobile phones and colour television. Between 1991 and 2001, there witnessed more than thirteen fold increase from Rs. 7.19 crores ($156 million) to Rs. 9, 684 crores ($2.1 billion). In the coming years, India would become a much better manufacturing base for the American firms.

Efforts are still going on for expanding the level of trade and economic relations that India and the United Stated enjoy at present. This is reflected in the number of official visit from the U.S. to India and vice-versa that is aimed at transforming economic relations through resolving the underlying trade disputes. Since 2001 up to 2005, more than hundreds officials have visited India for this purpose. According to Mr. Amit Mitra, Secretary General, Federation of Indian Chamber of Commerce and Industry (FICCI), "we are talking more than ever before and discussions are happening at the highest level." India from its side has also taken the most important step of eliminating quantitative restriction on a large number of products thereby opening ways for American manufacturers.[22]

Even after the imposition of restrictive measures, the U.S. was keen to engage in closer business ties with India. On 9 August 2001, the United States Trade Representative (USTR) Robert Zoellick announced that the U.S. would totally free India's trade for 42 products comprising of $543 million of exports under the U.S. Generalised System of Preferences (GSP) for developing countries. Such a move is important in terms of expanding economic and trade ties.

President Mr. George W. Bush had done what the former President Mr. Bill Clinton had failed to do vis-à-vis waiving of economic, military and technological restriction on 22 September 2002. Moreover, on 1 October 2002, the U.S. Department of Commerce had reduced the number of Indian organizations from the entity list from 150 to just 16.

In a bid to take advantage of the newly gained relationship after the relationship reached low ebb owing to India's nuclear tests, the American companies and the Indian counterpart signed a number of business agreements in three different places of India, worth $4 billion in March 2004 in the presence of the U.S. Commercial Secretary Mr. William M. Daley.[23] Trade relations have also improved due in part to removal of licensing requirements but not entirely. During the fiscal year 2003, which ended on September 30, total exports to India have also increased to 4.8 billion dollars witnessing a 25 per cent increase from the previous year.[24]

The conclusion of the High Technology Cooperation Group in 2002 and the Next Step in Strategic Partnership of 2004 has its positive impacts on the expanding trade relations. It has increased the level of the trade relations. This stems from the fact that the dual use licenses for India had climbed from 423 in FY 2002 to 912 in FY 2004. In value terms, it rose from $26.78 million in FY 2002 to $90.06 million in 2004. In the year 2004, 57 licenses were approved and 8 were denied.[25]

Followed by the decision of the U.S. government to restore the GSP in 2005 that was suspended earlier in 1992 for a large number of products exports to U.S. by India owing to the inadequate protection of Intellectual property rights in India. This has also resulted to denial of 785 agro-chemicals and pharmaceutical products that was otherwise eligible for GSP. Therefore, the restoration of GSP would open the way for the exports of agro-chemicals and pharmaceuticals from India. Such decision came only after India has made a progress in providing adequate and effective protection of IPRs.

3.5 India-U.S. Bilateral Merchandise Trade

Trade and commerce form a crucial component of the rapidly expanding multi-faceted relations between India and the U.S. In recent years, there has been a significant jump in export and import resulting in a huge trade turnover. The trade volume has moved from the US $5191 millions in 1991 to US $44,429 millions in 2008, registering a more than five hundred fold increase. Indian exports have contributed more than the India's import from the U.S. in reaching this level. India's exports to the U.S. have been increasing steadily over the years, 1991-2008, with an average annual growth rate of around 11 per cent per annum. Because of which the United States has been a major destination for Indian exports. India's exports commands a share of 1.6 per cent of total U.S. imports and is ranked 17th in the list of exporters to the U.S. Indian exports to the U.S. in 2008 amounted to $25,762 millions.

However, when it comes to import from the United States, India remains a relatively less significant export destination for the United States because of the slow growth of U.S.

export to India. However, the figure of the U.S. export to India in recent years has improved significantly. Since 2003, there has been a significant growth in the U.S. export to India, with 2007 reaching the highest growth rate of 74.33 per cent from the previous year. U.S. export to India in 2007 was US $17,592 million. Overall, the US exports to India have grown at an average rate of around 6 per cent annually.

Given the environment created after the cold war end and the presence of the complementarities of interest, the trade turnover is not so significant. This is reflected from the fact that India-U.S. trade is far behind the U.S.-China trade relations. This could be because both sides have market access barriers with each other. India had complained about the existence of high tariff peaks in food products, rules of Origin affecting exports of textile products, denial of GSP benefits to some critical sectors such as textiles, gems and jewelry, charges of anti-dumping duties in exports of Iron and Steel etc. While the United States had complained about the existence of high tariffs, higher transaction costs and the need to encourage trade facilitation, India having a large negative list of imports, remnants of the licensing systems in some sectors viz. motion pictures, lack of transparency in government procurement procedures, lack of a proper Intellectual Property Rights protection regime.[26]

American company view India as a lucrative market where they can sell their products and a better destination for investment. This is clearly evident from the fact that according to official U.S. trade statistics, bilateral merchandise trade has increased three times from a meager under $10 billion in 1996 to a huge $31 billion in 2006. India's ranking in terms of imports and exports have also improved. In 1996, India was the 32nd largest market for the U.S. export and the 25th largest source of imports. By 2006, India became 21st largest export market for the U.S. and 18th biggest supplier of imports. The bilateral trade volume between India and the United States in 2006 was more than that of the U.S. total trade with Israel, Nigeria and Thailand.[27]

The progress in economic and trade relations since 2001 may be attributed to the political and strategic understanding that both countries started enjoying after nuclear tests. With this, the annual growth rate of India-U.S. trade also improves. Merchandise exports from India to the U.S. grew by 21.4 per cent in 2002 compared to 2001, rises from $9.74 billion to $11.82 billion. This strong performance reflects the highest annual percentage growth in Indian exports to the U.S. over the past decade. Another reason for this could be the passing of several trade related legislations by India such as Trademark Bill, Geographical Indications of Goods and the Copyright Bill to meet WTO requirements. This came only when the U.S. brought the import restrictions on 2,700 tariff line items before the WTO dispute settlement panel.[28]

The last eight years has registered a twenty per cent growth rate, with 2007 registering the highest growth rate of more than thirty per cent. The credits for this should also go to the significant increase in imports from the United States. The U.S. export to India registered 74.33 per cent increase from the previous year. Total bilateral trade in 2004 crossed US $21 billion, having rises by more than 55 per cent since 2001 and doubled since 1998. The two-way trade has moved from US $13.5 billion in 2001 to the US $43.38 billion in 2008, registering three fold increases (See table 3.1 as shown below).

India-U.S. trade relations is at the threshold of significant improvement given the present level of improvement continues. This can be seen from the fact that India and the United States was successful in clinching the target set out four years back that by 2008 they would reach the figure of US $40 billion. They can score more than what they expect.[29]

Table 3.1: Merchandise Trade Between India and United States: 1991-2009 (in US $ millions)

Year	India's Exports to U.S.	Growth Rate (%)	India's Imports from U.S.	Growth Rate (%)	Trade Turnover	Balance
1991	3,192		1999		5,191	1,193
1992	3,780	18.42	1917	-4.10	5,697	1,863
1993	4,551	20.39	2,761	44.03	7,312	1,790
1994	5,302	16.50	2,296	-16.9	7,598	3,005
1995	5,736	08.20	3,296	43.55	9,032	2,440
1996	6,169	07.57	3,318	00.76	9,487	2,851
1997	7,322	18.70	3,608	08.80	10,931	3,715
1998	8,237	12.45	3,564	-01.20	11,801	4,673
1999	9,071	10.12	3,688	03.50	12,759	5,383
2000	10,686	17.90	3,663	-0.67	14,349	7,023
2001	9,737	-08.90	3,757	02.56	13,494	5,980
2002	11,818	21.38	4,101	09.20	15,919	7,717
2003	13,055	10.47	4,980	21.43	18035	8,055
2004	15,572	19.30	6,109	22.67	21,681	9,463
2005	18,804	20.80	7,919	29.62	26,723	10,885
2006	21,831	16.09	9,674	22.16	31,505	12,157
2007	24,073	10.26	14,969	54.73	39042	9,104
2008	25,704	06.77	17,682	18.12	43,386	8,022
2009	21,176	-17.61	16,462	-06.83	37, 638	4,714

Source: This is compiled by using

1. Trade in Goods (Imports, Exports and Trade balance) with India, available at <http://www.census.gov/foreign-trade/balance/c5330.html#1991>.
2. India-U.S. Trade relations, available at <http://www.indianembassy.org/indusrel/trade.htm>.
3. India-US trade, available at <http://indianembassy.org/newsite/indoustrade1.asp>.

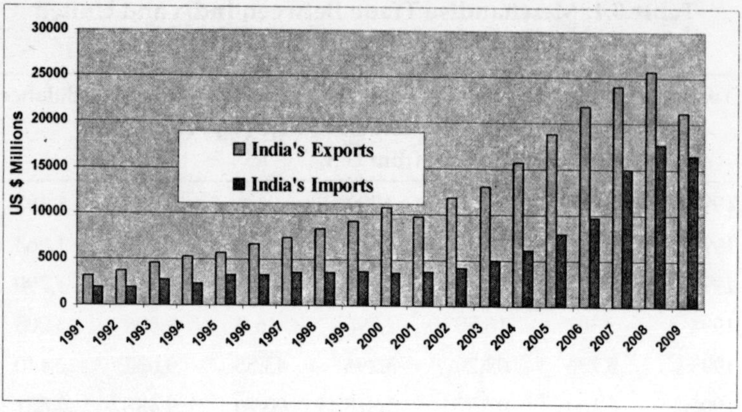

Source: Prepared using Table 3.1.

Figure 3.1: India-U.S. Bilateral Merchandise Trade (1991-2009).

From the table no. 3.1 and figure no. 3.1, one can conclude that

(a) With every passing year India's exports to the U.S. has been on rise except for the year 2001, where there was a decline in comparison to previous year.

(b) Exports to the United States have contributed more to the trade volume than the imports from the United States.

If India and the United States really wants to improve the level of trade relations they enjoy at present then they must have to work together sincerely to resolving the trade issues that underlie on the way to reaching a satisfactory level. Instead of complaining about the market barriers to each other, they should engage in a fruitful dialogue because these are not such issues that cannot be resolved.

3.5.1 Composition of India-U.S. Import and Export of Items

Unlike India-Australian import and export diversification,[30] there witnessed no such significant diversification in the India-U.S. import and export since the cold war end. There witnessed changes only in the rankings of the items exported and imported between the two countries. Market penetration is also missing in India-U.S. trade relations.

India's export to the U.S. comprises of Gems and Jewelry, textile and clothing product, machinery and mechanical products, Iron and steel and related products, carpets, organic chemicals and other materials, while the U.S. export to India are confined to electrical machinery and parts, optical and photographic accessories, precious stones, metals and pearls and other materials. Among the major items that India export to the U.S, textiles has the highest share of (25.9 per cent), Precious stones & metals (13.7 per cent), Iron & Steel products (9.7 per cent), Organic Chemicals (7 per cent), Machinery (6 per cent), Electrical Machinery (5.8 per cent), Pharmaceutical products (5.1 per cent). While Machinery has the highest share of (18.2 per cent) in terms of India's import from United States. This is followed by Aviation & aircraft (12.1 per cent), Precious stones & metals (10.5 per cent), Electrical Machinery (7.2 per cent), Fertilizers (7.1 per cent), Mineral fuel, Oil, etc. (6.8 per cent) and Optical instruments & equipment (6.7 per cent).[31]

In 1996-97, the chief commodities imported from the U.S. were Machinery and Mechanical Appliances, parts there off, Electrical Machinery and equipment and parts there off and other electronic goods, Organic Chemicals and Project Goods, while the major items exported from India to the U.S. were Gems and Jewelry, Textile Products, Marine Products, Carpets, Electrical Machinery and equipment and parts there off and other electronic goods. The same items were exported and imported during the year 2002 and 2003. This is one area where Indian and American officials have to seriously think over if they really want to have broader trade relations. This would result in an increase in import and export between India and the United States.[32] In the year 2001, Textiles top the lists of the items that were exported to United States with US $2827 millions, followed by cut and polished diamonds and jewelry with US $2642 millions. Engineering goods and machinery including electrical machinery and organic chemicals comes third and fourth with US $513 millions and US $323 millions respectively. However, in 2003, there was change in the ranking of the items exported to the United States, cut and polished diamonds and jewelry replaced textiles as the first rank in the list of items exported to the United States. This was due to the significant increase in the percentage growth of cut and polished items from 2001 to 2003 (49.84 per cent), while textiles registered a growth of just 22.88 percent during the same period (See the table no. 3.2 and 3.3). Figure no. 3.2 gives an overview of India's top five exports to the U.S. in 2003.

Table 3.2: Major Export Items From India to United States during the Period (2001-2004) (in US $ millions).

Items	Year			
	2001	2002	2003	2004
Textiles	2827	3213	3474	3950
Cut and Polished Diamonds and Jewellery	2642		3959	4516
Engineering Goods and Machinery including Electrical Machinery	513		731	1*
Organic Chemicals	323		408	518
Vehicles and Parts	127	181	215	303

Note: * signifies billion.

Source:

1. "India-US Trade", available at <http://www.indianembassy.org/Trade/Trade.htm>.
2. "India-US Trade", available at <http://www.indianembassy.org/Trade/Trade05.htm>.

Table 3.3: Major Import Items from United States to India during the Period (2001-2004) (in US $ millions).

Items	Year			
	2001	2002	2003	2004
Engineering Goods and Machinery including Electrical Machinery	1262	1494	1641	2131
Miscellaneous Chemical Products	101	283	491	
Precious Stones	212		411	583
Organic Chemicals	196		299	471

Source:

1. "India-US Trade", available at <http://www.indianembassy.org/Trade/Trade.htm>.
2. "India-US Trade", available at <http://www.indianembassy.org/Trade/Trade05.htm>.

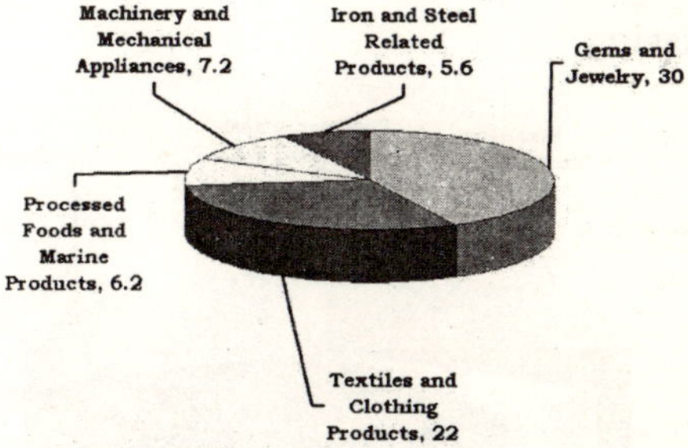

Figure 3.2: India's Top Five Exported Items to U.S. in 2003

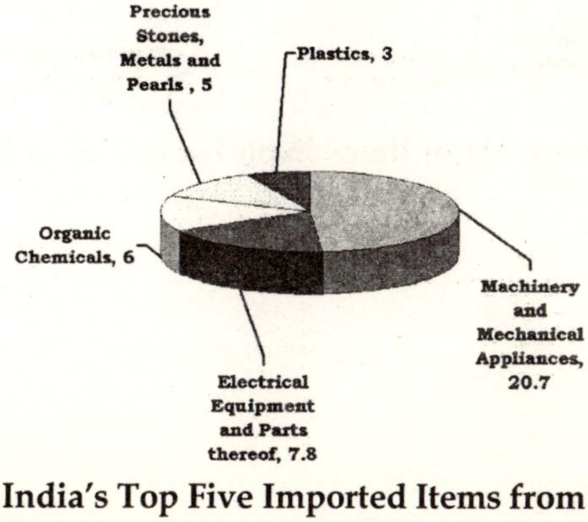

Figure 3.3: India's Top Five Imported Items from U. S. in 2003

Source of Fig 3.2 and 3.3: Jayanta Roy and Pritam Banerjee, "India and United States: Economic Analysis and Trade Strategy", Confederation of Indian Industry, July 2004, available at
<http://cii.in/documents/Trade_Globlizations?India USEconomicAnalysisandTradeStrategy.pdf>.

Among the major items that have been exported to the United States in 2009, textiles were on top with a share of 23 per cent. Followed by precious stones and metals with 21.5 per cent, pharmaceutical products with 7.8 per cent and machinery were at the bottom with just 5 per cent. While precious stones and metals have the largest share among the major items imported from the U.S with 14.2 per cent. Machinery comes second with 14.1 per cent, followed by aviation and aircraft with 13.7 per cent. In addition, optical instruments and equipment has the lowest share with 5.6 per cent (See Figure no. 3.4 & 3.5 as shown below). This clearly reflects that market penetration is missing.

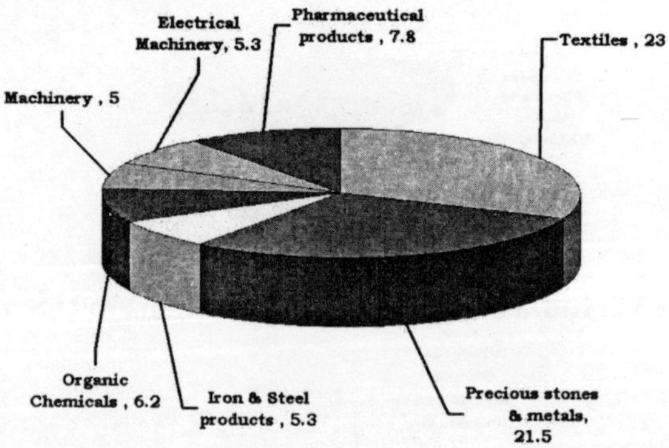

Figure 3.4: Major Items Exported to U.S. in 2009

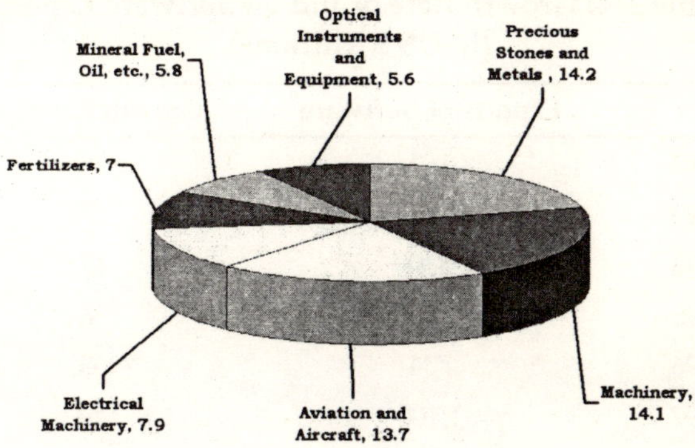

Figure 3.5: Major Items Imported from U.S. in 2009

Source of Fig. 3.5 and 3.6: India-US Trade, available at <http://indianembassy.org/newsite/indoustrade1.asp>.

3.6 India-U.S. Trade in Services

India has made significant improvement in trade in services with the United States. However, one area that has made a huge difference is the software service exports. Software services forms an important part of the India-United States economic relations. India export software services to more than sixty countries in which the United States alone accounts for two-third of the exports. The software product export to the U.S. has witnessed significant improvement in recent years. Because of which, India has been perceived at the forefront of the emerging knowledge economy. The overall Indian software exports have moved from US $164 million in 1991-92 to US $12,200 million in 2004-05 (for more details see table 3.4). The area of software services offers significant scope for cooperation between the two sides. Software services cooperation between India and the United States has the potential to bring both the two countries even closer.

Table 3. 4: Growth Rate of Indian Software Exports (in US $ Millions)

Year	Exports of Software	Growth Rate (%)
1991-92	164	28
1992-93	225	37
1993-94	330	47
1994-95	450	36
1995-96	734	63
1996-97	1,100	49
1997-98	1,759	60
1998-99	2,600	48
1999-2000	3,400	31
2000-01	5,300	56
2001-02	6,200	17
2002-03	7,100	15
2003-04	9,200	30
2004-05	12,200	33

Source: Subhash Bhatnagar, "Indian Software Industry", pp. 2-3, available at <http://www.iimahd.ernet.in/~subhash/pdfs/Indian%20software%20industry.pdf>.

India's total services exports has moved from $16.3 billion in 2000-01 to $87.7 billion in 2007-08, reflecting an increase of 438.03 per cent. Out of the total services exports, software exports share have gone up from two-fifths in 2000-01 to 46 per cent in 2007-08. However, in 2006-07 alone the share of software exports was 61 per cent. Other sectors that have also contributed to services export progress are business services, travel and transportation, etc. India-U.S. trade in services in 2005 was just $10.2 billion, but in 2007, the figure has doubled to $20.0 billion. Unlike Merchandise trade where the trade balance is in favor of India, trade in services is in favor of the United States. It is only recently, the situation has changed and started tilting in favor of India.[33] However, good news for both countries is that trade in Services is improving continuously year by year. (See table no. 3.5)

Table 3.5: India-U.S. Trade in Services, 2000-2005 (in US $ Billions)

Year	India's Exports	India's Imports	Trade Turnover	Trade Balance
2000	2.539	1.889	4.437	640
2001	3.003	1.815	4.818	1.189
2002	3.255	1.809	5.064	1.445
2003	3.760	1.972	5.732	1.788
2004	4.461	2.889	7.350	1.572
2005	5.193	5.018	10.211	174

Source: Michael F. Martin and K.Alan Kronstadt, "India-U.S. Economic and Trade Relations", CRS Report for Congress, Code RL34161, p. 38.

Today the United States has become the attractive destination for India's software exports. United States account for 61 per cent of India's total software exports valued at $6.3 billion during the period from 1991-2000. This is followed by Europe and Japan with 23 per cent and 4 per cent respectively. With expanding software services, India has also expanded its software development centre. With every passing year, software exports from India are increasing. In the first half of 2001, software exports increased by 63 per cent or $2.8 billion, representing 12.5 per cent of India's exports. It is expected that if the present trends of growth rate continues, India would have a much better share of world's IT market. By 2008-10, India plans to export $35-50 billion.

The contribution of the United States to India's software industry is highly laudable. Without the support of United States, it would be very difficult for India's software industry to reach at this stage. American companies that are involved in the global IT market have set up their development centers in India, while many others have acquired software developers and some other companies have developed joint alliances with the Indian companies. Besides, many non-IT companies outsource their software requirements to India. The number of Fortune 500 companies that outsource their requirements is increasing with every passing year. India has made significant improvement in the field of software development process that today it is well known for its achievement and many more to come. India's software industry is the leader in the global market.[34]

3.7 India-United States Investment Cooperation

Foreign investment to any country helps in overcoming a gap between the level of domestic savings and any required expenditure on investment to achieve employment and other development targets. It raises the standards of living of the people by improving labour productivity. It can also help the recipient country meet its needs of transfer of technology and technical skills. Foreign investment generally has two forms-one is the foreign direct investment and the other is foreign portfolio investment. The difference between the two lies only in the degree of influence.

Since the integration of the Indian economy to the international economic regime, there witnessed a sudden upsurge in the strategic thinking of India with regard to Foreign Direct Investment (FDI). Foreign Direct Investment is considered to be the engine of growth for the host countries. India's dire need for foreign investment coalesced with the initiation of certain policy changes such as reduction of restriction and controls over the entry of foreign firms, created a climate conducive for foreign direct investment. It seems India have realised that FDI play no less significant role than trade in the progress of Indian economic growth and development. Because of which, India had signed a number of bilateral investment agreements with foreign countries including United States to attract investment. Since then foreign direct investment to India has improved a lot. At the same time, Foreign Exchange Regulation Act (FERA) was amended to allow easier operation of firms in India with foreign equity. India also signed the Multilateral Investment Guarantee Agency (MIGA) convention to promote foreign investment. However, the most important factor that makes India a very hot destination for foreign investors are its market size, prevalence of domestic institutions and the enforcement of rule of law.[35]

Former Deputy Secretary of Commerce Mr. Bodman while speaking at the re-launch of the U.S.-India Commercial dialogue has said that, "in a country of over a billion people, $1.7 billion in direct investment is not just a drop in the bucket; it is a drop in the Ocean." He further added that India's immense potential in the global economy is very far from being realised. His statement reflects the lacking of attracting more foreign investment from investors and the eagerness of more investment by American investors for which India must have to take certain steps. Earlier Brownback has warned the Indian government to introduce more reforms thereby resulting in flow of more investment from the U.S. China was able to attract more investment from investors because of continuous reforms programs.[36]

3.7.1 U.S. Investments in India

The decision of the Indian government to increase its foreign investment equity limit from 40 to 51 per cent since July 1991 was a good move to attract more investment from the United States. Since then American firms has expressed keen interest in investing in India. In the year 1993, nearly half of all the investment approvals by India (approximately $1.2 billion) were from U.S. companies. It is more than doubled that of 1992 and roughly equal to the cumulative investment during the last four decades before 1991. American firms investment towards India has been on rise. The main area of attraction for American investors are power generation, telecommunication expansion and transportation modernisation,[37] chemicals, electricals, electronics, mechanical engineering and industrial machinery, making the U.S. India's most important source of foreign technology. By 1996, more than 1500 collaborations with the U.S. companies had been approved. At the same time Foreign Institutional Investment from the U.S. are active in portfolio investments.

To promote and expand more American investment toward India, both India and the United States signed an India-U.S. Investment Incentive agreement on November 1997. The agreement would facilitate investment support to the U.S. investors from Overseas Private Investment corporation (OPIC). The agreement enlarges the nature and scope of investment for the U.S. investors.[38]

Major US corporations that have made substantial foreign investments in India are Coca-Cola, Whirlpool, Ford, General Motors 3M, Honeywell, Pepsi, Proctor and Gamble and Reebok. While in the financial sector, major investors include Citicorp, GE Capital, and American Express.[39]

According to Table 3.6, the actual FDI inflows to India have increased twenty-four fold from US $143.6 million in 1991 to the US $33,028 million in 2008. During these periods, on three occasions the investment decreases- first in 1998 then in 2001 and 2003. Otherwise, the figure of overall FDI to India would have been different.

Among many countries that invest to India, the United States is the largest investor in terms of FDI approvals, actual inflows, and portfolio investment. The US investments cover almost every sector in India, which is open for private participants. The U.S. share in FDI has moved from US $11.3 million in 1991 to US $1797.16 million in 2008. FDI inflows from USA constitute about 8 percent of actual FDI inflows into India in rupee terms. In the very first year of the liberalisation regime, the share of U.S. FDI inflow to total FDI inflows in India was 7.87 per cent. The year 1993 witnessed the highest U.S. share of 25.34 per cent in FDI to total-actual inflow in India. The lowest the U.S. share has been in the year 2007 with just 4.02 per cent. Otherwise, the average U.S. share to total FDI in India is 10.60 per cent.

Although there is a huge gap in between the approval and actual inflow, but the ratio of cumulative U.S. FDI inflow to approval has accelerated in recent years indicating that FDI approved in the past years are materializing now. The last nine years witnessed continuous increase in the U.S. share of actual inflow to approval in India from 1996 onwards. The huge gap between approval and actual inflow reflects the huge potential and scope for improvement in the field of Foreign Direct Investment.[40]

Table 3.6: Share of US FDI in Total-Actual Inflow

Years	Total FDI ($ Mln)	US FDI ($ Mln)	US Share (%)
1991	143.6	11.3	07.87
1992	258.0	43.9	17.02
1993	582.9	147.7	25.34
1994	1048.5	118.9	11.34
1995	2172.0	215.6	09.93
1996	3021.0	271.0	08.97
1997	4579.1	736.6	16.09
1998	3377.2	347.1	10.28
1999	4016.1	431.2	10.74
2000	4498.1	418.4	09.30
2001	4281.1	367.6	08.59
2002	4434.5	282.8	06.38

Years	Total FDI ($ Mln)	US FDI ($ Mln)	US Share (%)
2003	3109.0	396.3	12.75
2004	3753.6	647.65	09.93
2005	4353.8	472.07	10.00
2006	11,122	732.34	06.59
2007	21,797	875.50	04.02
2008	33,028	1797.16	05.40

Source: See, "Standards and Conformance Cooperation Programme on 1st Indo-US Summit on Standards in Trade", Background Paper Prepared in collaboration between Ministry of Commerce & Industry Government of India, Confederation of Indian Industry, American National Standards Institute and US Trade and Development Agency, 16 February 2010, New Delhi, p. 4, available at <http://www.standardsportal.org.in/Pdf/US-Indiatrade_paper.pdf>.

From the table no. 3.6, we can conclude that the percentage increase in the share of the U.S. FDI to total actual inflows has not been impressive. This is due to the significant increase in the total actual FDI from other countries. This is not to say that the U.S. investment to India is not impressive. The U.S. investment to India has improved from US $11.3 millions in 1991 to US $875.50 millions in 2007, but has not been able to exploit its actual potential. The huge gap between approval and the actual inflow can be reflected from the fact that the actual cumulative FDI inflow in 2004 (up to August) was not even in par with what has been approved in 1995. However, it is good for India that the gap is narrowing in the last three to four years. If such a trend continues then one can expect a significant reduction in the gap between the approval and actual inflow. (See the table no. 3.7 and figure no. 3.6 as shown below).

Table 3.7: India's Cumulative FDI

Year	FDI Approved to USA	Actual Inflow to USA	Share of Inflow to Approval
1991	76	11	14.87
1992	547	55	10.10
1993	1676	203	12.11
1994	2788	322	11.54
1995	5035	537	10.67
1996	7908	808	10.22
1997	11785	1545	13.11
1998	12687	1892	14.91
1999	13538	2323	17.16
2000	14513	2742	18.89
2001	15607	3109	19.92
2002	16034	3392	21.16
2003	16718	3788	22.66
Up to August 2004	16853	4133	24.52

Source: India-U.S. Economic Relations, available at <http://www.indianembassy.org/Economy/economy.htm>.

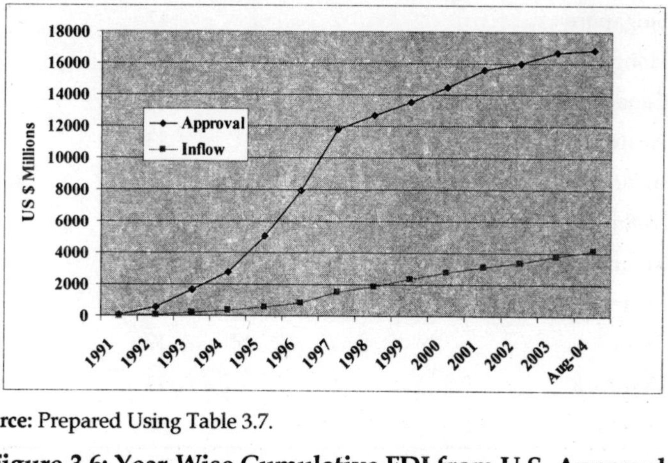

Source: Prepared Using Table 3.7.

Figure 3.6: Year-Wise Cumulative FDI from U.S. Approvals and Inflow (1991- August 2004).

3.7.2 Portfolio Investment

Also in portfolio investment, the U.S. is India's leading investor. During the academic year 1992-93, there was no FII registered with India. From a very limited FII to invest in India, today, as on 5 October 2007, we have 1110 FIIs registered under the Securities and Exchange Board of India (SEBI) (See table no. 3.8 below). Until 31 March 2006, there were 342 U.S. based FIIs registered with SEBI. United Kingdom comes second with 148 FIIs registered with SEBI, and the last on the list is Denmark with 11 FIIs (See table 3.9 below). As of 30 June 2004, the U.S. based FIIs have made a net investment of nearly $10.2 billion out of a total of $25.3 billion as on that date in the Indian capital markets, which accounts for about 40.5 per cent of the net investments made by the FIIs since 1993.

Table 3.8: Registration of FII

Country	FII
USA	342
UK	148
Luxembourg	84
Singapore	47
Hong Kong	30
Canada	26
Australia	23
Ireland	23
Netherland	23
Mauritius	22
Switzerland	19
France	17
Denmark	11
Others	87

Table 3.9: Country-Wise Registered With SEBI as on 31 March 2006.

Financial Year	Total registered at the end of the year
1992-93	0
1993-94	3
1994-95	156
1995-96	353
1996-97	439
1997-98	496
1998-99	450
1999-2000	506
2000-01	528
2001-02	490
2002-03	502
2003-04	540
2004-05	685
2005-06	993
As on Oct 5, 2007	1110

Source: Neeta Tripathi, "Foreign Institutional Investment Flows (FII) in Indian companies", Asia-Pacific Business Review (New Delhi), vol. IV(1), Jan-Mar 2008.

Today American companies are involved in a spectrum of economic activities that had never experienced before. It ranges from infrastructure to consumer goods and from information technology to consultancy services.[41] From table no. 3.10 as shown below, one can conclude that even though the U.S. portfolio investment in India is the highest, but the U.S. share is decreasing since 1998-99. Overall the U.S. share of FIIs has been satisfactory. Instability in the FIIs has been a case of concern where they need to work on.

Table 3.10: Year-Wise Foreign Institutional Investments

Years	Total FII ($ Mln)	FII from USA ($ Mln)	US Share (%)
1993-94	1634	781	47.80
1994-95	1528	894	58.51
1995-96	2036	856	42.04
1996-97	2424	1019	42.04
1997-98	1463	1005	68.69
1998-1999	-176	-9	5.11
1999-2000	2235	841	37.63
2000-01	2222	1174	52.84
2001-02	1702	533	31.32
2002-03	525	174	33.14
2003-04	8630	2863	33.17
2004-05	10172	2065	20.30
2005-06	9332	3266	34.99
2006-07	7100	2240	31.55

Source: See, "Standards and Conformance Cooperation Programme on 1st Indo-US Summit on Standards in Trade", Background Paper Prepared in collaboration between Ministry of Commerce & Industry Government of India, Confederation of Indian Industry, American National Standards Institute and US Trade and Development Agency, 16 February 2010, New Delhi, p. 6, available at <http://www.standardsportal.org.in/Pdf/US-Indiatrade_paper.pdf>.

3.7.3 India's Investment to U.S.

India is also known for investing to other countries. When India have made policy changes to attract investment from other countries, it has also made policy changes in overseas investment that was first undertaken in 1992, followed by further liberalisation in 1995. Since then there emerged certain policy changes from time to time and Reserve bank of India (RBI) replaced Ministry of Commerce to look after the overseas investment policy.[42] This step would help increase India exports and to provide Indian industry access to new markets and technologies thereby help them to become globally competitive. Among the major companies that have made significant investment in the U.S. are Tatas, Birlas, Essar, Mahindra and Reliance.[43]

India's Overseas Investment has witnessed significant improvement since 1996. The value of approved Indian Investment abroad has increased by more than five fold to US $2854.84 million between April 1996 and March 2006.[44] The U.S. has been one of the largest recipients of Indian investment, receiving roughly one-fifth of India's investments abroad. Indian investment to the U.S. is not restricted to IT, but now spreading beyond the IT sector to include other sectors, such as pharmaceuticals, healthcare, travel, luxury hotels, engineering services and manufacturing, such as the Mahindra's tractor factories in the U.S. Such an Indian investment to these sectors resulting in creation of 30,000 jobs. Among the Indian companies, Tata group is the largest investor in the U.S. Currently, the Tata group companies has 16 businesses and employs 19,000 people in the United States."[45]

Indian corporates/Registered partnership firms are allowed to invest in entities abroad up to 400 per cent of their net worth and are permitted to make overseas investments in any bonafide business activity.[46] The United States has been a better destination for India's direct investment in joint ventures and wholly owned subsidiaries. Since April 1996 to 2006-07, U.S. has received a total of US $3285.192 million. Followed by Russia with US $2839.629 million and United Kingdom comes third with US $2683.300 million. Still there are huge prospects for India's investment to the United States (See table 3.11 below).

Table 3.11: India's Direct Investment in Joint Ventures and Wholly Owned Subsidiaries to Five Major Countries (Amount US $ million).

Country	Year						
	April 1996- March 2002	2002-03	2003-04	2004-05	2005-06	2006-07	Total
U.S.A	1540.83	185.27	207.14	251.42	270.256	830.276	3285.192
Russia	1748.68	0.15	1.43	1076.17	1.168	12.031	2839.629
U.K.	410.62	34.53	138.48	71.852	158.270	1869.548	2683.300
Mauritius	618.34	133.35	175.59	149.38	322.665	1162.786	2572.111
Netherlands	157.92	15.92	30.18	30.65	284.619	1286.129	1805.418

Source: Available at <http://www.finmin.nic.in/the_ministry/dept_eco_affairs/icsection Annexure_6.htm>.

3.7.4 Hindrance to Foreign Direct Investment Inflows in India

India is lacking behind to China when it comes to attracting FDI due to the following reasons. Firstly, foreign investors are of the view that India is not the ideal destination for investments. This is fuelled from the perception that Indian bureaucracy is corrupt. Second factor is that decision making process on approvals has been very slow, resulting in a great financial loss to potential foreign investors. Thirdly, infrastructure facilities in India such as road transport and telecommunication has been below par, making it highly difficult for the foreign investors. Better infrastructure facility is the prerequisite for attracting investment from other countries. For instance, the China offers a better infrastructure facility than India forcing the investors to invest in their country. Fourthly, reliable and honest joint ventures as a potential partner for foreign investors are difficult to find in India. Last but not the least, the lack of political stability in India has also been the problem for the foreign investors.[47]

Lack of political consensus is leading to poor infrastructure facility. Many a times in India, due to lack of political consensus, efforts to improve the infrastructure facility remain unsuccessful. For instance, the resolve of the Indian Government for privatization of airports in Mumbai and New Delhi received opposition from airports workers and communist parties. Such a lack of political consensus forced the investors to have a second thought on it.[48]

According to a survey carried out by a key global consultancy firm in December 2000, government bureaucracy was the reason behind the lack of FDI in India. FDI is hampered by the higher transactions costs in India, compared to countries like China:

Anyone doing business in India runs up against what might be called institutional fiction. Whenever he ventures beyond an environment under his own control to one controlled by others, he needs to watch out. This happens every time he petitions a bureaucrat, signs a contract, goes to court or even turns a light switch.[49]

3.7.5 Good Prospects for Investment to India in Future

There are huge prospects for increasing investment to India given that the Indian economy continues to grow at the same pace that had witnessed in recent years. What the investors is looking for is a stable and resilient economy that shows positive impacts in times of crisis. According to a study carried out by the UNCTAD, the year 2008 was a significant one for India in terms of foreign direct investment. Last year, India witnessed a significant increase of 85.1 per cent of FDI inflows from the previous year i.e. 2007. It is noteworthy that this comes at the time when the global flows have declined from $1.9 trillion in 2007 to $1.7 trillion in 2008, registering more than 11 per cent decrease. Even China, which is known for attracting more investment from other countries including India, had registered only just 10 per cent increase in 2008 from the previous year. That does not mean China receives fewer amounts than India nor India would outclassed China in attracting more investment from outside investors. Nevertheless, this is to say that in terms of percentage increase India have registered more than China.

Another significant fact is that India's FDI inflows have reached half of what China has succeeded. Indian market continues to remain bright destination for investors in a recession-hit world.[50] According to Goldman Sachs, FDI to India will prosper in the coming years given that the momentum of the domestic demand remains resilient. According to the bank, the FDI flow to India during the period between September and January, when the credit crisis was at its peak, amounted to $9.2 billion, $1.3 billion higher than the amount received during the same period of last year.[51]

There is lot many areas where America is ready for investment once India removes the restriction imposed to these sectors. These include pensions, insurance, banking, and multi-brand retail in India. Allowing American investment in these sectors will bring greater efficiencies, better prices, new products, and more choices will be available to Indian consumers.[52]

3.7.6 Measures to attract more Investment

Given the wide gap between the approval and the actual inflows it becomes very imperative that to reduce the gap or filled the gap, certain steps must be taken. This includes:-

a. Create a suitable environment for the investors.
b. We must offer a large diversified market with a well-organized industrial base.
c. Create a policy of investment that is friendly to both the investors and the destination. That does not mean it should be against the interest of the nation.[53]

d. We must have to open as many high priority areas such as power, telecommunications, electronics, chemicals, biotechnology and others as possible for investment by other countries including the United States. India has opened its sector less than other developing countries.

e. The overall process of approvals for investment by other countries has to be very quick. Decision making process has to be very quick.

When all of these steps are fulfilled and given the presence of huge pool of scientific and engineering talent with a low cost labour force to the investors, there is no reason why India should lack behind to other countries.[54]

3.8 India-U.S. Institutional Trade and Economic Cooperation Framework

India and the United States have established an institutional framework that would take the economic and trade relations forward. The Institutional framework for India-United States economic and trade cooperation is carried out at two levels- one is at the government-to-government, while the other is at the business-to-business level. They meet each other on regular basis and discuss on how to promote, strengthen and expand the level of economic, and trade relations that both countries enjoy.

The visit of the then U.S. President Mr. Bill Clinton to India in March 2000 was a turning point in the history of India-U.S. relations that it opened the way for institutionalization of the economic and trade relations between the two countries. This comes in view of the enormous economic potential for enhancement of economic and trade relations between the two in the knowledge Age. Decision has been taken during his visit to establish bilateral economic dialogue. It will be closely monitored through a high-level coordinating group. This group will be led on Indian side by Deputy Chairman Planning Commission with Ministry of External Affairs support and the U.S. side will be led by White house with the assistance of State Department. Since then it has been expanded to include many other forums to look out for other matters.

U.S.-India Financial and Economic Forum	U.S. - India Commercial Dialogue	U.S. - India Working Group on Trade
India's Finance Minister	India's Ministry of Commerce and Industry	Ministry of Commerce of India and other concerned Ministries/Departments
U.S. Secretary of Treasury	U.S. Secretary of Commerce	U.S. Trade representative

U.S.-India Financial and Economic Forum: It will host a forum for discussion on finance and investment issues, macroeconomic and international economic developments at regular basis. The Forum has annual Cabinet level meetings at Finance Minister/U.S. Treasury Secretary level and sub-cabinet level discussions. The fourth Cabinet level meeting was held on 30 October 2007 in New Delhi. Issues of mutual interest in areas such as Financial Services, Banking, Insurance, Pensions, Security & Corporate Bond Markets were discussed during the meeting.

U.S.-India Commercial Dialogue: It aimed at strengthening business ties between the business communities of the two countries by sorting out commercial issues. For this, the dialogue will be held at the government-to-government levels and private sector meetings on a regular basis that will be participated by cabinet agencies and ministries from both sides. The validity of this Commercial Dialogue has since been extended up to March 2010.

U.S.-India Working Group on Trade: Here the representative of the two sides will discuss to enhancing cooperation on trade policy. It will also look into the matter of trade issues underlying between the two sides with the participation of other agencies.

Besides, both sides decided to set up a consultative group on clean energy and environment and establish to set up a US-India Science and Technology forum. In a follow up to the above-mentioned forum, many others were formed later.

Trade Policy Forum: The India-U.S. Trade Policy Forum was set up in 2005. It meets at the Ministerial and Senior Official level. Private Sector Advisory Group (PSAG) has been created at the third ministerial meeting of the forum in June 2006, as an adjunct to the trade policy forum. It will provide strategic direction and input to the forum.

India-U.S. CEOs Forum: The India-U.S. CEOs forum formed in 2006 aimed at providing the two Governments with private sector inputs for invigorating the economic partnership. The India-U.S. CEOs forum has submitted its second set of recommendations in April 2008 to both the Governments. Both Governments have prepared a list of feasible items based on the recommendations, which are being acted upon. All of these dialogues would only deepen the economic interaction between the two world's largest democracies.[55]

3.9 India-U.S. People-to-People Ties

The people-to-people ties have a significant role to play in bringing the two countries closer. In recent years, the strength of the American of Indian origin has moved up nearly two million. With the increase of population, they have made significant presence in every occupation in the United States. They have left marks in every field whether it may be academicians, entrepreneurs, doctors, lawyers, engineers and financiers. Out of the 72.3 per cent of Indian Americans work force, 43.6 per cent are employed in managerial and professional specialties.

As compared to other community and the national per capita income of $14, 143.00, they possess the highest income ethnic group with per capita income of $17,777.00. The poverty rate of 9.7 per cent is also lower than the national average 13 per cent and the annual buying power is around $20 billion.

The strength of the Indian residing in the U.S. has reached a particular level that they would be able to influence the political decisions of the United States better than the past. Recently, they have played a significant role in the smooth passage of the civilian nuclear cooperation agreement between India and the United States. Despite of the opposition from various quarter on proliferation ground, their hard-fought lobbying helped cleared the way for the U.S. Congress to pass the deal with overwhelming victory. In the coming years Indian-American community has a huge task ahead in ensuring the Americans that, the relationship with India is different from those with others.[56]

3.10 Impediments to India-U.S. Stronger Trade and Economic Ties

The expanding economic and trade relations are not without its problems. Although it is clear that India after 1991 has provided a huge market for the U.S. goods and services, but the presence of certain aspects hampers the further progress of the economic and trade relations. They are:

a. India imposes high tariff rate, high surchages and taxes on a variety of imports. Major non tariff barriers include sanitary and phytosanitary restrictions, import licenses, regulations that mandate that only public sector entities can import certain products, discriminatory government procurement practices and the use of export subsidies. A variety of restrictions are placed on foreign services providers and on the level of permitted FDI in certain industries.

b. India continues to maintain a number of inefficient structural policies, which affects its trade including price controls for many essential commodities, extensive government regulations over many sectors of the economy and extensive public ownership of businesses, many of which are poorly run.

c. India's soft protection of Intellectual property rights (IPRs) especially for patents and copyrights has angered many U.S. government officials. Unless India provide a stringent protection of IPRs, it is not possible for it to develop internationally competitive information technology industries. According to international intellectual property alliance estimates, due to IPR piracy in India, United States firms lost an amount worth US $468.1 million during 2002.

d. The issue of outsourcing of the U.S. jobs to India has the potential to delay the free trade agreement between the two countries. Outsourcing of services or manufacturing jobs to India is a two-way trade that would benefit American economy. Any measures by the American side to restrict outsourcing of jobs would circumscribe the prospects of stronger trade and economic ties.[57]

Therefore, for better and unhindered economic ties between India and the United States, trade related issues have to be resolved first through a series of dialogue. The U.S. government officials are of the view that with such trade and investment barriers, stronger U.S.-India trade and economic ties is hard to come by. Deputy U.S. Trade representative Ambassador Jon Huntsman on February 2003, asserted that progress in transforming U.S.-India economic relationship has been slow due in part of India's grudging attitude towards imports that produces "multiple, onion like barriers" to potential exporters.[58]

3.11 Global Financial Crisis: Its Implications on Indian Economy and on India's Trade Relations with U.S.

Here I would like to highlight the implications of the ongoing Global financial crisis to the Indian economy and the subsequent changes that have taken place in India-U.S. trade after the global meltdown. Like all other emerging economies, India too had smelled the impact of this crisis on its economy. India's GDP has come down more than what was expected earlier, reflecting lower industrial production, negative imports, deceleration in services activities, dented corporate margins and diminished business confidence.[59] The impact of economic slowdown to Indian economy is very clear from the fact that the GDP growth has come down to 7.8 per cent during April-September 2008 from 9.3 per cent in the same period of 2007.[60]

The International monetary fund (IMF) has projected that unlike in the past five years, both India and China will witness a low GDP growth rate of 5.1 and 6.7 per cent respectively in the year 2009.[61] The impact of the global financial crisis can also be seen from receding India-U.S. trade relations. India's trade with the U.S. has registered a three-fold increase from $13.7 billion in 2001 to $41.4 billion in 2007, but suffered a serious setback due to the global slowdown with growth coming down from 30.5 per cent in 2007 to 7.4 per cent in 2008. While initial trend shows that global financial crisis has a major impact on India's exports to the U.S. than India's imports from the U.S. indicating some resonance in domestic demand.

The growth of Indian exports to the U.S. has slowed down from 10.1 per cent in 2007 to 8.4 per cent in 2008, while that of the Indian imports has dropped from 74.3 per-cent to 6.1 per cent. But the recent figures of the last two months of 2009 shows that Indian exports have come down by 23.2 per cent, while imports has declined by 18.9 per cent.[62] This is further strengthened by the fact that there is a decline in import and export of items between the two countries from the previous year. Exports of cut and polished diamond and jewellery have declined from $5.6 billion in 2008 to $4.6 billion in 2009. Textiles exports to the U.S. fell from $5.42 billion in 2008 to $4.86 billion the same year. Moreover, Iron & Steel products, Organic Chemicals and pharmaceutical products have also climb down.[63]

3.11.1 India's Economy after the Recent Financial Crisis

A different projection has been given by different economic institute on India's GDP in the year following the financial crisis. The International Monetary Fund (IMF) has estimated that the Indian economy will grow by 5.1 per cent in 2009-10, while the World Bank has projected to grow by 4 per cent. However the ADB had estimated that the country's GDP expansion rate at 5 per cent.

Nevertheless, India's Chief economic adviser Arvind Virmani has said that the growth rate of Indian economy would be higher than what the three institutes has projected. He is of the view that the growth rate would be between 5.5 per cent and 7.5 per cent depending on when the U.S. economy bottoms out. He linked India's growth rate to the recovery of the U.S. from the current financial crisis. He told the reporters that if in case the U.S. economy bottoms out by September then the Indian economy would grow in the range of 6.5 per cent to 7 per cent. Otherwise, it would grow in the range between 5.5 per cent and 6.5 per cent.[64]

3.12 Prospects for India's Further Economic Reform

The prospects for further economic reform in India is so bright that it would result in India's better trade relations with the international regime and the United States in particular. Many Indian and foreign economic analysts and experts have speculated that India under the able leadership of Prime Minister Mr. Manmohan Singh will come out with a broader reform. This speculation is a result of the recent historic victory of the Congress party and its close allies without the support of Left parties that had declined to assist after the recent India's civilian nuclear cooperation agreement with the United States.

In the past, the left parties posed a serious roadblock to introducing significant reforms. Foreign direct investment cap in multi-band retail sector will also be liberalised to 51 per cent in a step-by-step and calibrated manner. It was not possible in the past due to objection by the left parties on the ground that it would cause job losses. However, with left parties not in the picture, it is up to the present government how fast they introduce the reforms programs. Another area where we can see an easing of FDI cap will in defence. Last year Indian Defence Minister Mr. A.K. Anthony had indicated that FDI in defence sector would be relaxed to 49 per cent on a case by case basis. The UPA led government has a huge task ahead to in terms of introducing reforms and achieving the objective of sustaining healthy economic growth and further reducing poverty.[65] Indian Prime Minister Mr. Manmohan Singh after the significant victory of his party has clearly indicated the eagerness to introduce more reforms that was long overdue to improve the economy of the country. He further added that "we cannot afford to miss the bus now. We cannot afford to lag behind the rising economies of the East."[66] This statement is further strengthened by commitment of Pranab Mukherjee who replaced P. Chidambaram as the next finance Minister of India. He has made it very clear on what will be included on the agenda. Reforms can be seen in the areas of education, energy and last but not the least increase investment in the field of infrastructure to 9 per cent of the GDP.[67]

3. 13 Futuristic Areas of India-U.S. Economic Cooperation

With the growing economic and trade relations between India and the United States, it also becomes necessary for both countries to identify future areas of strategic economic cooperation. There are number of areas where they can have close cooperation for the mutual benefit. These include infrastructure, IT, Telecommunication sector, energy, knowledge industries such as pharmaceuticals and biotechnology and in the field of education and healthcare.

Closer cooperation in the field of infrastructure can yield mutual benefits to both the countries. The Government of India is seriously taking the issue in terms of reviewing its policies to create an investor friendly environment in sectors such as roads, ports and airports. Private sector participation in management, green-field airports, terminals and shipping berths and capacity augmentation has been initiated.[68] Presently, India needs over $475 billion for investment in the above-mentioned areas over the next five years to sustain high-growth rate. This creates a great opportunity for the U.S. private companies that would bring huge benefit to both countries.[69]

The IT sector is India's fastest growing sectors with over 50 percent average annual compounded growth since 1991. Today, nearly two in five of the Fortune 500 companies outsource their software requirements to India. Abundant investment opportunities exist for further strengthening India-U.S. ties in the IT sector, especially, in areas like communication infrastructure, optic fiber cable, gateways, satellite-based communication wireless, IT-enabled services, IT enabled education, data centers and server farms, and software development.

The energy sector offers for exploitation a vast untapped potential to investors in hydro electricity, oil & natural gas and coal. Although several U.S. companies have been looking at the Indian energy market closely, progress has so far been very limited. With the introduction of Central Electricity Act 2003, the government of India has now liberalized the power sector. Private sector participation is permitted in generation, distribution and transmission. Considering the vast present and projected demand supply gap, there is tremendous potential for economic cooperation between the two countries in this area.

Pharmaceuticals, biotechnology and chemical industries also offer huge scope for closer cooperation. India is one of the largest manufacturers and exporters of pharmaceuticals. Given India's expertise in genotype drug design and the presence of a large pool of trained doctors and cost effective research & development (R&D) activities, it becomes imperative for India and the United States to think over it.[70] The huge prospect for cooperation between the two sides is indicated by increasing exports of Pharmaceutical products to the United States. India exports of such products to the United States grew from $896 million in 2007 to $1480 million in 2008.[71] These areas of cooperation will have a huge bearing on the growth of economic cooperation.

Educational cooperation is another very important area for cooperation between the two countries given the increase in the number of students enrolled in United States for higher education and vice-versa. For the last eight years, India has maintained its position as number one in terms of number of students enrolled in University and colleges of the U.S. This time India created the history by crossing 100,000 marks for the first time. This is a sharp increase from 94, 563 students enrolled in 2007-08, reflecting an increase of 9.2 percent. At the same time, the number of students from America has risen from 2627 in 2006-07 to 3146 in 2007-08.[72] Both sides should look forward to strengthening the educational exchange programme.

Healthcare is another area that can offers huge scope for cooperation. Both sides by cooperating in this area will bring huge benefit. In India, the market for healthcare was $38 billion in 2007, expecting to reach $79 billion by 2012 with a growth rate of 15 per cent per annum. What they need to do is extending healthcare services, building healthcare infrastructure and developing its related technologies.[73]

3.14 Conclusion

Overall India-U.S. trade and economic relations since the cold war end has registered a significant upward trajectory despite of long pending issues of nuclear proliferation, Kashmir problem, human rights and a trade related problems. This sends a very clear message that both sides are serious about the opportunity of developing closer, long-term commercial ties that would be mutually beneficial. Economic and trade relations and investment cooperation has a huge scope for improvement. However, the strong political commitment and bold policy initiatives are very much required to bring the present level of trade and economic relations commensurate with the existing potential. Adequate effort has to be made by both countries to harness this potential to their mutual advantage.

The post-cold war India-U.S. economic relations have witnessed continuous and imbalance trade relations that is in favor of India. However, the dramatic improvement that has been reached so far is nowhere near their perceived potential. Had there been no trade and economic issues such as intellectual property rights, lack of quick decision making process, dual-use technology trade and investment issues, the performance of the economic, trade and investment relations would have been much better today.

India and the United States have a long distance to be covered. This is reflected from the fact that even after more than one decade of bilateral economic relations, India's ranking in terms of list of countries exporting to the United States is very low. India contributes less than 20 per cent of the U.S. imports, while the U.S exports account for nearly 12 per cent of India's import of non-oil products. In addition, the bilateral trade between the two countries is less than 1 per cent of global trade. At last, one can also conclude that there are huge scopes for improvement in the trade relations between the two world's largest democracies.[74] To exploit huge untapped potential, both sides will need to have stronger collaboration and coordination which will help to deepen India-U.S. economic engagement. The partnership will gain strategic significance in the long run as it will stimulate innovation, spur job creation and promote sustainable and inclusive growth in both countries.

Today, as experienced never before, American companies are involved in a broad spectrum of economic activities ranging from industrial machinery to consumer goods, and from information technology to consultancy services. If the Bilateral investment treaty which both India and the United States are working closely together gets materializes then one can expect more investment from the U.S. to India and vice versa. Because it would provides legal protection against arbitrary and discriminatory government actions.[75]

For much better economic and trade relations, it is highly recommendable that both sides engage in economic dialogue that is aim at resolving the persisting trade and economic issues at the earliest so as to make sure that these issues does not come on the way to future progress and development. Unless these issues are not resolved, satisfactory progress is not likely to come soon.

Endnotes

[1] Jisnudatta Misra, "Growing Economic Factor in Indo-US Relations", in Vinay Kumar Malhotra and K.S. Purushothaman, India and the USA-Economic Relations and Literature (New Delhi: Anmol Publications Pvt. Ltd., 1998), pp. 90-91.

[2] R.N. Ghosh and M.A.B. Siddique, "A view of Indo-Australian Economic Relations: Trade, Investment and Aid", The Atlantic Journal of World Affairs (New Delhi), vol. 1(1), October-December 2005, p. 54.

[3] R.K. Wadhwa, "Globalisation of Economy and India", in V.D. Chopra (ed.), India's Foreign Policy in the 21st Century (New Delhi: Kalpaz Publications, 2006), pp. 308-10.

[4] Baldev Raj Nayar and T.V. Paul, India in the World Order: Searching For Major-Power Status (New-Delhi: Cambridge University Press, 2004), pp. 9-10.

[5] Ibid., p. 44.

[6] See, "Standards and Conformance Cooperation Programme on 1st Indo-US Summit on Standards in Trade", Background Paper Prepared in collaboration between Ministry of Commerce & Industry Government of India, Confederation of Indian Industry, American National Standards Institute and US Trade and Development Agency, 16 February 2010, New Delhi, p. 1, available at <http:/www.standardsportal.org.in/Pdf/US-Indiatrade_paper.pdf>.

[7] B.K. Shrivastava, "India's Relations with the US: Vision of a Global Partnership", in V.D. Chopra (ed.), India's Foreign Policy in the 21st Century (New Delhi: Kalpaz Publications, 2006), pp. 98-99.

[8] Vivek Chadha, Indo-US Relations: Divergence to Convergence (New Delhi: Macmillan India Ltd., 2008), pp. 130-31.

[9] Ibid., pp. 166-67.

[10] Manoj Pant in K.P. Vijayalakshmi, et. al., (eds.), Report on the National Workshop on Changing Contours of Indo-US Relations (Ban-

galore: International Strategic and Security Studies Programme and National Institute of Advanced Studies, 2006), pp. 62-63.

[11] Wayne Morrison and Alan Kronstadt, "India-U.S. Economic Relations", CRS Report for Congress, Code RS21502, Updated 25 February 2004, pp. 1-3, available at <http://fpc.state.gov/documents/organization/30233.pdf>.

[12] Manjeet S. Pardesai and Sumit Ganguly, "India and Energy Security: A Foreign Policy Priority", in Harsh V. Pant (ed.), Indian Foreign Policy in a Unipolar World (New Delhi: Routledge, 2009), p. 98.

[13] Devin T. Hagerty, "India and the Global Balance of Power: A Neorealist Snapshot", in Harsh V. Pant (ed.), Indian Foreign Policy in a Unipolar World (New Delhi: Routledge, 2009), p. 35.

[14] Wayne Morrison and Alan Kronstadt, n. 11, pp. 1-3.

[15] Chintamani Mahapatra, "India and the US: Evolving Economic Ties", Strategic Analysis (New- Delhi), vol. XXI(12), March 1998, pp. 1756-760.

[16] Rashmi Jain (ed.), The United States and India, 1947-2006: A Documentary Study (New Delhi: Radiant Publishers, 2007), pp. 224-25.

[17] Ibid., p. 216.

[18] Ibid., pp. 226-27.

[19] Ibid., pp. 222-23.

[20] Ibid., pp. 229-30.

[21] Colin L. Powell, "New Heights in Indo-U.S. Relations: U.S. Presidential Election, 2004", in P.K. Das, New Heights in Indo-U.S. Relations (Jaipur: Raj Publishing House, 2005), pp. 121-22, 126.

[22] Ibid., pp. 129-133.

[23] Rashmi Jain, n. 16, pp. 252-54.

[24] Ibid., p. 263.

[25] Ibid., p. 269.

[26] Jayanta Roy and Pritam Banerjee, "India and United States: Economic Analysis and Trade Strategy", Confederation of Indian Industry, July 2004, available at <http://cii.in/documents/Trade_Globlizations?India-USEconomicAnalysisandTradeStrategy.pdf>. <http://www.fas.org/sgp/crs/row/RL34161.pdf>.

28 Prem P. Gandhi, "India-U.S. Economic Relations: A Perspective", in Ashok Kapur, Y.K. Malik, et. al., (eds.), India and United States in a Changing World (New Delhi: Sage Publications, 2002), p. 332.

29 Pranay Kumar, "Indo-US trade: Bilateral Trade Target Needs to be Raised by 50 %", available at <http://www.cygnusindia.com/Indo-US%20Trade.pdf>.

30 R.N. Ghosh and M.A.B. Siddique, n. 2, p. 64.

31 See, "India-US trade", available at <http://indianembassy.org/newsite/indoustrade1.asp>.

32 Jayanta Roy and Pritam Banerjee, n. 26.

33 See, "India-USA Economic Relations: the Next Decade", Confederation of Indian Industry, June 2009, p. 12, available at <http://www.corecentre.co.in/Database/Docs/DocFiles/indiausa_economic.pdf>.

34 Prem P. Gandhi, n. 28, pp. 339-341.

35 R.N. Ghosh and M.A.B. Siddique, n. 2, pp. 70-73.

36 Badar Alam Iqbal, Indo-U.S. Economic Relations: Then and Now (Hyderabad: Icfai University Press, 2005), pp. 4-5.

37 Rashmi Jain (ed.), n. 16, pp. 217-19, 221.

38 Ibid., pp. 234-35.

39 See, "Standards and Conformance Cooperation Programme on 1st Indo-US Summit on Standards in Trade", n. 6, p. 4.

40 See Table 3.5 (Share of US FDI in Total-Actual Inflow). Also, refer to India-U.S. Economic Relations, available at <http://indianembassy.org/newsite/economyrelations.asp>.

41 See, "India-U.S. Economic Relations", available at <http://www.indianembassy.org/Economy/economy.htm>.

42 See, "Overseas Investment Policy", available at <http://www.finmin.nic.in/the_ministry/dept_eco_affairs/icsection/Overseas_investment_Policy.htm>.

43 See, "Standards and Conformance Cooperation Programme on 1st Indo-US Summit on Standards in Trade", n. 6, p. 6.

44 See, "Overseas Investment Approvals", available at <http://www.finmin.nic.in/the_ministry/dept_eco_affairs/icsection/Investment_Approvals.htm>.

[45] David C. Mulford Remarks to the 4th Indo-U.S. Economic Summit "Building Strong Partnerships" 18 September 2007, available at <http://newdelhi.usembassy.gov/pr91907.html>., and also refer to R K Chopra, "Indo-US Economic Relations", Paper Presented in a seminar on Indo-US Relations: The Changing Perspective at Yashwantrao Chavan Academy of Development Administration, Organised by Centre for Advanced Strategic Studies, Pune, 22nd October 2008, p. 44.

[46] See, "India - U.S. Economic Relations", available at <http://indianembassy.org/newsite/economyrelations.asp>.

[47] R.N. Ghosh and M.A.B. Siddique, n. 2, pp. 73-74.

[48] Weng Dehua, "Economic Reforms, Opening-Up and Attraction of FDI-India: Can it Be a Benchmark for China?", The Atlantic Journal of World Affairs (New Delhi), vol. 1(1), October-December 2005, p. 131.

[49] Baldev Raj Nayar and T.V. Paul, n. 4, pp. 99-100.

[50] See, "FDI Growth Up 85 % in 2008, Amid 15 % Global Decline", Financial Express (Pune), 22 May 2009.[51] See, "FDI Flow to India Will Remain Robust: Goldman Sachs", available at <http://www.indianembassy.org/India_Review/2009/May%202009.pdf>.

[52] Remarks of Carlos M. Gutierrez, Secretary of Commerce, to the U.S.-India Business Council Washington, DC, available at <http://www.iaccindia.com/speech_carlos_m_gutierrez.htm>.

[53] Rudra Prakash Pradhan, "Determinants of Foreign Direct Investment in India: A Post-Reforms Scenario", in Falendra K. Sudan (ed.), Globalisation and Liberalization: Nature and Consequences (New Delhi: Serials Publications, 2005), pp. 180-85.

[54] Ibid., p. 197.

[55] See, "India-US Economic Partnership", available at <http://indianembassy.org/newsite/press_release/2008/Sep/23.asp>. Also, refer to India-U.S. relations: A vision for the 21st century, New Delhi, 21 March 2000, available at <http://www.indianembassy.org/indusrel/clinton_india/joint_indua_us_statement_mar_21_2000.htm>.

56 Ashok Sharma, "Growing Influence of Indian American Lobbying on Indo-US Relations", World Focus (New Delhi), vol. XXIX(7), July 2008, pp. 262-63.

57 Gautam Adhikari, "U.S.-India Relations: Reports on AEI's Roundtable Discussions", American Enterprise Institute for Public Policy Research (AEI) Working Paper #112, 22 June 2005, p. 12, available at <http://www.aei.org/docLib/20050622_Indiareport.6.22.05.pdf>.

58 Wayne Morrisson and Alan Kronstadt, n. 11, pp. 4-5.

59 See, "Statement of the Annual Policy of the Reserve Bank of India", Financial Express (Pune), 22 April 2009.

60 Rajiv Kumar, et. al., "Indian Economic Outlook 2008-09 and 2009-10", Indian Council for Research on International Economic Relations (ICRIER) Working Paper no. 234, March 2009, p. 7, available at <http://www.icrier.org/pdf/WorkingPaper234.pdf>.

61 Ibid., p. 3.

62 P. Raghavan, "Changing Trends in Indo-US Trade", Financial Express (Pune), 22 April 2009.

63 See, "India-U.S. Trade", available at <http://indianembassy.org/newsite/indoustrade1.asp>.

64 See Financial Express (Punc), 22 April 2009.

65 See, Financial Express (Pune), 17 May 2009.

66 See, "Cannot Afford to Miss the Bus" Financial Express, Pune, 20 May 2009.

67 See, "Pranab Meets Top Officials, to Focus on 11 Growth Areas", Financial Express (Pune), 25 May 2009.

68 "India-U.S. Economic Relations", available at <http://www.indianembassy.org/Economy/economy.htm>.

69 See, "India-USA Economic Relations: The Next Decade", n. 33, p. 27, available at <http://www.corecentre.co.in/Database/Docs/DocFiles/indiausa_economic.pdf>.

70 "India-U.S. Economic Relations", available at <http://www.indianembassy.org/Economy/economy.htm>.

71 "India-U.S. Trade", available at <http://indianembassy.org/newsite/indoustrade1.asp>.

[72] See, "Indian Students in US Cross 100,000 mark", Times of India (Pune), 18 November 2009.

[73] See, "India-USA Economic Relations: The Next Decade", n. 33, p. 27, available at <http://www.corecentre.co.in/Database/Docs/DocFiles/indiausa_economic.pdf>.

[74] Prem P. Gandhi, n. 28, p. 333.

[75] See, "Standards and Conformance Cooperation Programme on 1st Indo-US Summit on Standards in Trade", n. 6, p. 12, available at < http://www.standardsportal.org.in/Pdf/US-Indiatrade_paper.pdf>.

INDIA-UNITED STATES RELATIONS: PAKISTAN AS A FACTOR

4.1 Introduction

Pakistan has been and continues to be the one of the major point of differences between the two world's largest and world's oldest democracies, India and the United States respectively. The disintegration of the Soviet Union resulted in the end of cold war no doubt created the climate suitable for the U.S. Administration to initiate an independent strategy towards India and Pakistan. Otherwise, the United States policy toward South Asia in the past almost five decades has been that of zero-sum game that neither serves the U.S. interest nor South Asian interest. An independent strategy toward both of India and Pakistan would better serve the interest of both sides. However, it was the former U.S. President Mr. Bill Clinton and his Administration obsession with the nuclear nonproliferation issue in South Asia that did not allow for the start of non-zero sum game policy toward India and Pakistan. This way Pakistan was the major beneficiary of the U.S. approach in the initial years after the end of cold war.[1] The chapter argues that the trajectory shift in the relationship between India and the United States should not be construed as the end of Pakistan factor. The United States would love to enjoy close relations with both South Asian rivals and not repeat the mistake committed in the past- engaging one at the cost of other.

If today the United States has declared that a 'strong and vibrant India will be most effective' partner in advancing the shared objective of promoting peace and stability in Asia, combating the menace of terrorism, preventing the proliferation of weapons of mass destruction and protecting the sea lanes of communication then it does not mean Pakistan has lost its relevance in the minds of American. Even after the disintegration of the Soviet Union, Pakistan continues to be strategically important in the changing international strategic and security environment. This is not a welcome development for India not because Pakistan is an enemy for India but because it would put a hindrance to a growing strategic relationship between India and the United States. Pakistan is never happy with the growing defence and security ties between the two world's largest democracies. Like China, Pakistan does not want to see India become a regional power assuming that it would foil its dream of occupying Kashmir which they claim to be their territory.

Although understanding between India and the United States on the need to transform the relationship to a broader level has improved, but Pakistan was successful in convincing its long time ally not to supply advance weapons and technology to India. Because of which, high technology transfer to India during the period of nineties and beginning part of the twenty-first century was limited.[2] On the other hand, Pakistan continues to receive military, political and economic support from United States that had brought serious security concern to India thereby undermining Asian security. The U.S. military assistance to Pakistan boosts up the morale of the latter in terms of challenging India.

India and the United States still have divergence over the aggressive attitude of Pakistan and its stand on the Kashmir dispute. India is not happy with the U.S. policy toward Pakistan that had prevented India from having deeper engagements with the United States. The U.S. has even supported Pakistan stance on Kashmir. It has even supported Pakistan in acquiring nuclear weapons capability that has not only aggravated Asian security. The U.S. support to Pakistan comes at the cost of Indian security. It is only recently, the U.S. shifted its policy from hyphenating to de-hyphenating. The present U.S. policy provides the options of having closer relations with a country of its interests. This is very well manifested after the turn of the twenty first century where the U.S. close ties with Pakistan did not come at the cost of the transforming relations between India and the United States. The relationship between the United States, India and Pakistan is no more zero-sum game. Today, the United States can enjoy closer relations with both South Asian countries based on their respective interests. However, still there are few areas where India needs to work out with the United States regarding Pakistan so that it does not circumscribe the prospects of future relationships.[3] How deep and breadth the relationship India enjoy with the United States in the coming decades, India cannot expect the United States to completely ignore Pakistan, its long time partner and will continue to be an important partner for other purposes where the U.S. has a huge stake including fight against terrorism, external influence, etc. The United States still believes that Pakistan has a lot to offer in the changing world scenario. This chapter will seek to study shift in the U.S. approach toward South Asia after the end of cold war. It also examines Pakistan's response to the growing relationship between India and the United States. Also it highlights the implications of the continuing U.S.-Pak relations to India. Lastly, but not the least, any shift in the

U.S. approach toward India-Pak disputes. Within this, the chapter will try to answer for these critical questions. Does the transforming relation between India and the U.S. mean an end to Pakistan factor? What are the main points of divergences between India and the United States over the Pakistan issue?

4.2 United States, India and Pakistan-Washed Away the Prospect for Improvement

The post-cold war period witnessed a significant shift in the United States policy toward South Asia. The strategic shift in the U.S. policy toward South Asia was a result of certain factors. First, the withdrawal of the Soviet forces from Afghanistan and disappearance of the Soviet Union resulted to the end of more than four decades of cold war rivalry. This is followed by the loosing relevance of Pakistan that is specially meant for containing communism and the deterioration of U.S.-Pakistan relations. Thirdly, the former U.S. President Mr. George H. W. Bush unwillingness to certify that Pakistan did not possess nuclear weapons. These factors no doubt brought some hope in the Indian strategic analysts about the prospects of India-U.S. relations that remained handicapped due to cold-war bipolar structure.

When Pakistan failed to met the satisfaction of the United States over the nuclear issue, Pressler Amendment was imposed upon Islamabad. Pakistan was annoyed by this move because it was not expecting the U.S., its cold war strategic partner, to take such step that works against its interest. With this, all forms of military assistance to Pakistan came to a halt, thereby resulting to a huge setback in U.S.-Pakistan relations. Pakistan criticised the United States for this loss saying that it was a result of its exhausted utility to America. But from the Indian point of view, it was a welcome development and that is what India was expecting from the United States.

However, despite of all these developments, the U.S. commitment to improve the relations with India after the cold war end could not take place freely due to the former obsession with India's nuclear weapons programme, human rights issues and the Kashmir dispute. This is further worsened by the double standard treatment meted to India. United States on the one hand prohibited the transfer of cryogenic rocket engine to India; while on the other hand, it was eager to start supplying certain types of commercial sales to Pakistan. The one time waiver of the Pressler amendment under the Brown amendment in 1996 dashed India's hopes for an end to Pakistan factor. As the amendment clears the way for further supply of military weapons and equipment to Pakistan. India again was not happy because it came at the time when the relationship between the two world's largest democracies is slowly gaining its confidence toward a purposeful one. How would not India remain unhappy by this unnecessary development when it would only burden India's security concerns? This is something what India was not expecting from the United States. It only sends a wrong message to India about the United States that the latter is not seriously concerned about India's security problems arising from Pakistan. For the sake of Pakistan, the United States was not cared about India's security.[4] Thus, the Bill Clinton Administration was not able to break past from its traditional the U.S. policy toward South Asia that has nothing to do with the present the U.S. interests.

4.2.1 What Makes Pakistan so Important For United States?

The strategic importance of Pakistan to the United States can be seen in the light of the latter interests and concerns in the former. The evolving U.S. interests and concerns after the cold war end and in particular after the turn of the twenty first century include combating and dismantling al-Qaeda and

Taliban in Afghanistan and also those terrorist organisations residing in safe heaven in Pakistan territory, preventing nuclear proliferation, democratisation of Pakistan and relations with the Islamic world. This was very clearly announced by former U.S. President Mr. George W. Bush in a Camp David summit held on June 2003.[5]

Unlike during the cold war period, the level of Pakistan's importance in the eyes of American has come down after the end of cold war. This does not mean the relevance of Pakistan to major powers has gone. Even after the end of cold war, Pakistan still continue to remain important for global powers including the United States, China and others due to its geo-strategic and geopolitical locations. Pakistan is located in crucial position which is surrounded by India in the east, China, Afghanistan and Oil and Gas rich Central Asia in the north and north-west and Iran and Persian Gulf to its west. The location of Pakistan would make it quite a difficult job for the United States to totally ignore it.

It is located at a very strategically important place that is the key to reaching other strategically important place. For the United States, if it want to reach these strategically resource rich countries, then it is possible through Pakistan. Secondly, Pakistan is strategically important because of its close proximity to Afghanistan, which has been one of the safest heavens for terrorism. Terrorism is increasingly becoming one of the serious challenges to peace and security of the international community in the twenty-first century. To achieve the objective of eradicating the problems of terrorism, the U.S. would have to take the help of Pakistan. Pakistan is ready to help out achieving this objective by allowing its territory to be used as bases for operation. And since the war against terrorism is not likely to end very soon, Pakistan will continue to be strategically important. Pakistan will continue to occupy an important place in the strategic perception of the U.S. Therefore, global geopolitical considerations of combating terrorism and other challenges will continue to be the driving factor for the U.S. closer security ties with Pakistan.[6]

Another factor as to why the U.S. would like to keep itself engaged with Pakistan is achieving its objective of a stable security in South Asia. Former U.S. Assistant Secretary of State for South Asian affairs, Mr. Karl Inderfurth in his speech before the U.S.-India council on 19 October 1999 has said that, "the US was not walking away from Pakistan because of a stable, democratic and prosperous Pakistan is in the interests of India and United States." This reflects the raising violence in Pakistan due to lack of good governance. Pakistan is facing a huge security problems arising from the increasing terrorist violence. At this juncture, if Pakistan is left alone then there is a possibility of Pakistan becoming a failed state. In another lecture he said that 'Pakistan has a potential to be a prosperous Islamic democrary and its serving as a gateway to Central Asia'. This was followed by what Chairman of the House of representative's International relations subcommittee on Asia and pacific, Mr. Doug Bereuter has said that by isolating Pakistan, Washington would be "effectively no longer seek to influence the course of events in Pakistan." All of these statements reflect the need for the United States to keep on engaging with Pakistan for the long-term perspective.[7]

Recently, the U.S. Administration has committed to get back the troops out of Afghanistan in the summer of 2011. Whether the U.S. Administration is able to achieve it in time or not is another question, but this commitment reflects the significant role that Pakistan will be playing in the months to come. The U.S. will have to be relying on Pakistan to achieving this objective.[8]

4.3 U.S. Support of India During the Kargil Conflict

Unlike in the past events, United States for the first time has come out in support of India during the Kargil conflict of 1999. This was a welcome development for India because this reflected an indication of a significant shift in the U.S. stand toward India and Pakistan. It seems that the United States has decided not to turn a blind eye towards Pakistan. The reason behind this prompt decision was that the relationship between India and the United States was growing and any wrong move would bring a heavy blow to the much needed relations.

In May 1999, both Pakistan regular and irregular forces deceived the Indian government by intruding illegally into the Indian side of the Line of Control (LOC) in a bid to gain the territory that has for long been claiming to be their own territory. Another reason was to attract international attention into the Kashmir dispute. Also, if successful would cut off the Ladakh area and Siachen region through interdiction of India's communications jugular in this remote region. More importantly, Pakistan was expecting support from its close patron United States.[9] India demanded complete withdrawal of the Pakistan forces from its territory. American feared that a conventionally weaker Pakistan may opt for nuclear forces that would bring highly disastrous implications to the security in the region. In its support to India, the then U.S. President Mr. Bill Clinton sent Commander in Chief of the Central Command, General Anthony Zinni and Mr. Gibson Lanpher, Deputy Assistant Secretary of State to Islamabad to pressurize former Pakistan President Mr. Nawaz Sharif and Army Chief Pervez Musharraf to withdraw its troops from the Indian side of the LOC. The U.S. had to intervene the matter because it perceives the possibility of escalating the conflict into a nuclear war between the two South Asian rivals. Under pressure, former Pakistan Prime Minister Mr. Nawaz Sharif had to finally withdraw its troops without achieving any objective of concessions from India over Kashmir.[10] The U.S. General Kinning in his address before the Sharif had stated that, 'if you don't pull back, you are going to bring war and nuclear annihilation down on your country'.[11]

What really helped the U.S. to turn in India's favour was due to the fact that despite domestic pressure for the war against Pakistan, India maintain restraint and did not cross the line of control which Pakistan was expecting India to commit such mistake. Washington acknowledged India for successfully handling the issue and not allowing the conflict to escalate into nuclear one. This saw shift in the U.S. perception that India is a responsible power and a stabilizing force in Asia.

What really matter for India is the shift in the U.S. policy towards South Asia? In one of his speech on 21 July, Mr. Daley said that, "In the past there have been attempts to impose intellectual constructs such as balance or even handedness on American foreign policy towards India and Pakistan. These days are over…America's relations with India and Pakistan are going to have their own separate vectors, trajectories and velocities."[12]

The kargil events of 1999 provided a clear evidence of what India has been claiming for the last many years about Pakistan sponsoring terrorism. This has no doubt brought in some understanding between India and the United States over the security concerns facing the former. The aggressive Pakistan attitude has led many U.S. legislators to calls for more pressurising the former to stop such illegal activities. These legislators include Mr. Gejdenson and Mr. Robert Wenler, has called for Congressional hearing on Pakistan's support for terrorist groups in Kashmir. However another legislator Pallone went a step ahead to urge for introducing legislation and even demanded the U.S. State Department to officially designate Pakistan as a state sponsor of terrorism. This way the result of the events of 1999 goes against what Pakistan was expecting.[13]

4.4 A Paradigm Shift in the U.S. Response Toward India and Pakistan

There witnessed a paradigmatic shift in the U.S. approach toward the two South Asian powers just before the end of the twentieth century and by the turn of the twenty-first century. Unlike in the cold war period where close relations with Pakistan come at the expense of India, the turn of the twenty-first century and in particular after the horrific events of 9/11, the United States was determined not to repeat the same mistake and instead would like to have deeper engagement with both sides. Such a shift in the U.S. approach is fuelled by the need to manage and achieve regional stability by ensuring that nuclear clash between the two South Asian does not happen. Since then there witnessed the U.S. greater interests in the region.

What played a part in helping to bring about a shift in the U.S. stand toward India and Pakistan? Two factors were the crucial to this shifts-one is that by the turn of twenty-first century, India was viewed by Washington as a growing economic and military power that has significant role to play and secondly, Pakistan despite of being its long-time close ally was perceived to be no where near India and is facing a problem of political and economic instability. There is also a possibility of it becoming a failed state. This is only aided by India's unconditional support to the U.S. national missile defence initiative in May 2001. All of these factors have led the U.S. to finally decide that Pakistan factor will not be permitted to circumscribe the long-anticipated India-U.S relations. And any India-Pakistan bilateral issue shall not be allowed to prevent the relationship from transforming.

Mr. Colin Powell, former U.S. Secretary of State, has stated in his testimony before the Senate Foreign Relations Committee in early 2001 that, "India soon to become the most populous country in the world has the potential to help keep the peace in the vast Indian Ocean area and its periphery. We need to work harder and more consistently to assist India in this endeavor, while not neglecting our friend in Pakistan."[14] How the U.S. managed to have balance relations with both India and Pakistan can be smelled from the following sub-sections.

4.4.1 New Phase in U.S.-Pakistan Relations After September 11

Before the events of September 11, Pakistan was undergoing an economic crisis due in part to the huge military spending that was aimed at India and also the Kargil conflicts with India. Pakistan was desperately looking for the U.S. support to bring its economic structure back in track. The events of September 11 brought some relief to Pakistan when it was declared by United States as a 'frontline state in achieving the objective of defeating Al-Qaeda and Taliban. The U.S. need for logistic facilities and intelligence information about the Al-Qaeda and Pakistan need for constant U.S. support coalesced to transforming the relationship between Pakistan and the United States. Pakistan due to its close proximity to Afghanistan offered the United States with two naval bases, three air force bases and its airspace. Moreover, it deployed more than 70,000 troops to the Afghan border and even launched more than 38 major successful operations to flush out foreign terrorists. The U.S. officials acknowledge Pakistan support in the fight against terrorism.[15] Pakistan support to the United States entails both opportunity and challenges. The opportunity is that of regaining the lost relationship. With this, the U.S. would be supplying arms and equipment assistance to Pakistan that has been stopped after the nuclear tests. While the challenge before Pakistan is that they have to cooperate with the U.S. forces in the fight against al-Qaeda and Taliban based in Afghanistan with whom it had a close traditional ties. For the sake of regaining the lost relationship with the U.S., Pakistan reluctantly will have to sacrifice ties with Taliban. However, the main rationale behind why Islamabad took such a huge step was to ensure that the United States is with them in dealing with India on Kashmir and other related issues. And also to ensure that it have a hold in Afghanistan by establishing a friendly regime in Afghanistan.[16]

Pakistan and United States signed 'defence cooperation agreement' in 2002 under which, Pakistan had allowed the U.S. to make use of its military equipment for training and other military exercises. The agreement was a turning point in that military and security relationship between the two countries started improving. In September 2003 alone, U.S. authorized Pakistan for the supply of the U.S. air traffic control radars to enhance surveillance capability worth $110 million. This was followed by the designation of Pakistan as a "major non-NATO ally" in March 2004. It has also given special status to Pakistan for supplying Pakistan with defence equipment, spare parts and also providing training to its forces. In April 2003, former U.S. President George W. Bush allocated Pakistan with $200 million as a security related assistance. The same year Washington also announced a five-year $3 billion aid package for Pakistan which commenced in 2005. According to former U.S. Secretary of State, Mr. Colin Powell, "the U.S. assistance package to Pakistan constitutes one of the 'largest U.S. assistance programmes' in the world."[17] As a result of which, since 2001 Pakistan enjoyed being the largest recipient of the U.S. security assistance including arms transfer. In the year 2006, Pakistan emerged as the biggest arms recipient from United States.

According to the U.S. Defence Department estimates, Pakistan under the regime of Mr. Pervez Musharraf has received nearly $1 billion in Foreign Military Financing and signed government-to-government agreement in the U.S. weapons worth $4.34 billion. And according to a Congressional Research Service report prepared by Richard Grimmet entitled *"US arms sale to Pakistan"* in 2006, among the developing countries, Pakistan emerged on top as the major recipient of arms from the U.S.[18] Also the U.S. Congress passed an act in December 2004 whereby it assured continued assistance to Pakistan after the termination of the five year package in 2009.

Pakistan was also able to enter into a defence deals with the United States under which there will long list of supply of arms and equipment to the former. Pakistan will purchase 44 F-16 fighter planes, eight P-3C Orion marine surveillance aircraft equipped with anti-submarine missiles and Harpoon antiship missiles. It has also decided to buy 700 air-to-air missiles. The delivery of the missiles will start in 2008. This way during the period between 2002 and 2006, the U.S. military sales to Pakistan amounted to $823 million. Despite of the lack of Pakistan sincerity in the fights against terrorism and not able to fulfill its demands, the United States continue to provide arms and equipment that has nothing to do with the actual purpose.[19] On 29 July 2008, the U.S. completed the delivery of 14 F-16 aircraft under the scheme of Excess Defence Article Programme. Also, the U.S. authorized the delivery of 20 refurbished T-37 training aircraft to Pakistan in August 2008. These are followed by the Washington commitment for the supply of AH-1F Cobra attack helicopters.[20] Hence, overall, since 2001, Pakistan has received US $7 billion under the U.S. Foreign military financing and coalition support funds programmes.[21]

How eagerly Pakistan was waiting for such opportunity is reflected in the fact that on 13 February 2002, former Pakistan

President Pervez Musharraf has stated that, "let me say that Pakistan and the United States have enjoyed very close military relations, military ties which go to the strategic level of cooperation in the past. And it is my pleasure to revive the same degree of relationship again with the United States." This was further supported by former U.S. Secretary of State, Ms. Condoleezza Rice statement that, "Pakistan has become a vital ally with the United States in the war on terror....at one time in our history we did not maintain and continue deep relations with Pakistan after having shared strategic interests during the cold war....the United States will be a friend for life."[22]

Given the kind of arms supply and assistance relationship that Pakistan enjoy with Pakistan, there should not be any doubt why India is seriously concerned about it. Many years back as Indian Air Marshal K. D. Chadha, former Chief of Air force has said "Pakistan's affiliation with the United States aroused "ambitions and delusions of grandeur" in Pakistan's power elite. Military officers exposed to American training and doctrines "began to see themselves as invincible superior beings. They held the Indian military forces... in derisive contempt. Arrogant, flamboyant and impregnated with American doctrinal proclivities, they were more than convinced that militarily India was a push-over."[23] This is followed by what former India's Defence Minister Mr. Pranab Mukherjee has said on 12 December 2004, in reaction to the 9/11 commission report that calls for supply of arms and equipment to Pakistan that the supply of sophisticated weapons such as F-16 aircraft, lethal missile arrangements and naval surveillance reconnaissance aircraft to Pakistan by the U.S. would jeopardize the peace process between the two countries. Defence Minister argument is based on the fact that these weapons are meant for big wars and not to fight terrorism.[24] From this view, we can only conclude that American assistance to Pakistan has only provided energy and power to deal with India. How Pakistan has suc-

Table 4.1: Pakistan's Major Arms Acquisitions From U.S. (1990-2005).

Sl. No.	Years of Delivery	Weapons Designation	Weapons Description	No. Ordered/ Delivered
1	1996-97	P-3C(update 2.75)	Orion maritime reconnaissance and strike aircraft	3
2	1996-97	Harpoon	Anti-Ship missiles for the P-3C Orions	28
3	1996-97	AIM-9L	AA Missiles	498
4	1996-97	M- I98	155 mm towed guns	24
5	1997	Bell- 209/ AH- IS	Helicopters	10
6	2000-01	Technology transfer for the assembly of M-113 A2	APCs	30
7	2003-04	S-70/UH-60	Helicopter Black Hawk	6
8	2003	T- 37 B*	Aircraft	19
9	2004	Mk- 15 Phalanx	CIWS	6
10	2004	BGM- 71 TOW	Anti-tank missiles	2,014
11	2004	Bell- 412 EP	Helicopters	26
12	2004	C- 130 E Hercules*	Transport aircraft	6
13	2004	Bell-205/ UH-1 H	Helicopters	26
14	2004	Bell-209/ AH-1F*	Combat Helicopter	40
15	2004	BGM- 71 TOW	Anti Tank missiles	2, 014
16	2004-05	P- 3C*	MP and Strike aircraft	8
17	2005	F- 16 A*	Multi-role combat aircraft	2
18	2005	AGM- 84 L/ RGM-84L	Air-Surface launched missiles	60/50
19	2005	C-130E Hercules	Transport aircraft Ex- RAAF	7
20	2005	SA-316 B Alovette-3	Light helicopter (second hand)	2
21	2005	AN/TPS-77	Air Surveillance radars	6

* US Excess Defence Articles which are normally transferred at a price less than 10 per cent of the original. For example the cost of each F-16 is a little over $ 6 million.

Source: Jasjit Singh, "Trends in Defence Expenditure", in Jasjit Singh (ed.), Asian Defence Review 2006 (New Delhi: Knowledge World in Association with the Centre for Air Power Studies, 2006), pp. 91-94 and Shalini Chawla, "Pakistan's Conventional Arms Acquisitions: Priorities and Prospects", Air Power Journal (New Delhi), vol. 3(1), Spring 2006, pp. 127-30.

cessfully and consistently procured the required advanced arms and equipment from the United States during the period between 1990 and 2005 is given in Table 4.1. It also gives a clear indication that U.S. has keen interest in Pakistan for promoting its interests.

4.4.2 Pakistan as a Major Non-NATO Ally

Although Pakistan and the United States does not share a clear convergence of interests regarding combating terrorism, but the events of 9/11 changed the fortune for Pakistan. The United States under the Mr. George W. Bush Administration was fully aware of the close linkage between Pakistan's Inter Services Intelligence (ISI) and Taliban in Afghanistan[25] but ignored it for use of military facilities available in Pakistan in the fight against terrorism. Such U.S. stand has no doubt significantly enhanced the significance of the location of Pakistan. By June 2004, former U.S. President Mr. George W. Bush had officially declared Pakistan as a major non-NATO ally (MNNA). Such designation were given only to allies who are very keen on working with the U.S. forces but need not necessary belong to North Atlantic Treaty Organisation. This status was a welcome development for Pakistan but a setback to India's security concerns.

This has no doubt opened the way for strengthening Pakistan's defence forces. Under this designation, Pakistan was able to participate in certain counterterrorism initiatives, purchase and supply of arms and equipments, receive economic and military assistance, training of the Pakistan forces and last but not the least it can even use American financing for the purchase of certain defence equipment.[26]

In a bid to take advantage of the situation, Pakistan sends a long list of items for supply to the United States. These includes submarine based communication equipment, UHF-to-UHF, frequency scanners and UHF-to-satellite communication systems, night vision googles, thermal imaging devices, deep navigation equipment, GPS systems for Pakistan Air Force (PAF) and ground based radars. Going by the demands of equipments by Pakistan, many wonder as to why it is demanding for such equipments and where it is going to be used. What aroused concern in India is by the additional demands put forward by Pakistan to United States when the latter has extended enough economic and military assistance since the start of the Operation enduring freedom.

However, the Pakistan Foreign Minister Mr. Khurshid Ahmed Kasuri during his visit to China has said that, "the purpose of granting MNNA decision by the U.S. Administration is to facilitate the purchase of military equipment by Pakistan from the United States, particularly to assist us in the fight against terrorism." In response to the Foreign Minister statement, many American diplomats did question Pakistan for its lack of sincerity in the fight against terrorism. They even admit that Pakistan is not going to take the case seriously and hand over Mr. Osama bin laden or Mr. Zawahari to United States. Instead, Pakistan would only take advantage of the U.S. need for a partner in the fight against terrorism.

On the other hand, the United States assured India for what it had done that the status will not result in any significant sale of high-value military hardware like F-16 fighter bombers and depleted uranium munitions.[27]

4.4.3 De-hyphenation of U.S. Relations with India and Pakistan

If on the one side Pakistan was closely engaging with the U.S. in the fight against terrorism then India on the other hand had lost nothing. India's relations with the United States also improved significantly than ever before in the past. The event of 9/11 was a turning point for India too. Security understanding between India and the United States also improves a lot.

The decision to go with Pakistan in the fight against the terrorism was taken along with the commitment to strengthen the ties with India. India had no complain about the growing U.S.-Pak ties but was not satisfied with the U.S. selective approach in the fight against terrorism. Because, the U.S. global war on terrorism (GWOT) did not encompass terrorist problems facing India, abetted and supported by its neighboring state Pakistan. It is very much certain that the U.S. would hesitate to pressurise Mr. Pervez Musharraf Government for the time being since they are engaged in fight against terrorism in Afghanistan.

In response to India's agitation, former U.S. President Mr. George W. Bush came out strongly to saying that U.S. fight against terrorism would be global in character and would not have double standards. This was followed by a series of terrorist attacks in India in 2001 and 2002 including the one in Indian Parliament in December 2001. After these events, the U.S. did not remain quite but responded positively to pressurising Pakistan to stop such activities. For the first time, the U.S. acknowledged the alleged linkage between the terrorist groups operating in Kashmir and in Pakistan state.[28] The U.S. State Department's Patterns of Global Terrorism report of 2001 even questioned the credibility of Pakistan when it stated that, "Questions remain, however, whether Musharraf's "get tough" policy with local militants and his stated pledge to oppose terrorism anywhere will be fully implemented and sustained."

In acknowledgement of India unconditional support to the United States after the events, U.S. former President Mr. George W. Bush on 23 September 2001, lifted the sanctions that were imposed during the Clinton period. This move was a welcome development for India as this would ensure the transfer of defence equipments and strengthen the military-to-military ties. This was followed by signing of the General Security of Military Information Agreement (GSOMIA) in early 2002 that would only strengthen the weapons transfer between the two countries. This is not the end in itself. Many more developments have come about after this.[29] (More details can be seen in Chapter 2).

Today when the relations between India and the U.S. are growing in a way that has never existed before, the U.S. is willing to accommodate India's security concerns arising out of Pakistan aggressive attitude while not losing its security ties with Pakistan. It is quite clear that the more the relationship becomes stronger, the lesser will be the divergence over Pakistan. The U.S. administration is very much willing to see amicable relations between the two South Asian rivals that would offer the opportunity of closely strengthening the relationship with both countries without worrying about the pressure from one side about the other. The task ahead of India in the coming years should be to concentrate on getting closer to the United States while not concerned about the tone of the relationship with Pakistan because for the U.S., relationship with Pakistan is the key to achieving its security and strategic objectives which is also important for India. However, at the same time India should also ensure that Pakistan is not using its relationship with the United States against India. For instance, India has in the past and present not objected to weapons transfer to Pakistan but will continue to object to their quantity, quality and type. It continues to be relevant for India what India's former Prime Minister Ms. Indira Gandhi has said many years back before her visit to Washington in 1982 that, "We don't want the U.S. to give up its friendship with Pakistan. But we don't see why that should affect its attitude toward us." This is followed by what India's former India's Ambassador to Washington, Mr. P.K. Kaul has said, "Pakistan will always remain a problem, but instead of making it the key determinant one should make it one of fifty terms." If India and United States is really serious about getting the relationship stronger then both sides must have to stick to this formula. Then continue to work hard to removing the divergence over Pakistan. The U.S. would be required to stop appeasement of Pakistan that has no doubt endangered India's security concerns. India in any way should not come under any U.S. pressure to make concessions to Islamabad.[30]

4.5 India's Concern over the Growing U.S.-Pakistan Arms Supply Relationship

India has for many decades been complaining for the growing arms supply relationship between the United States and Pakistan. This is because of the fact that the whole world knows that the intention behind Pakistan acquiring arms from the U.S. is to meet the challenges posed by India and to create a roadblock to India becoming a regional power. Many a time when India raised the issue, the United States was not ready to accept it on the ground that Pakistan is a close ally in the fight against terrorism. This way Pakistan had really benefited from the United States supplying arms and equipments needs.

However, recently, it was for the first time disclosed by the former Pakistan President Mr. Pervez Musharraf when he said that 'military aid provided by the United States to Pakistan for the war against terror during his tenure had been used to strengthen defence against India'.[31] Former Pakistan president admission does not bring an end to the issue, unless the U.S. is convinced of what India has been facing for the last many years.

The recent Af-Pak strategy does fail to address India's concerns over the issue. Mr. Bruce Riedel, former CIA official, whom U.S. President Mr. Barack Obama had entrusted with the responsibility of tackling the Af-Pak strategy has said that, "there is no foolproof guarantee against Pakistan transferring

U.S. technology to its advantage against India." He further added that military assistance provided for one purpose can be inherently used for another purpose because it is 'fungible' in nature. However, Riedel has said that, "the U.S. will investigate allegations of technology transfer of American equipment provided to Pakistan thoroughly."

To take advantage of the situation, Pakistan is creating such situation and in the name of fighting terrorism, they are demanding advanced weapons and technologies including drones form the United States. Only when it is pressurized, Pakistan has reacted to it, otherwise they provided the safe heaven to the terrorist. Therefore it becomes critical for India to convince the United States that such illegal usage should not take place in the name of fighting terrorism that posed a serious threat to India's security.[32]

4.6 Pakistan Response to the Growing India-U.S. Strategic Relationship

Pakistan expresses apprehension over the growing India-U.S. ties in general and booming defence and security ties in particular. It has criticized India for trying to disrupt U.S.-Pakistan ties, thereby strengthening its preeminent position in South Asia. Pakistan does not want the growing India-U.S. multifaceted strategic relationship to take place because it believes that the growing relationship would undermine its ambition of strengthening defence cooperation with the United States that holds the key to deterring India. Without the support of the United States, it perceives that the existing conventional weapons imbalance would be widened thereby resulting in India achieving its regional hegemony. Also Pakistan is feared about loosing the United States that has always come out in support of it in Kashmir issue. If Pakistan has developed relations with the United States then it is for none other than to pressurise India to give up its claims and pursue its legitimate interests of defeating India.

Pakistan has even criticized Washington for being close to India and showing disinterest to it.[33] In recent years, India and the U.S. has reached a significant number of agreements that would no doubt put the relationship to a stronger footing. These includes Next Step in Strategic Partnership (NSSP) of 2004, Defence Framework agreement of 2005 and July 18 Civil Nuclear Cooperation Initiative (more details on all of these initiative has been given on chapter 2 and 6). These developments were the results of the former U.S. President George W. Bush commitment to intensify collaboration with India across the wide range of regional and global issues that is consistent with the rise of India as a world power. These had led many Pakistani analysts to claim that the U.S. has recognised India's 'sphere of influence' in Asia. While other Pakistan analysts claim that these agreement represents a threat to Pakistan's economy and security. They presume that these would strengthen India's armaments on the ground that the United States would provide the latest technology and equipment needs to India.

The recent Pakistan response to the landmark civilian nuclear cooperation between India and United States clearly shows that it would not allow India-U.S. ties to move closer. Pakistan has raised a serious of questions over the paradigm shift in the U.S. non-proliferation policy that had opened the door for India to exchange nuclear fuel and reactors with the international community. On 12 April 2006, former Pakistan President Mr. Pervez Musharraf convened a meeting to discuss on the implications of the civil nuclear agreement. Later the Pakistani National Command Authority then stated that, "In view of the fact that the agreement would enable India to produce significant quantities of fissile material and nuclear weapons from unsafeguarded nuclear reactors, the NCA expressed firm resolve that our credible minimum deterrence requirements will be met."[34]

Pakistan perceives that the growing India-U.S. ties would entails the following security threats to Pakistan security as:

a. it would bring down the level of relationship that Pakistan enjoy with its long time strategic patron the United States, that holds the key to supply of modern technology to Pakistan.

b. it would result to loss of Pakistan image in the eyes of the United States thereby Pakistan expectation from the United States to pressuring India to resolving the Kashmir dispute would become obsolete. With this Washington would play very less crucial role in resolving the dispute.

c. it would give way to the United States pressuring Pakistan in meeting the challenges posed by terrorism based in the Pakistan-Afghan border. This would be a welcome development for India and a huge setback for Pakistan.

d. it would create instability in the South Asian region because of the imbalance that would be created due to the U.S. tilt toward India in the conventional and nuclear facilities. This would compelled Pakistan to look for better and lasting alternative to meet the security challenges that would be posed by the growing India's military and nuclear capabilities.

e. the increasing number of multifaceted exercises between the armed forces of India and the United States would improve the operational ability and capability of the Indian forces and also would be much better prepared for any kind of military operation.

f. the closer India-U.S. ties is the key to Indo-Israel defence and security cooperation thereby only worsening the security situation in South Asia. India is moving closer to engaging with Israel for the defence needs. With this India would be receiving advanced technology from Israel. For instance the release of Phalcon radar systems and other equipment to India by Israel through the consent of the United States.[35]

g. it perceive that the relationship would strengthens India's hegemonic ambitions in South Asia and dash away Pakistan effort to prevent India from becoming a hegemonic power in South Asia.

h. it would ensure India play a bigger role in South Asian matters. Pakistan is never in favour of India playing a bigger role in South Asian issues and problems.[36] For instance Pakistan feared India most likely to play bigger role in the reconstruction of Afghanistan. In this regard, India has pledged to provide $565 million in reconstruction aid and $50 million for the new national assembly building. This is due to the fact that Pakistan wants strategic depth in Afghanistan for its security purposes.[37]

4.7 India and Pakistan Position over the Kashmir Dispute

Kashmir issue has been and continued to be one of the major issues of contention between India and Pakistan that remain unresolved for many decades. Both the countries have taken a very different stand over the dispute. Pakistan has so far not changed its demand over the Kashmir which is not quite possible for India to agree. But from time to time it has changed the strategy on how to capture the territory from India. The long standing border dispute that has not shown any prospect for resolution has only sent a wrong message to the international community that resolution is the key to progress in bilateral ties between the two South Asian powers. This is not true because Pakistan has not shown any eagerness to improve ties with India through discussion and instead they were engaged in illegal activities of proxy war that threatens India's security.[38]

The resolution of the Kashmir issue would require both sides to make certain changes to their policies of the past that holds the key to further progress. Both sides must have to understand the fact that their previous policies and stand was not able to provide the strategic breakthrough. They have to adopt a positive approach to the resolution of the Kashmir dispute. Their rigid stand and not showing any flexibility in their respective stand has only worsened the possibility of bringing solution. First, the resolution of the Kashmir issue would require understanding and reduction of mistrust between the two countries. To ensure understanding, normalization of the conflictual situation has to be erased from their minds. Both sides must engage in economic and other cooperation that would no doubt bring close understanding between the two counties. Unlike India-China relations, India's relations with Pakistan did not enjoy close economic relations. Peace must be restored between the two countries. For which Pakistan on its side must abandon its support for militancy, ensure that it is not engaged in proxy war against India that has a serious consequences in the border region. India on its part must ensure that there is good governance in the state that listens to the grievances of the citizens and work for the prosperity of the state. Lack of good governance has given way to agitation of the local people.

Pakistan in particular has not shown any political commitment in the past. It seeks to resolve the issue by force and through the outside support rather than dialogue, while India on the other hand seeks to resolve bilaterally through consensus. Whenever India agreed to enter into a fruitful dialogue but it was the Pakistan double standard stand that circumscribed the possibility of success. For instance the summit meeting between former Prime Minsiter of India and Pakistan, Mr. Atal Bihar Vajpayee and Mr. Nawaz Sharif respectively at Lahore in February 1999 was not able to bring out fruitful result due to alleged invasion by the Pakistan military into the Indian territory. This was followed by the attack on the Indian Parliament in December 2001 that comes just after the General Pervez Musharraf visit to India for the Agra summit in 2001. These events did not allow the climate to be created for the successful solution of the dispute.[39]

Also, Pakistan military leadership obsession with the Kashmir dispute has also been one of the main determinants to creating a climate suitable for resolution. Too much of military influence and the resulting weakness in political leadership has not allowed for the Pakistan government to assert its political will for peace with India. Start from General Zia-ul-Haq to General Musharraf and even today there witnessed no change in their stand on Kashmir problem. It was General Zia-ul-Haq who began to call Kashmir as the core dispute and all other relations with India would be dependent on the solution of the core dispute. This was followed by what former Pakistan General Pervez Musharraf has said that 'even if the Kashmir issue is resolved, Kargils would happen.[40] Pakistan Prime Minister Mr. Shaukat Aziz during his visit to Hongkong has declared that until the Kashmir issue is resolved, economic relations with India could not fully restored. Such stand precludes the possibility of any resolution. For the sake of Kashmir, Pakistan wants to normalize the relations with India and nothing else.[41]

4.7.1 India and Pakistan Came Very Close to Resolving the Kashmir Dispute

Once the 2001-02 crises between India and Pakistan ended in April 2003 when former Indian Prime Minister Mr. Atal Bihari Vajpayee offered bilateral talks to his Pakistani counterpart Mr. Zafarullah Khan Jamali[42] and the latter announcement of a ceasefire along the Line of Control. Since then, both sides are seriously thinking of resolving the bilateral disputes including the Kashmir issue, resulting in both sides agreeing to resume the composite dialogue. Both sides held a series number of talks at the official level and non-official level. Discussion on the bilateral disputes between the two countries improved after the replacement by Mr. Manmohan Singh as the new Prime Minister of India in 2004.

In a bid to resolve the long standing bilateral disputes, both sides reached an agreement on five broad areas- no change in the current division of Kashmir into Pakistan and Indian areas, creation of soft border along the Line of Control that would ensure greater freedom of movement of people and goods, greater autonomy and self-governance for both India and Pakistan administered parts of Kashmir, the establishment of a consultative mechanism across the Line of Control and lastly, demilitarisation of Kashmir.[43]

At the New Delhi summit held in April 2005, General Pervez Musharraf in a sharp departure from its past stand recognised that borders cannot be redrawn though the LoC could not become the permanent border between the two countries. Moreover the joint statement issued at the conclusion of the summit meeting declared that the peace process was not irreversible.[44]

This was the period where both military and non-military Confidence Building Measures (CBMs) improves. For instance Agreement on Advance Notification of Ballistic Missile Tests–brought into effect in 2005, establishment of a Communication

Link between Pakistan Maritime Security Agency and Indian Coast Guard–brought into effect in 2005. Both the rail services between Attari and Lahore, and air linkages between the two countries were resumed in 2004. This was followed by the resumption of Samjhauta Express, which runs between Delhi and Lahore in 2005, and the first bus service between Srinagar and Muzaffarbad also started this year. Joint Economic Commissions and Joint Business Councils were reactivated in 2004. Moreover, Foreign Ministers of both countries agreed to a series of Kashmir-specific CBMs to facilitate crossing the LoC in 2008.[45] Nevertheless, the effort did not so far pay-off owing to continuing Pakistan aggressive attitude toward India and its involvement in terrorist violence in India.

4.7.2 U.S. Stands on Kashmir Since the Cold War End

The U.S. stand on Kashmir issue in the past has been influenced by the cold war dimension where Pakistan was a close ally for the U.S. in the fight against communism. India is not satisfied with the consistent the U.S. stand on Kashmir that is against the interests of India. From the Indian side, it has been made very clear during the visit of General Corus and Admiral Kelso to New Delhi that Kashmir is and always remain to be part of India. This was in response to the questions raised by the American officials against India's stand on Kashmir dispute. Indian Foreign Secretary during his visit to the U.S. in March 1992 has responded very strictly that neither the U.S. nor Pakistan should expect India to compromise on its unity and territorial integrity. He made it very clear to the U.S. officials that any practical compromise had to necessarily take into account the ground realities and the tremendous changes that had occurred since 1947. He further stressed the fact that it would be futile to pressurize India to go back in time and start discussing the Kashmir issue in the pre-partition context. In any way India would adopt a valid stand.[46]

The visit of Foreign Secretary to Washington was a successful one because it was only after this visit one can witnessed a shift in American position on Kashmir. This is reflected in the hearing held by the Sub-committee on Asia and Pacific Affairs of the House Committee on Foreign relations in March 1991 when Ms. Teresita Schaffer, Deputy Secretary of State, stated that the U.N. resolution requiring a plebiscite in Kashmir, which the U.S. had strongly supported in the past, were no longer tenable and it now favored bilateral negotiations to solve the problem within the framework of the Simla Agreement of 1972. It is only this time U.S. talk of bilateral solution to the problem.[47]

Nevertheless, the problem aroused when U.S. Deputy Secretary of State for South Asia, Mr. John Malott, without any concerned about the negative consequences of such statement went for a public declaration in his talk at India International Centre, New Delhi that the U.S. policy toward Kashmir will be guided by three principles- one is that the U.S. considers all of Kashmir to be disputed territory, on both sides of the LoC. The other two principles dealt with bilateral negotiation between India and Pakistan and the willingness of the U.S. to assist in the process if that is desired by both sides. India felt unhappy with the first principle that has gone against the spirit of Simla agreement.[48] This was further worsened by the statement of the newly appointed as the Assistant Secretary of State, Ms. Robin Raphel, that in the U.S. policies and perceptions, Jammu and Kashmir remained a disputed area. She went on to elaborate that the U.S. did not consider the Instrument of Accession signed by the maharaja of Kashmir in October 1947, making Jammu and Kashmir a part of India, politically or legally valid. She even questioned the legitimacy of Kashmir accession to India which did not find favour in India. India was highly disappointed by all of these statements because it came at the time when the relationship has just started expanding after the Soviet disintegration.[49] But when India raised an issue against her statement, the U.S. officials made it very clear that Washington did not view the issue in constitutional and legal terms but in terms of the existing ground realities and express that the only the U.S. interest is to avoid any form of war between the two Asian giants in the name of Kashmir.[50]

However, very soon the U.S. Administration realised the mistake committed on its part. In a bid to not allow such issue to become a roadblock, the U.S. State department arranged a meeting between Mr. Peter Tarnoff and the Indian Ambassador Mr. Siddhartha Shankar Ray in which the former assured India that the U.S. still consider the Simla Agreement as a basis for resolving the Indo-Pak differences over Kashmir. Finally the U.S. had to return back to its previous position.[51]

Since then the U.S. Administrations have even tried their best to resolving the issue but without success due to its one-sided stand taken that is favorable to Pakistan. This has led American Scholar Mr. Stephen Cohen to admit that, "the U.S.-Pakistan alliance is widely believed to have militarized Pakistani politics and foreign policy through the connection between the Pakistan Army and the United States, making it impossible for Delhi to come to accommodation with Islamabad over Kashmir."[52]

However, the U.S. stand in Kashmir in the coming years is likely to be determined by the following factors:

a. India's growing economic and military relationship with the U.S.

b. The level of Pakistan's relevance to the United States and

c. India's stand in the key international affairs.[53]

4.7.3 Future U.S. Role in Resolving the Dispute

However, with the recent the U.S. Administration committed to sustained engagement with both countries, the focus has shifted from direct and active intervention to promoting a composite dialogue between India and Pakistan. America today realized that one sided stand only exacerbate the issue rather than resolving it. The U.S. intervention would come only after the consent of the two countries. But U.S. should help both countries in finding the common ground for the problem.[54]

The former U.S. Administration led by President Mr. George W. Bush dislike of mediation in resolving the Kashmir dispute has given way to facilitation between the two countries. The U.S. will not give up working closely with both countries on the issue because of the fact that both are nuclear power countries that came very close to large scale war in two occasions after the detonation of nuclear tests by both countries. The U.S. knows very clearly that given the stand taken by both sides, the resolution of dispute is not likely to take place very soon, so there is a need for the U.S. role in preventing another major crisis from occurring. This was very clearly spelt out by former U.S. Ambassador to India Mr. Robert Blackwill that 'the United States would facilitate two-party talks between India and Pakistan, but that it would not provide substance, a road map, or a blueprint'. A task force sponsored by two important American foreign policy institutions subsequently recommended (in September 2003) that the administration appoint a high-level official to aid and abet the India-Pakistan dialogue, especially on Kashmir, and assume a more "forward leaning" posture in attempting to deal with India-Pakistan crises before they start.[55]

However, the resolution of the Kashmir dispute has nothing to do with the U.S. It is up to the South Asian rivals on what steps they take on the issue and their seriousness. The role of the U.S. should be only to ensure that both sides engage in a serious and purposeful dialogue that would prevent any unwanted incidents from happening. Given the aggressive nature of Pakistan, the United States should pressurise Pakistan to stop abetting cross border terrorism that would create an environment for the start of the purposeful dialogue. So far, it has been very clear that Pakistan proxy war and cross border terrorism has only delayed the prospects of resolution. Both sides should be encouraged to maintain understanding, increased trade and confidence building measures (CBMs).[56]

4.7.4 Internationalisation of the Kashmir Dispute

Against the spirit of the bilateral Simla agreement, Pakistan wants international attention to resolving the long-standing dispute. It is looking for support from other major powers whose interest's lies in South Asia including the U.S., China and other Islamic countries. In a bid to take advantage of the long-term strategic partnership with the United States, Pakistan had tried its best to take the former to the Kashmir dispute so that the issue turns out to be in its favour. Pakistan wants the U.S. intervention on the issue, but so far the U.S. has refrained itself from getting directly involved in the resolution of the dispute. However, in future the U.S. involvement in the resolution cannot be ruled out owing to the U.S. perception of Pakistan as a long-term close strategic ally.[57]

As far as China is concerned, since the cold war end, its stand has moved from self determination to peaceful solution of the dispute via bilateral negotiations owing to improving relations with India.[58] It is never in favor of internationalising the Kashmir dispute. Besides these, Pakistan expects support form Organisation of Ialamic conference (OIC) on the Kashmir dispute. On 18 February 2004, the Secretary General of the OIC made an offer to mediate in the Kashmir issue at the UN Rights Commission meeting at General, but India rejected this offer.[59]

Pakistan's interest coalesced with the interests of major powers, have led to internationalisation of the Kashmir dispute. The sincerity of Pakistan and major powers is questionable that have only delayed the end to this problem. Earlier it was U.S. that helped Pakistan to be in competition with India, but today China is helping Pakistan so that India's dream of becoming a major power remains unfulfilled. The major powers have in the past only tried to take advantage out of this conflict for advancing their own interests. This situation continued till the end of the twentieth century.[60]

Mr. Sisir Gupta, a renowned scholar on Kashmir issue clearly outlines how the external influence has only worsened the possibility of early resolution to the dispute in the way that, "Although China and U.S. shared the belief that India could be kept under check through Pakistan, the reasons for their doing so might have been different. In the case of America, the underlying assumption behind many of its foreign policy postures was in its supreme confidence in itself. This was consequently a broad western stance of siding with the so-called weaker powers in regional contests, e.g., Malaysia against Indonesia, Pakistan against India, and Israel against Arabs.

He further elaborated that in the case of china... its geopolitical stakes in preventing India from becoming a major power were so high that it began to perceive a great deal of interest in the ability of Pakistan to act as check on India.[61] If they really want to provide a breakthrough then they would need to change their approach that is pro-Pakistan rather than balancing approach that is in the interests of both India and Pakistan. The recent years has witnessed changed in the approach of major powers particularly the United States due in part to the productive ties with India and the increasing role India is going to play in the twentieth century.

China has emerged as the major and reliable source of supply for Pakistan after the then the U.S. President George H. W. Bush (Senior) declined to certify that Pakistan is not undergoing nuclear weapons programs, as required under the US laws. With this, the U.S. military aid to Pakistan also comes to a standstill.[62]

4.8 Indo-Pak Relations After the Mumbai Attack

The recent Mumbai incidents have only aggravated the already not so good relations between India and Pakistan. Since then understanding between the two countries has come down to a much lower level. The attack was carried out with a well planned by ten perpetrators from Pakistan in which 164 innocent people were killed and injuring more than 300 peoples. The attack created havoc in the financial centre of India and the State capital of Maharashtra. The rationale behind the attack seems to be to create instability in the financial status of India.

The Indian government claimed that all the perpetrators belong to Pakistan, while Pakistan was not ready to accept, asking for evidence that shows that they belong to Pakistan. Since the Pakistan government was not ready to accept what India had to say, so there is no question of taking action against those involved in this heinous activity. Angered by the response of Pakistan, India cancelled any forms of dialogue with Pakistan. This way, the events put a brake to ongoing composite dialogue that is meant for resolving the bilateral problems including the Kashmir issue. This had only strengthened India's position that unless there is a positive response from Pakistan regarding cross border terrorism to India there can be very little hope for a composite dialogue. Pakistan must seriously take the issue and ensure that they are not involved in such activities and also that their territory is not used for such illegal activities by the perpetrators. India's positive response to Pakistan demand for peaceful dialogue after the Mumbai events would require Pakistan to take stringent action against those involved in such heinous activities. This would help ensure that India is ready for composite dialogue.

The events no doubt brought the United States close to understanding on the need to tackle the state supporting terrorism. But still there lacks understanding on how best to achieve this when the United States does not view Pakistan as a state sponsoring terrorism but instead consider it as a partner in combating terrorism. The need for Pakistan support in tackling the Al-Qaeda and Taliban in Afghanistan did not allow for stringent action against Pakistan. But one area that has witnessed significant improvement is in sharing of intelligence.[63]

4.9. U.S.-India Relations after the Mumbai Attack

Ashley Tellis participated in one of the recent RAND study in which he points out that, "The Mumbai attack demonstrates that jihadist organizations based in Pakistan are able to plan and launch ambitious terrorist operations, at least in neighboring countries such as India. Put in the context of previous terrorist attacks in India by Pakistani-based or local jihadist groups, it suggests a continuing, perhaps escalating, terrorist campaign in South Asia. Beyond India, the Mumbai attack reveals a strategic terrorist culture that thoughtfully identified strategic goals and ways to achieve them and that analyzed counterterrorist measures and developed ways to obviate them to produce a 9/11-quality attack. For 60 hours, the terrorists brought a city of 20 million people to a standstill while the world looked on. The attack put into actual practice LeT's previous rhetoric about making the Kashmir dispute part of the international jihad. In so doing, LeT has emerged, not as a subsidiary of al-Qaeda, but as an independent constellation in the global jihad galaxy. Indeed, with al-Qaeda central operational capabilities reduced, the Mumbai attack makes LeT a global contender on its own."[64] His point reflects the seriousness and the need to tackle the problem comprehensively and cooperation among the like minded nations.

From both the Indian and American perspective, the events of 26/11 really bought in urgency to tackle the issue of terrorism at the global level. Both New Delhi and Washington stand to gain considerably from improving counterterrorism cooperation owing to the fact that unlike Pakistan, India is very much eager and sincere to root out terrorism that would increasingly pose problems for the international community. However, this would require removing the lingering distrust that stems largely from the U.S. reluctance to include terrorist organizations base in Pakistan that has been the main concerns for India's security. The events provided a golden opportunity for both countries to wipe away the past understanding and look forward to closely working to strengthening counter-terrorism cooperation that includes sharing of intelligence,[65] cyber-terrorism, etc. The question that needs to be asked to the American officials is that whether the time has not come for the Washington to come out strongly to ensuring that terrorism is not used to advance its foreign policy goals. India would look forward to receiving strong commitment from United States in meeting the challenges posed by the terrorist violence abetted by Pakistan. This is not to say that the United States stop engaging close relations with Pakistan which according to the United States hold the key to achieving the objectives of eradicating terrorism from Afghanistan-Pakistan border.[66]

In a bid to strengthen India's bilateral partnership with the U.S. in the field of counter-terrorism, Indian Home Minister Mr. P. Chidambaram visited the U.S. on September 2009 that was aimed at identifying areas for mutual cooperation with focus on procurement of advanced technology and sharing of information and best practices in investigation and prevention of terrorist attacks.[67] Really, the seriousness to tackle the issue of terrorism and its related activities has improved significantly between India and the United States in recent times.

4.10. US Af-Pak Strategy

The U.S. President Barack Obama after sixty days of inter-agency review had announced a "comprehensive new strategy for Afghanistan and Pakistan that is aimed at disrupt, dismantle and defeat of al-Qaeda both in Pakistan and Afghanistan. The strategy reflects two aspects-one that there is a seriousness to deal the issue before it escalate into a bigger one that posed a significant challenges to the international community and the United States in particular. Secondly, it reflects the close linkages between terrorist organisation residing in Afghanistan and Pakistan.[68]

The Af-Pak strategy launched in March 2009 would be comprised of both military and civilian approach. When more number of military forces will be dispatched for this purpose, at the same time there will be release of more civilian oriented funding based on the assumption that such objective could not be achieved by military force alone.[69]

Many commentators have raised the arguments in this context that coercive action must be taken against terrorist residing in Afghanistan. This would require pressurising Pakistan to act sincerely against terrorist residing in Af-Pak border. What is quite challenging for the United States is ensuring Pakistan that combating terrorism is also in the interests of Pakistan. This is because of the fact that there is a clash of interest between the U.S. and Pakistan. Pakistan doesn't seriously consider combating terrorism as a key to their Progress, development and survival. It is very important that the U.S. pressurise

Pakistan to come out with full commitment vis-à-vis violent insurgency in Baluchistan, North Western Frontier Province and FATA. The situation in Pakistan has reached a level of non-ignorance from which there is always a possibility of moving towards a failed state or rogue state.[70]

Unlike in the past, this time the U.S. administration under the leadership of Barack Obama has put a condition to the money that will be transferred to Pakistan. The money transferred will be based on result-oriented. To ensure accountability, the U.S. administration has argued for transparency about where and how the money is utilised.[71]

However, the success of the U.S. Af-Pak strategy is most likely to be delayed given the fact that Pakistan, who is a key ally in the fight against terrorism, seeks a strong Taliban in Afghanistan to offset the rising Indian influence there. Pakistan has not given up the hope of creating anti-Indian, pro-Pakistan government in Afghanistan for their interests. Pakistan does not want to see India expanding its influence in Afghanistan, which according to Islamabad would help the Kashmir issue to turn in their favour. This is the missing link between the United States and Pakistan that has only favoured Pakistan and a setback for India. It was during the visit to Islamabad by the U.S. Director of Intelligence Mr. Mike McConnel in 2008, a Pakistani General has told that "we must support the Taliban so that there is a government friendly to Pakistan in Kabul. Otherwise India will reign." With such stand it is less likely that Pakistan would take steps sincerely to dismantle Taliban in Afghanistan and Pakistan and al-Qaeda. On the basis of this, Pakistan has criticised India for over involvement in Afghanistan.[72] It is up to the U.S. Administration on whether it comes under the pressure of Pakistan to stop India playing a key role in the reconstruction of Afghanistan or pressuring Islamabad to take stringent action against Taliban and al- Qaeda.

4.10.1. Recent Developments-U.S. Pressurising Pakistan

In one of the recent developments, the U.S. President Barack Obama has put the Pakistan President in a dilemma. In his letter to the Pakistan President Mr. Asif Ali Zardari, the U.S. President Mr. Barack Obama has sent a clear and stringent message to Pakistan either they continue to use insurgents as a tool or receive military and economic assistance from the U.S. This is in response to the growing seriousness of the security situation in an around Pakistan and Afghanistan. From the Indian point of view, it is good to learn that U.S. has continued to pressurising Pakistan to ensure that it no longer pursue a policy of supporting terrorism as a foreign policy tools.

The U.S. President Obama has called upon Pakistan to be stringent and remain committed in its dealing with terrorist organisation operating in an around Pakistan. The list includes Al-Qaeda, Afghan Taliban, Lashkar-e-Taiba (LeT), Pakistan Taliban and other. This is further tightened by the interaction between the U.S. National Security Advisor, James Jones with the Pakistan officials. During his interaction, James Jones has made it clear to Pakistan that, 'if Pakistan cannot deliver, he (U.S.) may be impelled to use any means at its disposal to rout insurgents based along Pakistan's Western and Southern borders with Afghanistan'.[73] He further added that no matter how many troops the President commits to Afghanistan, the strategy will founder unless the safe haven inside Pakistan is dealt with.[74]

The U.S. President Mr. Barack Obama is seriously concerned about the threat posed by the growing extremist activities in an around the Af-Pak region. Eradicating the menace of terrorism in this region has been the top most priority of the U.S. President for the time now. This is reflected from what he has said that, "This is no idle danger…no hypothetical threat…In the last few months alone, we have apprehended extremists within our borders who were sent here from the border region of Afghanistan and Pakistan to commit new acts of terror. The danger will only grow if the region slides backwards and Al-Qaeda can operate with impunity...And the stakes are even higher within a nuclear armed Pakistan because we know that Al-Qaeda and other extremists seek nuclear weapons and we have every reason to believe that they would use them." It seems that the U.S. President Barack Obama is convinced that the success of eradicating the menace of terrorism lies in pressuring it to act into it with full commitment. It was during his speech at the U.S. military Academy at West Point, the U.S. President Barack Obama has said, "we will act with full recognition that our success in Afghanistan is inextricably linked to our partnership with Pakistan. We are in Afghanistan to prevent a cancer from once again spreading through that country. But the same cancer has also taken root in the border region of Pakistan. That is why we need a strategy that works on both sides of the border." That is why the U.S. President Barack Obama is keen to pursuing a policy of pressuring Pakistan to act against terror on the one hand and extend every help to Pakistan so as to ensure that the main objective is achieved.[75] India shall not be annoyed by this developments because it is not in the intention of India that the United States totally ignore Pakistan but it shall be in the interests of India that the United States keep itself engaged with Pakistan and at the same time ensuring that Pakistan has stop using the extremists as a foreign policy tools against India.

4.11 Conclusion

Pakistan factor will continue to remain the main determinant to the growing India-U.S. strategic ties as long as there is a lack of a convergence of perception between India and the United States regarding Pakistan and Indo-Pak issue is resolved. U.S. stand on Pakistan illegal activities has a huge stake on India-U.S. strategic relationship. But what is most important is how India and the United States take care of the issue in terms of not allowing such issues to circumscribe the further prospects of the long term strategic ties. India on the one side view Pakistan as a real problem to its security concerns while U.S. still and is most likely to continue to perceive Pakistan as a close ally in the fight against terrorism. Because of which, the U.S. is not worried about whatever steps Pakistan take. It is not an easy task for the United States to totally ignore Pakistan that holds the key to some of the U.S. long-term interests.

But given the kind of relations that India enjoy with the United States in the past one decade, one can only say that the past zero-sum policy of U.S. is not likely to repeat once again. It should also be in the interests of the United States too that Pakistan factor does not impede the future prospects of India-U.S. ties. Today India has a crucial role to play for U.S. long-term interests. Therefore, what India should do is to keep itself engaged with the U.S. in common areas of interests and at the same time take the U.S. into confidence on our security concerns.[76] With increasing terrorist violence in and around India sponsored by none other than Pakistan, the U.S. long time close ally, there is a need for closer understanding between India and United States to tackle the challenges posed by terrorism without making any discrimination. The time has come for the United States to reconsider and think seriously the problem facing India that has a global repercussion. The problem created by the terrorist events facing India is not just a problem for India but for the whole of international community. Given this fact, both India and the United States must have to more or less agree to a secure, stable, democratic and a civilian controlled Pakistan state that seeks to live in peace with its neighbours. This can only come about when the U.S. is seriously concerned about India's problems and stop applying its traditional policy of appeasing Pakistan by providing military arms and equipment, training to its forces, etc. Such a huge different stand in future may not allow the two countries to prosper with ease.[77]

Since, it is not in the interest of Pakistan to see India-U.S. relations to keep on growing. Therefore Pakistan will be looking for every possible means to exploit the free and safe passage of India-U.S. relations. For instance, the recent Pakistan response to civil nuclear cooperation between India and the United States is a proof of how Pakistan would try to prevent India from becoming a regional power. However the dehyphenation policy offers very little room for the Pakistan to influence the United States against India. And on the other side, offers India very good opportunity to keep growing its relationship with the United States. This is very much reflected in what U.S. Secretary of State Condoleezza Rice has said during her interview with Mr. Shivraj Prasad that, "we have tried very hard, as a matter of fact, to make the point that this is not a hyphenated relationship." She further added that the U.S. ties with each South Asian partner ought to be viewed on their own terms. But the success of the dehyphenation policy of the U.S. toward India and Pakistan is yet to come. Since, it fails to ensure that Pakistan aggressive attitude toward India has ended.[78]

Endnotes

[1] Ashley J. Tellis, "The Merits of Dehyphenation: Explaining U.S. Success in Engaging India and Pakistan", Washington Quarterly (Washington, D.C.), vol. 31(4), Autumn 2008, p. 22.

[2] Christopher S. Raj and Chintamani Mahapatra, "US Strategic Response to Emerging Problems in Asia", International Studies (New Delhi), vol. 41(3), July-September 2004, pp. 286-87.

[3] Rajiv Sikri, Challenge and Strategy: Rethinking India's Foreign Policy (New Delhi: Sage Publications, 2009), p. 191.

[4] See Arthur G. Rubinoff, "Legislative Perceptions of Indo-American Relations", in Ashok Kapur, et. al., (eds.), India and the United States in a Changing World (New Delhi: Sage Publications, 2002), pp. 435-36 and Monish Tourangbham, "The Pakistan Factor in India-US Relations: Is it Finally Muted?", World Focus (New Delhi), vol. XXIX(7), July 2008, pp. 274-75.

[5] Stephen Philip Cohen, The Idea of Pakistan (New Delhi: Oxford University Press, 2005), p. 301.

[6] Shalini Chawla, "Pakistan's Conventional Arms Acquisitions: Priorities and Prospects", Air Power Journal (New Delhi), vol. 3(1), Spring 2006, p. 114.

[7] Pramit Pal Chaudhuri, "The Pakistan Factor", in Kanti Bajpai and Amitabh Mattoo (eds.), Engaged Democracies: India-U.S. Relations in the 21st Century (New Delhi: Har-Anand Publications Pvt. Ltd., 2000), pp. 134-36.

[8] Srinath Raghavan, "The Eternal India-Pak-US Triangle", Asian Age (Mumbai), 23 December 2009.

[9] See Abhay R Karve, "Indo-US Strategic Relations: Moving from Estrangement to Engagement", Paper submitted to the National War College, National Defense University, p. 42.

[10] Dinshaw Mistry, "Tempering Optimism about Nuclear Deterrence in South Asia", Security Studies (Philadelphia, PA), vol. 18(1), January-March 2009, pp. 156-58.

[11] Hafeez Malik, US Relations with Afghanistan and Pakistan: The Imperial Dimension (Karachi: Oxford University Press, 2008), p. 119.

[12] Pramit Pal Chaudhuri, n. 7, pp. 132-33.

[13] Robert M. Hathaway, "Coming of Age: Indian-American and the US Congress", in Ashok Kapur, et. al., (eds.), India and the United States in the Changing World (New Delhi: Sage Publications, 2002), p. 397.

[14] C. Raja Mohan, "A Paradigm Shift toward South Asia", Washington Quarterly (Washington, D.C.), vol. 26(1), Winter 2002-03, pp. 141-44 and also see Ashley J. Tellis, n. 1, pp. 23-25.

[15] Touqir Hussain, "US-Pakistan Engagement: The War on Terrorism and Beyond", Regional Studies (Islamabad), vol. XXIV(1), Winter 2005-06, p. 9.

[16] C. Raja Mohan, n. 14, pp. 144-45.

[17] Shalini Chawla, n. 6, pp. 120-23.

[18] Saileja, "Indo-US Defence Co-operation", World Focus, vol. XXIX(7), July 2008, p. 259.

[19] Zafar Nawaz Jaspal, "The Indo-US Strategic Relationship and Pakistan's Security", South Asian Strategic Studies Institute Research Report 9, December 2007, p. 29, available at <http://www.sassi.org/pdfs/The%20Indo-US%20Strategic%20Relationship%20and%20Pakistan's% 20Security%20.pdf>.

[20] See, "Central and South Asia", in The Military Balance 2009: The Annual Assessment of Global and Military Capabilities and Defence Economics (London: Routledge, 2009), p. 330.

[21] Ibid., p. 341.

[22] Zafar Nawaz Jaspal, "Enhanced Defence Cooperation between the United States and Pakistan", Strategic Insights (Monterey, CA), vol. VI(4), June 2007, available at <http://www.ccc.nps.mil/si/2007/Jun/jaspalJun07.asp>.

[23] Stephen P. Cohen, India Emerging Power (New Delhi: Oxford University Press, 2002), pp. 273-74.

[24] Manohar Singh Batra, "India-Pakistan Relations in the Twenty-First Century", in V.D. Chopra (ed.), India's Foreign Policy in the 21st Century (New Delhi: Kalpaz Publications, 2006), p. 169.

[25] Mel Gurtov, "The Bush Doctrine in Asia", in David P. Forsythe, et. al., (eds.), American Foreign Policy in a Globalised World (New York: Routledge, 2006), p. 302.

[26] Zafar Nawaz Jaspal, n. 22.

[27] A B Mahapatra, "Implications of MNNA Status for Pakistan and the Subcontinent", Defence Digest (New Delhi), vol. 3(6), May-June 2004, pp. 39-41.

[28] C. Raja Mohan, n. 14, pp. 146-47.

[29] Monish Tourangbham, n. 4, pp. 275-76.

[30] Satu Limaye, "The Changing Place of Pakistan in US-India Relations", Contemporary South Asia, vol. 1(1), 1992, pp. 118-24.

[31] See, "US Funds were Diverted to Prop Defence Against India", Times of India (Pune), 14 September 2009.

[32] See, "Af-Pak Strategy Doesn't Address Tech Transfer?", Times of India (Pune), 22 September 2009.

[33] Zafar Nawaz Jaspal, n. 22.

[34] Stephen Blank, "Geostrategic Implications of the Indo-American Partnership", India Review, vol. 6(1), January-March 2007, pp. 2-3.

[35] Zafar Nawaz Jaspal, n. 19, pp. 31-33.

[36] Mavara Inayat, "US-Indian Strategic Partnership: Implications for Asia and Beyond", Regional Studies (Islamabad), vol. XXIV(2), Spring 2006, pp. 27-28.

[37] Ibid., p. 31.

[38] Milind Thakar, "Coping with Insecurity: The Pakistani Variable in Indo-US Relations", in Gary K. Bertsch, et. al., (eds.), Engaging India-U.S. Strategic Relations with the World's Largest Democracy (New York: Routledge, 1999), p. 227.

[39] See, "India/Pak Relations and Kashmir: Steps Toward Peace", International Crisis Group Asia, Report No. 79, 24 June 2004, pp. 2-3.

[40] Kalim Bahadur, "India-Pakistan Relations", in V.D. Chopra (ed.), India's Foreign Policy in the 21st Century (New Delhi: Kalpaz Publications, 2006), pp. 147-49.

[41] Ibid., p. 152.

[42] Ashutosh Misra, "India-Pakistan Peace Process: Gatheing Momentum", in S.D. Muni, (ed.), IDSA Asian Strategic Review 2007 (New Delhi: Academic Foundation, 2008), p. 79.

[43] Hilary Synnott, Transforming Pakistan: Ways Out of Instability (London: Routledge, 2009), pp. 143-44.

[44] Kalim Bahadur, n. 40, p. 151.

[45] Samarjit Ghosh, "Two Decades of Indo-Pak CBMs: A Critique from India", IPCS Issue Brief 132, September 2009, pp. 1-2.

[46] Subhash Shukla, Foreign Policy of India (New Delhi: Anamika Publishers, 2007), pp. 39-42.

[47] Ibid., p. 44.

[48] Reeta Chowdhari Tremblay, "Indo-US Relations and the Kashmir Issue", in Ashok Kapur, et. al., (eds.), India and United States in a Changing World (New Delhi: Sage Publications, 2002), pp. 522-23.

[49] Subhash Shukla, n. 46, p. 49.

[50] Ibid., pp. 51-52.

[51] Reeta Chowdhari Tremblay, n. 48, p. 524.

[52] Abhay R. Karve, n. 9, p. 41.

[53] Subhash Kapila, "United States Obsession with the Kashmir Issue: An Analysis", South Asia Analysis Group (Noida), Paper no. 403, 30.01.2002, available at <http://www.southasisanalysis.org/papers5/paper403.html>.

[54] Saleem Kidwai, "US and South Asia: Post 9/11 Scenario", in Saleem Kidwai (ed.), US Policy toward South Asia: Focus on Sixty Years (New Delhi: Academic Excellence, 2008), p. 37.

[55] Stephen Philip Cohen, n. 5, p. 322.

[56] Saleem Kidwai, n. 54, pp. 44-45.

[57] Chintamani Mahapatra, "US Factor and the Kashmir Issue", Journal of Peace Studies (New Delhi), vol. 8(4), July-August 2001, p. 44.

[58] M C Bhandari, Solving Kashmir (New Delhi: Lancer Publishers and Distributors, 2006), p. 319.

[59] Ibid., pp. 222-25.

[60] Ashok Kapur, "Major Powers and the Persistence of the India-Pakistan Conflict", in T.V. Paul (ed.), The India-Pakistan Conflict: An Enduring Rivalry (New York: Cambridge University Press, 2005), pp. 131-33.

[61] Ibid., p. 144.

[62] Jasjit Singh, "Trends in Defence Expenditure", in Jasjit Singh, (ed.), Asian Defence Review 2006 (New Delhi: Knowledge World in Association Har-Anand Publications Pvt. Ltd.with the Centre for Air Power Studies, 2006), pp. 90-91.

[63] Hilary Synnott, n. 43, pp. 139-41.

[64] Ashley J. Tellis, "Lessons From Mumbai", Testimony presented before Committee on Homeland Security and Governmental Affairs, United States Senate, 28 January 2009, p. 9, available at <http://www.carnegieendowment.org/files/0128_tellis_mumbai_testimony1.pdf>.

[65] Lisa Curtis, "After Mumbai: Time to Strengthen U.S.-India Counterterrorism Cooperation", The Heritage Foundation, No. 2217, December 9, 2008, p. 1, available at <cbi.nic.in/newsarticles/newsreport/backgrounder.pdf>.

[66] Ibid., p. 8.

[67] Annual Report 2009-2010, Ministry of External Affairs, Government of India, p. 94.

[68] Hilary Synnott, n. 43, p. 116.

[69] Ibid., pp.162-63.

[70] Ibid., pp.166-68.

[71] Ibid., p. 175.

[72] Selig Harrison, "From Kabul to Kashmir", Indian Express (Pune), 20 November 2009 and Fareed Zakaria, "The Prize is India", Indian Express (Pune), 23 November 2009.

[73] Karen Deyoung, "Stop Using Lashkar, Insurgenst for Policy Goals, Obama Warns Pak", Indian Express (Pune), 1 December 2009.

[74] David E. Sanger and Eric Schmitt, "Pakistan: What Obama Left Unsaid", The Hindu (Hyderabad), 3 December 2009.

[75] K. Subrahmanyam, "The Speech Within the Speech", Indian Express (Pune), 3 December 2009.

[76] Polly Nayak, "U.S. Security Policy on South Asia since 9/11- Challenges and Implications for the Future", Occasional Paper Series, Asia Pacific Center for Security Studies, February 2005, pp. 11-12.

[77] C. Chrisitine Fair, "The Mumbai Attacks and Indo-U.S. Relations", The Hindu (Hyderabad), 24 November 2009.

[78] Ashley J. Tellis, n. 1, pp. 36-37.

INDIA-UNITED STATES RELATIONS: CHINA AND GREAT POWERS AS A FACTOR

5.1 Introduction

The constructive relationship that started soon after the cold war end had witnessed significant upward trajectory by the dawn of the twenty-first century, that today, both countries have more convergences of interests than the divergences of interests. The convergence of interests has been the driving force behind the prospering India-U.S. strategic relationship. With this, both India and the United States have seen more understanding on the underlying regional and global issues. That does not mean complete convergence on regional and global issues. Such developments have led many to perceive that the rationale behind the growing relationship is aimed at containing China that has the potential to threaten both India and the United States.

The expanding relations should not be construed as moving together for the containment of China. Mr. Ashley J. Tellis in his testimony before the Senate Foreign Relations Committee on April 2006 has refuted the claim made by many Indian and American Officials that an India-U.S. expanding relation is aimed at containment of China. He is of the view that a policy of containing China is neither feasible nor necessary for the United States at this point of time. He further added that it remains unclear whether it would be in the interest of India to become a part of any containment policy vis-à-vis China.

Here one may ask a question and that is whether India and the United States are really interested in the containment of China. If yes, then what would they gain out of it. Also both countries must recognize the implications of this step to regional and global peace and security. Therefore, before evolving any such containment strategy, India and the United States must have to rethink its short-term and long-term implications of such strategy. If the U.S. is really interested in the containment of China then India must have to ensure that it does not become a victim of the U.S. policy of containment that has nothing to do with India's interests. As India's interests require co-operative relationship with China or any other countries.[1] It reminds us one of the arguments made during the 1980s by the first Bush Administration when it contended that the U.S. should export sensitive dual-use equipment to Saddam Hussein in order to build up Iraq as counterweight to Iran. Later on Iraq became the victim of the U.S. under the Junior Bush Administration by making false claim and the fact is that Iraq no more serves the U.S. interests.

Mr. Ashley J. Tellis was quite right when he say during his testimony before the Senate Foreign Relations Committee that, "a strengthened bilateral relationship does not imply that India will become a treaty bound ally of the United States at some time in the future. It also does not imply that India will become a meek, complaint and uncritical collaborator of the U.S. in all its global endeavors. Rather India's large size, its proud history, and its great ambitions, ensure that it will always pursue its own interests- just like any other great powers."[2] Former U.S. Deputy Secretary of State, Mr. Robert Zoellick in his speech in China on 21st September 2005 has said that 'Washington recognizes the growth of China as a world power is non-stoppable and that China's cooperation is necessary for addressing regional and global concerns'. Deputy Secretary of State views reflects about what should be the U.S. position toward China and the role China would play in future given the regional and global insecurity.[3]

This is further accentuated by what the former U.S. Secretary of State Ms. Condoleezza Rice in her speech in Tokyo in 2005 regarding the role of U.S.-India relationship vis-à-vis China had said that, "I really do believe that the USA-Japan relationship, the USA-South Korean relationship, the USA-India relationship, all are important in creating an environment in which China is more likely to play a positive role than a negative one." She further added that these alliances are not against China; they are alliances that are devoted to a stable security, political and economic and indeed, values-based relationships that put China in the contest of those relationships and on a different path to development than if China simply untethered, simply operating without that strategic context."[4] Ms. Condoleezza Rice Statement seeks to clear the misperception underlying India-U.S. relationship vis-à-vis China.

Since the strategic partnership is not aimed at identifying good partner and bad partner, the relationship with the U.S. should not at any level pose a problem to India's relationship with other countries with whom it share interests such as Russia, Japan or China. It will always be in the interests of India to seek to have good relations with other countries. Really, this is important from the Indian point of view if it has to achieve major power status. From the Indian side, Mr. Pranab Mukherjee has said, "We are no longer bound by the cold war paradigm where good relations with one power automatically entailed negative consequences with its rivals." His comments reflects that India today stand poised at the threshold of having closer relations with all major powers that would strengthened India's interests. This is further accentuated by the fact that during the cold war the U.S. and Soviet Union were rival super powers. Because of which India's tilt toward the latter did not allow India to have closer relations with the U.S. Today, the situation is quite different that the U.S. and China enjoy closer ties with each other. Therefore, there should not be any problem for India to engage with both countries that have significant positive consequences for India. India has a lot to gain out of it. India's strategic analysts Mr. C. Raja Mohan is of the view that India must offer reasonable assurance that its partnership with the U.S. is not directed against China in order to ensure that it joins the Asian balance of power without causing unnecessary turbulence is pertinent.[5]

Containment of China would result to serious strategic and economic implications to India. India must keep in mind the fact that today China and the U.S. also shares a lot many common interests that may at some point of time in future forced both countries to work closer together. Therefore, India should prefer to work for its own interests, rather than coming under someone pressure.[6] The chapter argues that if India is seriously considering about containing China then the kind of India-China relations that we have witnessed so far after the cold war end would not have seen. On the basis of which, the growing India-U.S. relationship should not be construed as countering China. The chapter seeks to find out the answer of the following central questions. Does the growing India-U.S. relationship aimed at containing China? Why containment of China is not a feasible option? The chapter seeks to ensure that the relationship is not aimed at containing China by analyzing the bilateral relations between India, the United States and China. It also examines the implications of India-U.S. relations to Russia and Japan and their response to it. And lastly, what are the possible areas of strategic cooperation between India, the United States and China, Russia and other countries.

5.2 Why India-U.S. Containment of China is Less Likely to Happen

There are many reasons as to why containment of China is less likely to happen. Today India and the United States have a much better interactions with China than ever before in the past. And where there is a convergence, there must also be a divergence. The same is the case with India and the United States stance towards the containment of China. Although India and the U.S. have the same concerns over the growing Chinese power and its expanding influence, but still they have the differences over other issues involving China that would seriously undermine India's strategic security. The growing relationship between India and the United States should not become the sole ground for the containment of China.

India expressed concern over the Chinese equipping Pakistan with nuclear and missile technology and other weapons needs. India perceives this as helping to maintain strategic balance between the two South Asian giants, thereby worsening the security situation in South Asia. However, the United States remain non-committed to the growing military ties between China and Pakistan that would seriously threaten India's security. The reason may be due to the fact that Pakistan has really benefited from the American arms and equipment supply in the past and also at present.[7] And also that the U.S. Deputy Assistant Secretary of State for Non-Proliferation, Mr. Robert Einhorn has made it very clear when he say that, "We are terribly concerned about the behavior of Iran. Pakistan of course is a friend of the US and we wish to have good bilateral relations with Pakistan. We also recognise China as a good friend of Pakistan and we don't intend to interfere in anyway with their close relationship." And instead China and the United States together has opposed India's nuclear programme.[8] Therefore, it becomes very important for India that it looked at China factor from its own mirror rather than looking at from the mirror of the U.S. thereby avoiding getting involved in an unnecessary events that would only increase India's concerns over China.

It would be quite interesting to know why the U.S. should be ready to take such a huge step when China today is the second largest holder of treasury bonds with nearly $400 billion next only to Japan with some $841 billion. Chinese exports to U.S. are five and half times more than what the former imports from the U.S.[9] Also the United States has in the past and present been investing heavily in Chinese economy. If today, China has become an economic powerhouse, then it was with the support of the United States. How can a nation think of containing a country where more than one hundred U.S. owned multinationals companies are doing business? The American businesses would lobby hard against any of the American move to counter China. Because, they understand the significant losses that would be incurred as a result of such move. The economic relations would be seriously affected if the U.S. and India directed their relations against China.[10] The United States have a much better trade relations with China than ever before in the past. It is much ahead of what it enjoys with India. Given this fact, India and the United States would want to have closer relations with china. If the United States were to contain China then it would not have helped the latter to become a partner in the thermonuclear energy research and in the building of more nuclear reactors in the country.[11]

From table 5.1 one can observe that Containment of china is less likely to happen given the kind of convergence that China enjoys with both India and United States. China enjoys some point of convergence with India that is against the wish of the United States such as the creation of the multipolar world and human rights. At the same time, the United States also share areas of convergence that goes against India's interest like U.S. and China stance towards India's long time enemy Pakistan and South Asian stability (there is always a possibility of U.S. and China coming together to pressurizing India for resolving the Kashmir dispute).[12] As Chinese Foreign Minister Mr. Tang Jiaxuan has said, "the international community should encourage direct dialogue between India and Pakistan in a more balanced and fair manner, which is the most effective way to lead South Asia toward peace and stability." The United States and China seeks to maintain a balance between India and Pakistan so that the Line of control is not changed unilaterally and also by violence.[13]

Table 5.1: Areas of Convergence and Divergence between India and U.S., India and China and U.S. and China.

Name of the Pairs	Areas of Convergences	Areas of Divergences
India and United States	Combating terrorism, promoting democracy, ensuring regional and global security, preventing nuclear proliferation.	India signing NPT, CTBT and Pak factor.
India and China	Combating terrorism, establishment of a multipolar world order, human rights.	Border dispute, Tibet issue, Sino-Pak collaboration, China's regional influence.
United States and China	Combating terrorism, preventing nuclear proliferation, ensuring regional and global security.	Taiwan issue, Chinese military modernisation.

Source: John W. Garver, "The China-India-U.S. Triangles: Strategic Relations in the Post Cold War Era", The National Bureau of Asian Research (NBR) Analysis (Washington), vol. 13(5), October 2002, pp. 5-56.

5.2.1 Whether Containment of China is in the Immediate Interests of United States

This section would like to highlight what the American officials had to say vis-à-vis containment of China. Many American officials are not in favor of containing China, instead they have suggested for more engagement with China, given the role that China would play in the twenty-first century. Also the international community demanded close cooperation between the U.S. and China rather than confrontationist relations for the betterment of international peace and security. One of the main argument of this chapter is that the long term strategic interactions between India, U.S. and China would hold the key the regional and global peace and security. The U.S. would need China's help in meeting the twenty-first century challenges. As Mr. William Overholt had commented that, "these two great civilizations must now engage each other-for better or for worse-to a degree that has never before occurred', since 'much of the future of humanity will hinge on whether both sides can approach this engagements with appropriate gravity and earnest efforts to understand one another's real motives'.[14]

Former U.S. Secretary of Defence, Mr. William Perry had concisely summed up China's growing presence as one where 'China is fast becoming the world's largest economic power and that combined with its UN permanent five states, its political clout, its nuclear weapons and a modernizing military, make China a player with which the U.S. must work together'.[15] This is followed by the statement of former U.S. Assistant Secretary of defence, Mr. Nye's who had argued for 'deep engagement' with China where 'it is wrong to portray China as an enemy. Nor is there reason to believe that China must be an enemy in the future....enmity would become self-fulfilling prophecy'. This view was again supported by Chief, Secretary of Defence Mr. William Perry when he said that containment was the wrong option, alienating China and damaging America's own security interests. Instead, the U.S. should engage China, not contain it.....we believe that engagement is the best strategy to ensure that as China increases its power, it does so as a responsible member of the international community'.

Then comes the turn of former Secretary of State, Mr. Madeleine Albright who also spelt out the similar view when he say that how 'no nation will play larger role in shaping the course of twenty-first century Asia than China with its huge population and vast territory, China's emergence as a modern, growing economic and military power is a major historical event'. And as such a containment policy for China would be a mistake, would, in fact, guarantee an outcome contrary to American interests. A policy of containment would divide our Asian allies and encourage China to withdraw into narrow nationalism and militarism'.[16] From all of this statement and views, it becomes very clear that containment of China cannot be in the immediate interests of the United States owing to the need for China in meeting serious challenges in the twenty-first century.

5.2.2 Options Available for India and United States

As far as China is concerned, both India and the United States must be very careful before taking any such steps. Taking a confrontationist approach or the containment approach against China would be counter-productive for both India and the United States. It should be in the interest of both countries that they encourage China rise in positive direction that doesn't pose any threat to both of them rather than in a negative one. This way they can receive maximum benefit out of the expanding relations, economically and militarily.[17]

Both India and the United States should find out way for cooperation in areas of common international concern where

China has a significant role to play given its economic and military prowess. Ensuring international peace and security has been the common major objective of the three countries. Cooperation among the three countries is the key to achieving this very objective. It should be in the interests of India, the United States and China that they avoid getting involved in the strategy of containment of each other country that would have negative implications.[18]

For India, Beijing negative response to the growing relationship with the U.S. should not back-out India from moving further ahead when it is in the national interest of India. It is always in the interest of India that it continue to enjoy close relations with both the major powers of the world- the United States and China. At the same time, India should ensure that shadow of India-U.S. relations does not figure in India-China relations. This way India can enjoy closer relations with both the United States and China. The level of cooperation may be different due to the level of understanding gained between these countries.[19] Diplomatically, India is playing a great game to ensuring that it continue enlarge close relations with both super powers that hold the key India becoming a global power.

5.3 Chinese Stance on India-U.S. Relationship

The end of cold war brought a significant shift in the relationship among the states. They are no more bound by the cold war dimension where a close relationship with one superpower does not allow it to have closer relations with the other side. The United States is not the only country with whom India has expanded its relations. It has expanded relations with Russia, France, Australia, Japan, etc. India is a rising power in the world which is still in the process of development that needs the support of other countries and in particular to the United States owing to the pre-eminent power. India would never want the growing relations with the United States to come at the cost of its relations with any of the abovementioned countries including China. India would like to have balance relations with each of these countries. For instance, India enjoys a strategic partnership with Russia which has a clash of interest with the United States. However, in some cases, it may tilt in favor of one country depending upon the convergence of interests and a close understanding.[20]

China is closely watching the prospering India-U.S. relations with suspicion because it is against the interest of it. China perceives that the expanding multifaceted relationship between India and the United States is finally aimed at the containment of China. Beijing perception arises owing to the fact that both India and the United States have clash of interests with the former. This is further accentuated by the fact that both India and the United States have a close convergence of interests. China doesn't want to see India become a major great power in the world and the relationship with the United States is the key to India achieving this objective. It also believes that the relationship would alter the regional balance of power. Beijing apprehension is fuelled by the growing defence and security relations between India and the United States. Also the military-to-military ties since the last one decade has improved significantly (more details on this aspect has been written in chapter 2). Both countries have conducted a series number of unprecedented and increasingly substantive combined exercises involving all the three branches of the armed forces. Beijing concerns over a regular India-U.S. joint naval Malabar exercise off the Indian coast is owing to China's growing dependence on oil imports transiting the Indian Ocean.

A Beijing concern over the expanding India-U.S. relations is well placed by Mr. Yang Yunzhong at the Jinan Military Academy when he critically said that, "The rapid developments between US-India relations will exert profound influence on the political and security environment of the Asia-Pacific region and the world. The U.S. now views India as a leading player in South Asian affairs and a rising world power, not just a source of regional problems. Both economically and militarily, India is gathering momentum and this provides the U.S. more diplomatic and strategic angles to play in the region. Among the benefits for the U.S. is the fostering of an anti-China stronghold, south-west of China." Mr. Yang views reflect the fact that China is seriously concerned that the growing relationship has the potential to restrict Beijing influence in Asia-Pacific region.

The landmark ten year defence framework agreement signed recently between India and the United States outlining the future areas of cooperation is viewed with suspicion in China. The content of the agreement raised the eyebrow of the Chinese officials. The areas of cooperation includes expand the two-way defence trade, increasing the opportunities for technology transfer and co-production that remain non-starter for many years, expand collaboration in missile defence and last but not the least establishment of a bilateral Defence Procurement and Production Group.

Beijing came out very strongly against the pact and perceives that this step is aimed at the U.S. armed forces conducting exercises and training in the Indian Ocean. This will improve operational capabilities of the U.S. forces in the region, widen its influence and obtain important strategic advantages.[21] As another Chinese scholar Mr. Zhang Lijun thinks, 'most importantly, India is the best bet to restrict a future strong China, as per U.S. regional security strategy in Asia'. Also Mr. Zhang Guihong said, "U.S.-India strategic partnership in South Asia and the Indian Ocean, and U.S.-Japan military alliance in East Asia and West Pacific Ocean are the two major concerns for China in the new big power games in the Asia-Pacific region." Such a perceptions only reflects that China is serious worried about the growing India-U.S. relationship.[22]

Many India and American Strategic analysts have refuted the claim made by Beijing as not reasonable. As former U.S. Under-Secretary of Commerce, Mr. Juster in his speech in Mumbai on 20 November 2003 has said that, "A strong and vibrant India will be the most effective in advancing our shared objective of promoting peace and stability in Asia, combating global terrorism and stemming the problem of Weapons of Mass Destruction." In addition to this, according to a report prepared by the U.S. based Council on Foreign Relations, "U.S.-India military-to-military cooperation is evolving along lines that the pentagon has established with many non-allied but 'friendly' countries and the policy challenges is to continue this enhanced cooperation and where possible, to enlarge its parameters'.[23] Chinese claim of the growing India-U.S. relationship as moving in the direction of containment of the former is baseless because this is not the first time United States has come out in support of any country. If the United States has expressed its intention to help India become a major power then it is in keeping with the changing world scenario and the role that India is most likely to play for the international peace and security. If the U.S. is willing to help India to become a major power then it is not aimed at undermining Beijing role and instead the move would reduce the responsibility of both the U.S. and China. What the Chinese should not forget is the fact that despite of having fought a war and a clash of interest, the United States has come out in support of it during the cold war period. The United States has provided them with technology and capital support. The U.S. support has played an important part for the Chinese to become a world power. Today when the United States is ready to help India to become a world class power, Beijing is making false claim so that India does not get the benefit of the relationship. Such a Chinese selfish claim should not dissuade India from engaging closely with the

United States the sole super power in the world. India stands at the threshold of huge strategic gain from this relationship.[24]

It was during his visit to New Delhi in March 2008, the U.S. Defence Secretary Mr. Gates made it very clear in the context of the growing military-to-military ties that, "I don't see our improving military relationship in this region in the context of any other country, including China. When you look at the kinds of activities that we are engaged in and the kind of exercises that we conduct...these expanding relationships don't necessarily have to be directed against anybody."[25] Also that United States is not the only country with whom India engage in a joint military exercises. India also conducts regular naval exercises with IOR and Southeast Asian navies. What China should not forget is that it was in the year 2004, India held its second joint exercise with its People's Liberation Army Navy (PLAN). The exercise provided an opportunity for the two Asian giants not only to assess one another, but also to extend a hand of rapprochement in the face of existing circumstances that cause the Chinese to feel encircled by the United States.[26]

5.4 Understanding the Bilateral Relationships between United States, China and India

This section would examine the bilateral relationships between United States and China and India and China, starting from the end of cold war to the present. This would give an overview of how the relationship have shaped during this period.

5.4.1 Post Cold War U.S.-China Relations

Upon assuming office, former U.S. President Mr. Bill Clinton was expecting some improvements from China regarding human rights issues. For which he even threatened to invoke the MFN status (now called normal trade nation status) if China fails to meet to his demands. Despite such threatened message, China was not ready to accept it. Instead, the Chinese Ministry of Foreign Affairs issued an official statement claiming that the U.S. Government had violated the three communiqué and trade agreements between the two countries and considered it as interference in China's internal affairs. The statement urged the Clinton Administration not to link the MFN status to that of the human rights issues. Later the U.S. Administration realised the futility of such a linkage and had publicly declared that in future it would not follow such a policy and instead would broadened the engagement in broad areas. United States enjoy a closer engagement with China during the President Clinton period.

The then U.S. President Mr. Bill Clinton's policy of closer engagement with China did not find favor when he was replaced by former U.S. President George W. Bush. This is reflected in what President George W. Bush has regarded China as a strategic competitor. Unlike Mr. Clinton, he took a tough stand against China.[27] He was very much concerned about the growing Chinese military power that has the potential to threaten Taiwan and even challenge the U.S. pre-eminent position. With this, there emerged suspicion and distrust about each other. China, on the other hand was also disturbed by the U.S. sympathy towards Taiwan. Beijing apprehension were only aggravated by the events of American bombing of the Chinese embassy in Belgrade in 1999 and the collision of American navy surveillance plane and a Chinese fighter jet in 1991. What is to be noted is that despite of these events, the two countries did not come to a direct conflict. This also reflects the eagerness on the part of the two countries to improve the relations.[28]

5.4.1.1 U.S.-China Relations Since 9/11

Like India-U.S. relations, Sino-American relations also have improved since the horrific events of 9/11, when the U.S. World

Trade Center and Pentagon were attacked by the terrorist. Although both sides adopt confrontationist policies, but Washington and Beijing recognise that their national interests are best served by avoiding direct confrontation. Both sides are expanding cooperation where their interests converge. They follow parallel policies of pragmatic and mutual engagement. The closer engagement since 9/11 is a reflection to realization on the part of the two countries the benefit that would be gained by closely cooperating together. Also both countries hold high level talks on political and security issues. The first such talk was held between Vice Foreign Minister, Mr. Dai Bingguo and Deputy Secretary of State, Mr. Robert Zoellick on 1 August 2005.[29] The events of 9/11 did no doubt open the way for keeping aside the divergences and look forward to closely cooperating against the threat posed by the terrorist and others. The Chinese leader without any concerned about the past events was very quick to capitialise on the golden opportunity that it had agreed to extend unconditional support and also exchange intelligence information about the events. The U.S. acknowledged China for extending the much needed unconditional support after the attack. This way, the 9/11 event brought back the relations between the two countries on track.[30]

Understanding between the two countries on the security challenges facing the world has improved since then. This is indicated by President Bush dropping of its earlier perception of China as a 'strategic competitor' and instead trying to find out ways for possible cooperation in the areas of common long-term concern such as combating terrorism and preventing proliferation of weapons of mass destruction. United States wants China to play the role of a global partner, able and willing to match its growing responsibilities to its international responsibilities.[31]

It was during his visit to Washington, Chinese President Mr. Hu Jintao had pointed out that the two countries 'share important common strategic interests in a wide range of areas including economic cooperation and security and on major international and regional issues'. He further added that 'China and the U.S. are not only mutual Stake holders, but also should be constructive cooperators'.

Also it was during the then the U.S. President George W. Bush visit to Beijing on 20 November 2005, Chinese President Mr. Hu Jintao told that both China and the US should work 'gradually to realize trade balance and properly handle frictions and problems' emerging from trade and economic cooperation through dialogue. Later on, it was in Washington on 20 April 2006, Mr. Hu Jintao stressed that the 'mutually beneficial and win-win china-U.S. economic cooperation benefits the growth in the Asia-Pacific region and the rest of the world.[32]

However the expanding relation is undermined by the sharp divergences on various economic and security issues. These include Taiwan crisis, human rights, trade and Intellectual property rights, etc. The U.S. and China have a sharp divergence on Taiwan issue. China is closely watching the closer relations between the United States and Taiwan with suspicion. China is not satisfied with the kind of military support that is being provided to Taiwan by United States. This is reflected in the fact that it was during the Taiwanese President Mr. Lee Teng Hui's visit to the U.S., which from Beijing standpoint, according to David Shambaugh, "has breached it greatest sensitivity- Taiwan." This was further clarified by what the former Prime Minister of Singapore, Mr. Lee Kuan Yew has said that, "China considers any U.S. interference over the issue of Taiwan (as well as Tibet) a hostile act against Chinese national unity.[33] The Taiwan issue has the potential to transfer cooperation into confrontation. China has made it very clear that it would not shy away from using force should Taiwan declare independence. This is a strong message to both the Taiwan and the United States. China has never not ruled out the possibility of the U.S. intervention during the Taiwan crisis.[34]

5.4.1.2 Latest Developments

Recently, during the meeting between the U.S. President Mr. Barack Obama and Chinese President Mr. Hu Jintao, both leaders pledged to further strengthen the bilateral relations and agreed for cooperation on global challenges such as climate change and financial crisis. Mr. Hu said during the meeting that, "China and the U.S. share broader common interests and broader prospects for development in the face of the complicated and ever changing international situation." He further added that China is ready to work with the U.S. to seize these opportunities and deepen their cooperation to push forward bilateral relations in a sound and healthy way.

Chinese leader also said that the relationship between the two countries are on the whole showing a sound momentum of development and the two countries are joining effects to build a positive, cooperative and comprehensive relationship for the twenty-first century. In addition, Chinese President Hu Jintao has put forward four steps to further strengthen and deepen the ties. These include maintain close high-level exchanges, strive to complete the task set out after the first China-U.S. strategic and Economic dialogue held in July 2009, strengthen cooperation on major regional and international issues and lastly but not the least, step up cultural and people-to-people exchanges. On its part, the U.S. President Barack Obama has also committed to strengthen the close ties between the two countries.[35]

Despite of the consistent Taiwan approach since 2007 for the supply of 66-F-16 C/D Block 50/52 fighters to replace aging F-5s, the United States has declined to approve and release it. The reason is very clear; the U.S. does not want to aggravate the improving relations with China. This is also very well reflected in the fact that Wallace Gregson, the U.S. Assistant Secretary of Defense for Asian and Pacific security affairs said, "Although I'm not going to address that issue in detail, I can assure you, this Administration will not waver in its commitment to provide those defense articles and services necessary for Taiwan's self defense." This was made during the recently concluded annual U.S.-Taiwan defense Industry conference. The statement clearly indicates that the U.S. Administration is determined not to allow the relationship with China to fall down.[36]

5.4.2 India-China Relationship After the End of Cold War

The platform for start of Sino-Indian relations after the cold war end has been laid by former Indian Prime Minister Mr. Rajiv Gandhi during his visit to China in 1988. The visit was a historic one because it came after the gap of 34 years by any Indian Prime Minister. Soon after the cold war end, it was former Indian Prime Minister, late Mr. Narasimha Rao who visited China in 1993 where the two countries signed an agreement to maintain peace and tranquility along the Line of Actual Control. Three years later, Chinese President Mr. Jiang Zemin visited India in 1996 and signed an agreement on Confidence Building Measures (CBMs) in the border areas.[37]

The slowly improving relationship passed through a rocky stage when India cited China as the rationale behind its exposing nuclear capability. In his letter to the U.S. President Bill Clinton, former Indian Prime Minister A B Vajpayee had said,

"...we have an overt nuclear weapons state on our borders, a state in which committed armed aggression against India in 1962. Although our relationship with that country has improved in the last decade or so, an atmosphere of distrust persists mainly due to the unresolved border problem. To add to distrusts, that country has materially helped another neighbor of ours to become a covert nuclear weapon state."

China was dismayed with India's reference of her as the reason for tests. However, India despite of this event was not ready to lose relations with China. Very soon India's national security advisor came out to fill the lotion to the fractured relations that happen after the tests. He tried to calm down the anger of China by stressing that India did not regard China as an enemy and that it would like to solve all problems through substantive dialogue in the spirit of friendship and cooperation. This was followed by the statement of Indian External Affairs Minister Mr. Jaswant Singh who also made a statement that India was committed to improving its ties with China so that all outstanding issues were resolved in accordance with the five principles of peaceful co-existence. Very soon, the two countries resumed cooperation and brought back the relations on the track by holding the Joint Working Group meeting on April 1999.[38]

5.4.2.1 *Relationship By the Turn of Twenty-First Century*

Since the dawn of the twenty-first century, relationship between India and China are growing rapidly that is very well manifested by the growing consensus and the convergence of interests that today both countries have a closer understanding on regional and global issues. Both sides today view their relationship as the key to regional stability and security. This is a significant development owing to the fact that both countries have an unresolved territorial dispute and other issues. However, the resolution of the boundary dispute will take some time before it is successfully completed. But what is more important is the commitment on the part of the two countries that the boundary dispute and other issues shall not be allowed to come on the way to the prospering bilateral relations.

Both countries were committed to resolving the border dispute thereby strengthening the relationship. High-level Official interactions between the two countries are on upswing giving way to better understanding on the border disputes.[39] The former Indian Prime Minister A B Vajpayee visit to Beijing in 2003 brought an end to three decades old Sikkim dispute when China agreed to recognise Sikkim as an integral part of India and even issued a maps showing Sikkim as part of India. In response, India recognised Tibet as part of Chinese territory. This was followed by the re-opening of the trade route between India and Tibet via Nathu-la Pass in Sikkim.

In a bid to resolve the remaining border dispute, both sides unanimously agreed to appoint a special representative whose task would be to seek to resolve the problem step by step in three phases. They are identification of political parameters, then negotiation of specific mutual territorial concessions and actual delineation and demarcations of the new boundary. By the time Chinese Prime Minister Mr. Wen- Jiabao visited New Delhi in April 2005, the first step in the resolution of the border problem has been completed. Both India and China have come very close to resolving the border dispute when both sides agreed to hold border talks based on agreed political parameters and guiding principles rather than going by the legal and historical claims of the two countries. Despite of showing seriousness, both countries was not able to provide the strategic breakthrough.[40]

The 11 point agreement signed between the two countries during the visit of Mr. Wen Jiabao to India was the most important step toward resolving the border dispute. The agreement says that India and China are desirous of "qualitatively upgrading the bilateral relationship at all levels and in all areas while addressing differences through peaceful means in a fair, reasonable and mutually acceptable manner." It further added that, "the two sides are seeking a political solution of the boundary question in the context of their overall and long-term interests."[41]

Keeping aside the border dispute, both India and China have also started military relations. Since the security dialogue between India and China started in 2000. Both India and China conducted a bilateral naval exercise in 2004. In a bid to further strengthen the bilateral military relations, both countries were engaged in a first ever joint military counterterrorism exercises in late December 2007.[42]

However, the recent Chinese claim of Arunachal Pradesh would only give rise to delaying the border dispute resolution and distrust over each other's intentions. This seems to reflect that China is not in a hurry to solving the problem at the earliest. At this critical juncture, Indian Prime Minister Manmohan Singh and Chinese Premier Wen Jiabao meet on 24 October in Hua Hin. During the hour long meeting, both sides did not discuss on the Arunachal Pradesh issue but ensured that differences between them on a range of issues should not be allowed to act as impediments to the growing relations.[43]

The relationship between India and China in the coming years is most likely to witness both cooperation and engagement. They will be trying their best to expand the level of political and economic understanding so as to avoid any form of conflict and also serve the interest of both countries. Therefore, from the above analysis of the growing relationship between U.S.-China and India-China, it indicates that neither India nor the United States has been willing to closely align against China.[44]

5.4.2.2 Why Sino-Indian Border Dispute Remain Unresolved?

Both sides have claimed each other for not succeeding to resolve the border dispute. But, it was the lack of consistent

Chinese stand on the issue. They keep on shifting its position from time to time which had only aggravated the chances of breakthrough. The efforts that has been made since the cold war end in general and by the dawn of the twenty-first century in particular has been thwarted by the new Chinese claim to the Indian state of Arunachal Pradesh repeatedly in 2006, 2007 and 2008. The first such claim was made during the Chinese President Hu Jintao's visit to India in 2006. Before this, China had never claimed the whole of Arunachal Pradesh to be part of their territory. The only part they were claiming was the Tawang area. This sends out a wrong impression to India that they are not in a hurry to resolve the dispute. This way the Indian officials were not very clear about the Chinese intentions. Their claim of Arunachal Pradesh is not reasonable. India will only stick to the McMahon line that has been offered to it in April 1960.

Beijing is taking more time to resolve the border issue for its own benefit. Another factor that has also worsened the possibility of resolving the issue is the Chinese linking of the border settlement with the Tibet issue. They perceive that the early border settlement will have its implications on the status of the Tibet. So, they are waiting for the Tibet issue to be resolved first. This will only delayed the process of border dispute settlement. Unless they show any seriousness, India should not step forward to resolving the border dispute because, resolving the dispute should be in the interests of both countries.[45]

Indian Strategic affairs analyst Mr. Brahma Chellaney was quite right when he said that, "keeping India engaged in endless and fruitless border talks is a key Chinese objective so that Beijing, in the meantime, can change the Himalayan balance decisively in its favor through accumulation of military power and greater infrastructure development."[46] Therefore, it becomes very clear that resolution of the ongoing border dispute in future can take place if and only if both sides are ready to make some changes in its stand on the dispute. And also the lack of political commitment is only delaying to provide result.

5.4.3 Factors That May Take India Closer to United States

Containment of China is not in the immediate interests of neither India nor the United States, but there are certain factors that may propel India to move closer to engaging the United States in a way that has never experienced before. India and the United States share deep and serious concern about the rising Chinese military power. For the United States, China remains the only regional power that has the potential to seriously challenge or deny the U.S. role in Eurasia. At the same time, strategically India is also seriously concerned about the Chinese illegal military arms and equipment rapprochement with Pakistan that has the potential to threaten India's security and also undermine India's ambitions to play a key role in Asian continent.

According to a Ministry of Defence annual report 2008-09, "the possibility of enhancing connectivity with Pakistan through the territory of Jammu and Kashmir, illegally occupied by China and Pakistan, and with other countries, will also have direct military implications for India." The report further added that, "Beijing White Paper on National in 2008 stated objective of developing strategic missile and space-based assets, rapidly enhance its blue-water Navy and systematically upgrade infrastructure, reconnaissance and surveillance and operational capabilities in border areas 'will have an effect on the overall military environment' in the neighbourhood India."[47] The more the China have a closer relations with Pakistan, the rationale will be for India to enjoy closer relations with the United States.

These days, Beijing is increasingly making an effort to influence India's neighborhood for its long-term benefits. These include the development of the Gwadar Port off the Baluchistan coast, closer military ties with Myanmar and also its developmental projects in Bangladesh. These are viewed with suspicion in India.[48] India is strategically concerned about the 'string of pearls' strategy employed by China to extending its areas of influence very close to India's border. These include Pakistan in the north-west, Nepal, Bangladesh and Myanmar in the north-east, and Maldives and Srilanka in the South. India's inimical relations with both China and Pakistan have given way to the closer cooperation between the latter two countries. The "all-weather" and time-tested China-Pakistan strategic partnership has been taken further forward recently. Their joint interest of containing India from becoming a regional power in South Asia and gaining increasing weight on the international stage has contributed to strengthening the China-Pakistan strategic partnership, based on the premise that the enemy of one's enemy is one's friend. Pakistan got maximum benefit out of this. India is seriously concerned about China providing arms and equipment's needs to Pakistan that has nothing to do with its security concerns. They have transferred to Pakistan weapons designs and nuclear fissile material. Beijing has equipped Islamabad with JF-17 aircraft and JF-17 production facilities, F-22P frigates with helicopters, K-8 jet trainers, T-85 tanks, F-7 aircraft, small arms and ammunition. It has also built a turnkey ballistic missile manufacturing facility near Rawalpindi and helped Pakistan develop the 750-km-range, solid-fuel Shaheen-1 ballistic missile[49] (Details of the weapons supplied to Pakistan are shown in table 5.2).

Table 5.2: China's Major Arms Supply to Pakistan during the Period From (1990-2005).

Sl. No.	Years of Delivery	Weapons Designation	Weapons Description	No. Ordered/ Delivered
1	1990-2001	Red Arrow (called Baktar Shikan by Pakistan)	Anti-tank missiles	8,600
2	1991-99	Technology for the licensed production of T-69-II	Main Battle tanks	250+
3	1991-98	M-11	Short range ballistic missiles	80+
4	1992-97	T-85II, T-85IIAP and Type 85 III	MBTs	264, 3 & 1
5	1993	F- 7P	Combat aircraft	40
6	1994	K-8	Trainer Aircraft	6
7	1994-2001	QW-1 Vanguard portable	Portable Surface-to-air missiles (called by Pakistan as Anza-2)	560
8	1995	Armoured Combat vehicles		20
9	1996	Technology for Hatf SRBM		
10	1996-97	LY-60 N	Ship-to-air missile system + missiles	2+96
11	1997	C-801/802	Ship-to-Ship missile system	4
12	1997	C-802	Ship-to-Ship missile	32
13	1997-2001	Type-347G	Fire control radar	3
14	1998	130 mm Guns	Large Calibre artillery systems	27
15	2000	130 mm Guns of Type 59- 1	Large Calibre artillery systems	60
16	2001-01	Technology transfer for the construction of Jalalat-class FAC	Missile- armed	2
17	2000-01	C-802/CSS-N-8	Anti-ship missiles	24
18	2000-08	K-8	Fighter/trainer aircraft	75-100
19	2002	F-7 MG	Combat Aircraft	57
20	2001-02	F-7 PG Aircraft	Combat Aircraft	46
21	2002-06	Jiangwei	II class frigates	4
22	2003-04	122 mm D-30 (Howitzer)	Large caliber artillery systems	143
23	2003	A-5	Combat Aircraft	6
24	2004	Type 85	Main battle tank	10
25	2004	Type-347G	Fire control radar	2
26	2004	C-802/CSS-N-8	Anti-ship missile saccade	16

Sl. No.	Years of Delivery	Weapons Designation	Weapons Description	No. Ordered/ Delivered
27	2004	PL-12/SD-10	BVR AAM	
28	2005	C-803	Anti-Ship missile	32
29	2005	PL-12/SD-10	BVR air-to-air missile	
30	2005	FM-80/ HQ-7	Surface-to-air missile	64 (for Jiangwei frigates)
31	Deliverably possibly starting 2007-08	FC-1/JF-17	Multi-role combat aircraft	150*

* China-Pakistan joint venture.

Source: Prepared using Jasjit Singh, "Trends in Defence Expenditure", in Jasjit Singh (ed.), Asian Defence Review 2006 (New Delhi: Knowledge World in Association With the Centre for Air Power Studies, 2006), pp. 91-95, B. R. Deepak, India & China 1904-2004: A Century of Peace and Conflict (New Delhi: Manak Publications Pvt. Ltd., 2005), p. 368 and Srikanth Kondapalli, "Pakistan in China's Security Perceptions", in Swaran Singh (ed.), China-Pakistan Strategic Cooperation: Indian Perspectives (New Delhi: Manohar Publishers, 2007), pp. 74-75.

The China-Pakistan strategic partnership is aimed at foiling India's bid to emerge as a major power in the world and to maintain a balance between the two South Asian rivals. To contain India, China has supplied Pakistan with conventional arms, nuclear weapon capability and ballistic missile know-how. Besides, there are also credible reports about the presence of Chinese troops and personnel in Pakistan-controlled in India's state of Jammu and Kashmir. China's policy of equipping Pakistan serves dual purposes- one is that it helps Pakistan to maintain balance with arch rival India, thereby challenging India's conventional military strength and secondly, it pressurises India from taking any such steps that is not in favor of China. This way arms supply relationship between China and Pakistan has serious negative implications to India. These developments have compelled many strategic analysts in India to view that Beijing has a continuous and an uninterrupted support to Pakistan as a policy of encirclement of India. Also it seeks to ensure that Beijing successfully proceeds with its efforts to achieve its objective and delay India's ability to challenge China. India's suspicions were further aggravated when China developed a naval base in Gwadar in Karachi. Given this posture, Chinese claim of India-U.S. defence cooperation directing towards them is not justified. The recent Chinese expansion should not become an offshoot to the growing India-U.S. defence and security ties that holds the key to international peace and security. But the Chinese move would only destabilise the Asian security rather than bringing stability to the region[50] and gain more and more weights in the international system.

As the relationship gets stronger with every passing year and the Beijing's ensuring security guarantee for Islamabad has only brought significant change in the latter perception towards the former. Pakistan gives strategic importance to its partnership with China. This was very well reflected in the words of Dr Shireen Mazari, "The Peking has not only repudiated to back down on its defence pledges to Islamabad, in spite of Western pressure, but has been about especially responsible for permitting Pakistan a modicum of sufficient defence ability and nuclear development clearly makes China absolutely essential for Pakistan's survival., Pakistan has become extremely casual about its relations with China." Despite U.S. imposition of Pressler Amendment upon Islamabad, China continue to extend support to Islamabad nuclear weapons programme. China was closely working with Pakistan over the development of 9300 Mw power plant at Chasma. Moreover, China has been accused for transferring 500 ring magnets for Pakistan's nuclear facilities.[51]

China's anti-Indian stand is very well reflected in the recently concluded nuclear deal with Pakistan. Under the deal, China would be lending Pakistan with $207 million to buy two more reactors- Chasma-3 and Chasma-4. This deal is directed toward the successful conclusion of India-U.S. civil nuclear deal to show that if United States can offer nuclear deal to India then why cannot we offer to our close ally, no matter whether it goes against the wish of the international community and in particular to India. When the United States under the leadership of former President Mr. George W. Bush has out rightly rejected Pakistan demand for a nuclear deal, China has come out in support of its long time close allies Pakistan for establishing two more reactors at the Chasma atomic complex in Punjab. This step is aimed at maintaining a nuclear parity between India and Pakistan and also to ensure that India is engaged in a tussle with Pakistan that would restrict New Delhi from moving ahead and shift its focus from China.[52]

However, India is most unlikely to adopt a confrontationist stand against its Asian giants, China owing to the fact that it would keep the options alive of closely engaging with all the major powers of the world, which it perceive is the key to it becoming a major power in the world.

5.5 China's Military Modernisation

U.S. increasing concerns over the China's military modernisation is spelled out explicitly in the Pentagon's annual report on the Chinese military as, "China does not now face a direct threat from another nation. Yet it continues to invest heavily in its military particularly in programs designed to improve power projection. The pace and scope of China's military build-up are, already, such as to put regional military balance at risk. Current trends in China's military modernisation could provide Beijing with a force capable of prosecuting a range of military operations in Asia- well beyond Taiwan-potentially posing a credible threat to modern militaries operating in the region".

According to American perspective, Chinese military modernisation started in early 1990's, in a bid to gain great power status. Its move was fastened by the Revolution in military affairs and high-tech power and capability displayed by the U.S. during the Gulf war in 1991. Since then, Chinese civilian and military leadership was very serious about strengthening Chinese military capabilities of PLA. With the demise of Soviet Union, China has been relieved from the Soviet threat and has revised its security strategy to meet the challenges that comes from the PRC's borders. Since 2003, Chinese view that the Sea Lanes of communications (SLOCs) through Southeast Asia and across the Indian Ocean as the key to its security. Chinese military buildup is aimed at meeting the challenges that come on the way to resolving the Taiwan crisis. For which they have projected that the opposition may be from U.S. side. China's rapid military modernisation is a cause of concern to India too. For the United States, it poses a serious threat to its super power position, while for India owing to its close proximity and border dispute which it had with China. In an effort to bridge the gap, China had started modernizing its navy and air force.[53]

Recent years had witnessed a military modernisation process in China that would bring a significant change in the nature of its military power. The Chinese air force commander stated on 9 November 1999 that "Beijing would begin transforming the service from a territorial defence force into a more aggressive one with greater capabilities to attack well beyond China's forces." Moreover, the U.S. Secretary of Defence's annual report to the Congress stated:

The PLA's transformation features new doctrine for modern warfare, reform of military institutions and personnel systems, improved exercise and training standards, and the acquisition of advanced foreign (especially Russian) and domestic weapon systems. Several aspects of China's military development have surprised U.S. analysts, including the pace and scope of its strategic forces modernization. China's military expansion is already such as to alter regional military balances. Long-term trends in China's strategic nuclear forces modernization, land and sea based access denial capabilities, and emerging precision- strike weapons have the potential to pose credible threats to modern militaries operating in the region.[54] The Chinese military modernisation drive can be observed from its official defence expenditure shown in table 5.3 which keeps on improving from one year to another. China has increased its defence budget to US$106.4 billion in 2012, registering 11.2 percent jump from 2011 budget. The Chinese defence budget is much higher as it does not include the expenditure on areas like space which have significant military utility. Additionally, China's internal security budget has also been increased to US$ 111 billion for 2012 surpassing the defence budget amid growing unrest in Tibet and Xinjiang.[55] China's military modernisation drive is an ongoing process which would take years. Through this modernisative, they want to ensure that their forces are equipped with advanced high-tech weapons.

To keep India on dark, Beijing is making a false claim that India's eagerness to play a major role and its cooperation with the major powers such as the U.S. in the Indian Ocean is aimed at thwarting any outside power's would threaten its sea-borne energy. In the name of which, it is expanding its naval capability by equipping them with aircraft carriers, missile destroyers and nuclear attack submarine.[56]

Table 5.3: China's Official Defence Expenditure Statistics (in billions Yuan)

Sl. No	Year	Official Def. Exp. (bn Yuan)	Population (mns)	Armed forces	Total Government Exp. (bn Yuan)
1	1991	33.03	1,132.07	3,200	379.39
2	1992	37.78	1,148.59	3,200	442.39
3	1993	43.25	1,171.71	3,200	472.74
4	1994	52.06	1,190.00	3,200	582.00
5	1995	63.70	1,201.00	2,900	680.91
6	1996	72.00	1,210.47	2,935	790.29
7	1997	81.26	1,211.21	2,935	923.30
8	1998	93.47	1,221.62	2,840	1,079.71
9	1999	107.64	1,231.00	2,800	1,318.65
10	2000	120.75	1,236.00	2,800	1,588.44
11	2001	144.20	1,242.00	2,500	1,890.09
12	2002	170.77	1,260.00	2,500	2,2005.17
13	2003	190.78	1,270.00	2,500	2,464.94
14	2004	247.70	1,280.00	2,500	2,848.68
15	2005	283.80	1,290.00	2,250	
16	2006			2,300	

Source: Jasjit Singh, "Trends in Defence Spending", in Jasjit Singh (ed.), Asian Defence Review 2006 (New Delhi: Knowledge World in Association with Centre for Air power Studies, 2006), pp. 54-55.

5.6 Long-Term Implications of the Containment Strategy

Any move directed at the containment of the China must first assess the short-term and the long-term implications to the international security. The close relationship between India, the U.S. and China are the key to international peace, security and stability. This is reflected in what former U.S. President George W. Bush had said after meeting Chinese counterpart Mr. Hu Jintao that "both the USA and China share extensive common strategic interests under the new international circumstances. A good U.S.-China relationship is of strategic importance to the maintenance and promotion of peace, stability and development in the Asia-Pacific region and the world at large. Both the nations agree to address the bilateral relationship from a strategic and long-term perspective and to move forward for development of constructive and cooperative China-U.S. relationship in the 21st century."

For the U.S., relationship with China is important given its economic and military capability, to meet the twenty-first century challenges. It includes fighting terrorism, ensuring international peace and security. The U.S. would need the support of China in meeting the challenges posed by the nuclear programmes of North Korea and Iran.[57] If the growing relationship is really aimed at hedging China then there is no doubt that it would have its implications on the international security. The responsibility of the security and safety of the international community is before them given their convergence of interest on various security challenges facing the world. If the responsible state are engaged in the containment of each other for the sake of their interests rather than cooperating each other in eradicating such problems then what to say about the international peace and security.

The containment strategy would give way to counter containment that would be highly disastrous and costly, plus the objective of achieving the regional and global security would be under threat. As former U.S. Defence Secretary of Defence, Mr. William J. Perry and Assistant Secretary of Defence, Mr. Ashton B. Carter has said that, "Hedging is contagious....and hedging can beget more hedging in a dangerous spiral."[58]

The South Asian security and stability would be seriously undermined by adopting containment strategy. As such this step would only help to deepen the ongoing defence and strategic ties between Pakistan and China with whom India does not share very close relations. This is reflected from the fact that unlike the United States, China has continued to engage in close relations with Pakistan even after the end of cold war. Beijing would only tighten its stand on ensuring security guarantee for Islamabad. This would only mean that India should be prepared both mentally and physically to face a two-pronged problem directing from both east and west location. And also the possibility of resolving the border problems would be under threat.[59]

5.7 India-U.S. Strategic Relations: Implications to Russia

Does the growing relationship between India and the United States would have any implications to India's relations with other major powers of the world? As mentioned at the beginning of the study that the relationship between India and the United States is neither aligned nor aimed at any third country. India will continue to remains committed to strategic autonomy of its foreign relations. India's relationship with other major powers of the world will be decided based on New Delhi interest rather than dictated by the U.S. interest because India's interest is not subjugated to the U.S. interest. The relationship is for the mutual benefit of the two countries and that it will cooperate only when treated as an equal and also where its own interests are directly involved.[60]

India in the twenty-first century will continue to embark on a path toward pursuing independent foreign policies keeping in mind its respective national interest and aspirations to become a global power. The growing India-U.S. multi-faceted relations will have no negative implications to the traditional India-Russian ties. If India has taken a step forward to expanding defence and security relations with the U.S. then it is not at the cost of any of its ties with other countries including Russia, China or Japan. India has so far successfully managed to closely engaging with both counties that today both the US and Russia considers India to be their natural ally. India has a lot to gain out of the strengthening relationship with both the U.S. and Russia. Like U.S, Russia occupies an important place in India's foreign policy. With Russia we have a close understanding on major regional and global issues of our concerns. India enjoys a multi-dimensional strategic partnership with Russia. Russia has no problem to India's closer ties with the United States. It all depends on India how it manages to handle the relationship.

Indian Prime Minister Manmohan Singh has made it very clear to the public the importance of expanding close relations with Russia in a way that,

> "Relations with Russia are a key pillar of our foreign policy, and we regard Russia as a trusted and reliable strategic partner. Ours is a relationship that not only stands independent of any other, but whose significance has grown overtime. Our partnership covers areas such as defence, civil nuclear energy, space, science and technology, hydrocarbons and trade and investment."[61]

India's ties with thc U.S. will in any case not circumscribe its long-standing and a strategic partner Russia that holds the key to India's overall military and energy security and its quest for great power status. Unlike the U.S., Russia has been the major supplier of arms and equipment needs to India without any hesitation. Also it accepts India's pre-eminence in the region. It is very much keen to see India play a major power role in the world. Russia better understand the security challenges facing India from its neighboring countries. Russia has come out in full support to the much needed successful conclusion of the civil nuclear cooperation between India and the United States. Russia was eagerly waiting for such opportunity, as it would strengthen the cooperation between the two countries. It was during the recent visit of Indian Prime Minister Mr.

Manmohan Singh to Russia, both countries sign as many as six agreements, the most important being a civilian nuclear energy agreement under which Russia will set up more nuclear reactors in India, transfer the entire range of nuclear energy technologies. How much Russia is committed to such cooperation is reflected from the fact that it has promised to supply nuclear fuel even after the deal is called off. Russians have also promised India with enrichment and reprocessing rights.[62]

Unlike China, Russia is not much concerned about the depth of India-U.S. relations. In an interview with Hardnews magazine, Mr. Vyacheslav I. Trubnikov, Russian ambassador to India has said that 'Why should we fear close relations between New Delhi and Washington?'. He further pointed out that Russia too had 'considerably intensified' its cooperation with the U.S. in recent years even though their positions 'do not coincide in all respects'. This move should no doubt make India feel better and secure in terms expanding relations with both countries. Russian response reflects the basic understanding that it share with India. Russia better knows that it is in the interests of India that it expands its relations with other major powers of the world.[63]

5.8 India-U.S. Strategic Relations: Implications to Japan

Unlike China, Japan enjoys a prosperous relationship with both the United States and India. As we all know that Japan is a strategic ally for the United States. Japan's engagement with the United States is much deeper and broader than India is to the United States. Therefore, there should not be any problem for Japan by the strengthening strategic ties between India and the United States. The growing role that India is expected to play in the twenty-first century world in terms of ensuring regional and global security and in particular to security in the

Indian Ocean, should no doubt ease Japan's reactions to the strategic relationship between India and the U.S. India has in recent years successfully dealt with the problem of piracy. Another reason is that Japan is very much aware of the fact that India's relationship with China is almost unpredictable. Japan views that India has the capability to counter Chinese hegemony both in economic and military aspects.[64]

In his talk delivered at the United Service Institution (New Delhi), Mr. Masahiro Akiyama, Vice Minister of Japan Defence Agency highlighted the need for India and Japan to keep on engaging with the U.S. His view reflects that there should not be any problem to Japan by the growing relationship between India and United States.[65]

India and Japan have in recent years gained close understanding on the importance of maritime security, since both countries depend on sea for trade. Security of the sea holds the key for their economic progress and development. It was during his address to the Federation of Indian Chambers of Commerce and Industry in January 2003, the Japanese Foreign Minister Mr. Yoriko Kawaguchi had stated that 'cooperative maintenance of the security of maritime traffic in the sea-lanes that stretch across the Indian Ocean and the Strait of Malacca are among the security and defense issues, which deserve our increased attention'.[66] Both Tokyo and New Delhi have agreed to take up joint security measures including exercises between the Indian navy and the Japan Maritime Self-Defence Force (JMSDF), military-to-military exchanges and high-level dialogue.

With increasing energy security challenges and the need to sustain their economic growth, Tokyo and New Delhi may be compelled to cooperate and play a mutually beneficial role in the security of IOR. In this context, India is expanding its cooperation with countries such as the U.S., Japan, France and others. This step is aimed at safeguarding the various gates to the Indian Ocean. India's growing role in the Indian Ocean should not be perceived wrongly. India have demonstrated the positive role it can play when in 2003, the Indian Navy escorted the U.S. ships carrying goods. Also during the Tsunami incidents, India has demonstrated its search and rescue capabilities.[67]

The United States, India and Japan have a keen interest in ensuring stability of the India Ocean. The joint military exercises in the India Ocean should not have any problem to Japan security, since it is aimed at ensuring security in the region. It would be incorrect to say that the growing India-U.S. cooperation would destabilise the region through increasing the possibility of competition between India, China and Southeast Asian littoral states.[68] This is owing to the fact that India along with the United States, Japan and others countries have carried out joint naval exercises on September 2007. This exercise was aimed at maintaining good order at sea in the Indian Ocean region rather than targeting at any country that would result in creating instability in the region. It would help in increasing understanding among these countries on issues of mutual interest including providing security to sea-lanes in IOR (Indian Ocean region).[69] Also that India has a significant role to play in the protection of the sea lanes of communication.

5.9 Strategic Areas of Cooperation between India, China, United States, Russia and Japan.

The international community would benefit from the strategic cooperation between India, China, the United States, Russia and Japan on wide range of regional and global issues. These include fighting terrorism, preventing the proliferation of weapons of mass destruction, peace keeping operations, maritime security, security of the sea lanes of communication, climate change, etc. If there are areas of divergences among these countries, there are also areas of convergences that are most likely to bring these countries together. Really, the changing international security environment requires cooperation between these three countries rather than confronting each other. The relationship among these countries holds the key to international peace and security.

Former U.S. President Mr. George W. Bush has expressed optimism about the prospects for the major powers avoiding conflict. This was indicated very clearly in the Administration 2002 National Security Strategy report that, "today the international community has the best chance since the rise of the nation-state in the seventeenth century to build a world where great powers compete in peace instead of continually prepare for war. Today the world's great powers find ourselves on the same side- united by common dangers of terrorist violence and chaos." This is followed by what former U.S. Ambassador Mr. Richard Haass, Director of Policy Planning in the State Department during the Bush tenure has said in 2002 that, 'war between the great powers is almost unthinkable'. Moreover, the U.S. Secretary of Defence Donald Rumsfeld has noted in June 2004 that 'future dangers will less likely be from battle between great powers, and more likely from enemies that work in small cells, that are fluid and strike without warning anywhere, anytime- enemies that have access to increasingly formidable technology and weapons'. These views reflect the need for constant cooperation among the major powers that holds the key to international peace and security. They should stop projecting each other as a threat and instead come together to finding ways on how to tackle the challenges facing them and the world.[70]

If the United States today wants to have broader relations with both India and China that holds the key to international peace and security. Chinese leaders are also eager to work closely together with the United States and India. According to the Chinese officials and policy advisers, the Chinese leadership has concluded that the only China, as a rising power, can avoid conflict with the dominant power, the U.S. is not only to eschew challenging the current hegemon but also to forge a close partnership with it. Also the Chinese leaders have assured the U.S. officials that it does not seek to reduce or eliminate the U.S. presence, including military, in the Asia Pacific region and that China wants to cooperate with the U.S. on a wide range of issues of strategic importance to both countries.[71] Therefore, as the year rolls by there will be need for more and more cooperation among the major power countries on the global challenges facing the international community.

5.10 Conclusion

From the above analysis, one thing is very clear that the interests of India and the United States may be better served by being friends rather than becoming allies. India, the United States and China have both common and divergent interests that would make it quite difficult for the first two countries to adopt containment strategy against the third one. There may be cases in future where India and China would come together against the United States particularly when it adopts a policy that is strictly unilateral or interventionist. And also there is a possibility of the United States and China coming together to pressurising India on nuclear issue and on Kashmir dispute with Pakistan. This is further accentuated by the fact that there has been a significant thaw in the relationship between the three countries after the cold war end. This is not to say that there will not be any conflict between the three countries.[72]

The growing relationship between India and the United States does not mean India would come under the U.S. pressure to agreeing to hedging China with whom India had a border problem that remain unresolved for the last more than four decades. Also India had a share of common interests with China on many aspects. India has in the past resisted the U.S. attempt to take the former in its side to pressuring China. For instance India express unwillingness to the United States proposal of setting up a Center for Asian Democracy and vote against Beijing or at least abstain on China's human rights record at the UN Commission on Human Rights.[73]

If on the one side India has resisted the U.S. pressure to come with it against China but on the other side there is always a possibility of U.S.-China cooperation in pressuring India vis-à-vis South Asian security and signing the NPT and CTBT. India has very good reason as to why it cannot move along with the United States to contain China. After the 1998 exposition of nuclear capability by India and Pakistan, the United States and China under the leadership of President Bill Clinton and President Mr. Jiang Zemin respectively, together issued a joint statement stressing the need for both countries to jointly tackling the security situation in South Asia. The U.S. President Bill Clinton urged Beijing to play a bigger role in ensuring the peace and security in the South Asian region.[74]

Any negative approach on the part of India and the United States vis-à-vis China would have regional and global implications. Therefore, it is important that India and the United States pursue a moderate and subtle approach toward China that sends a positive message and also that it satisfy the interests of the two largest democracies, India and the Unites States.[75]

India and the United States instead of adopting a hedging strategy must find out ways of strategic cooperation with China. The U.S. relations with India and China are much better than ever before in the past that today they have a broader interaction on regional and global issues. On the other hand India's relation with China is also on the upswing in recent years.

Therefore a stable and prosperous relation between the U.S. and China should be in the interests of India. Otherwise, India would face a difficult situation of having to choose sides among the two countries in a conflict that would take India in an advantageous situation.[76] It is very much important for India that it keep the options alive for its closer engagement with other countries of the world that would serve its interests.

Endnotes

[1] See Ashley J. Tellis Testimony before the Senate Foreign Relations Committee on, "U.S.-India Atomic Energy cooperation: Strategic and Nonproliferation Implications", 26 April 2006, p. 5.

[2] Adil Sultan Muhammad, "Indo-US Civilian Nuclear Cooperation Agreement: Implications on South Asian Security Environment", The Henry L. Stimson Center, July 2006, p. 21.

[3] M.K. Bhadrakumar, "Russia-US relations: Impact on Asia's Strategic Stability", in Maharajakrishna Rasgotra, (ed.), The New Asian Power Dynamic (New Delhi: Sage Publication in Connection with Observer Research Foundation, 2007), p. 262.

[4] V R Raghavan, "Indo-US Strategic Partnership: China as a Factor", U.S.I. Journal (New Delhi), vol. CXXXVII(570), October-December 2007, p. 499.

[5] Ibid., p. 505.

[6] Karthika Sasikumar, "India's Emergence as a 'Responsible' Nuclear Power" International Journal (Canada), vol. LXII(4), Fall 2007, p. 838.

[7] V R Raghavan, n. 4, p. 502.

[8] Venugopal B. Menon, "India-China Relations: Critical Issues", in Rajen Harshe and KM Sethi (eds.), Engaging with the World: Critical Reflections on India's Foreign Policy (New Delhi: Orient Longmans Pvt. Ltd., 2005), pp. 164-65.

[9] V.P. Dutt, "Foreign Policy in the 21st Century: An Overview", in V.D. Chopra (ed.), India's Foreign Policy in the 21st Century (New Delhi: Kalpaz Publications, 2006), p. 26.

[10] Chintamani Mahapatra, "The United States and the Asian Powers", in R.R. Sharma (ed.), India and Emerging Asia (New Delhi: Thousand Oaks: London: Sage Publications, 2005), p. 165.

[11] K Subrahmanyam, "Indo-US Relations in the Coming Decades", U.S.I. Journal, vol. CXXXV(561), July-September 2005, p. 371.

[12] Zhang Guihong, "US-India Strategic Partnership: Implications for China", International Studies (New Delhi), vol. 42(3&4), July-December 2005, pp. 286-89.

[13] Zhang Guihong, "U.S. Security Policy Toward South Asia and its Implications For China: A China Perspective", The Henry L. Stimson Center, January 2003, p. 19.

[14] David Scott, China Stands Up: The PRC and the International System (London and New York: Routledge, 2007), p. 112.

[15] Ibid., p. 115.

[16] Ibid., p. 123.

[17] Harinder Sekhon, "America's Role in Asia", in Daljit Singh (ed.), Political and Security Dynamics of South and Southeast Asia (Singapore: Institute of Southeast Asian Studies, 2007), p. 39.

[18] V R Raghavan, n. 4, p. 496.

[19] Ibid., pp. 500-01.

[20] David Shambaugh, "The Evolving Security Order in Asia: Implications for US-India Relations", in Alyssa Ayres and C. Raja Mohan (ed.), Power Realignments in Asia: China, India and United States (New Delhi: Sage Publications, 2009), p. 139.

[21] Monika Chansoria, "Indo-US Relations: Assessing the China Factor", World Focus (New Delhi), vol. XXIX(7), July 2008, pp. 270-71.

[22] David Scott, n. 14, p. 157.

[23] Chintamani Mahapatra, n. 10, pp. 173-75.

[24] K Subrahmanyam, n. 11, pp. 360-65.

[25] Karl F. Inderfurth, "U.S.-India Relations", in The Asia Foundation, America's Role in Asia: Asian and American Views (San Francisco, 2008), pp. 266-67, available at <http://asiafoundation.org/resources/pdfs/19IndiaARA2008.pdf>.

[26] P K Ghosh, "Maritime Security Challenges in South Asia and the Indian Ocean: Response Strategies", Paper Presented at the Conference on Maritime Security in Asia, Honolulu, Hawaii, 18-20 January 2004, available at <http://www.southchinasea.org/docs/ghosh,%20maritime%20security%20challenges%20in%20S Asia%20&%20Indian%20Ocean.pdf>.

[27] Jia Qingguo, "Learning to Live with the Hegemon: Evolution of China's Policy Toward the US Since the End of Cold War", Journal of Contemporary China (United Kingdom), vol. 14(44), August 2005, pp. 398- 401.

[28] Harry Harding, "The Evolution of the Strategic Triangle: China, India, and the United States", in Francine R. Frankel and Harry Harding (eds.), The India-China relationship: Rivalry and Engagement (New Delhi: Oxford University Press, 2004), pp. 334-35.

[29] Paul H. B. Godwin, "China as a Major Asian Power: The Implications of its Military Modernisation- A View from the United States", in Evelyn Goh and Sheldon W. Simon (eds.), China, the United States and Southeast Asia: Contending Perspectives on Politico, Security and Economics (New York and London: Routledge, 2008), pp. 148-51.

[30] Jia Qingguo, n. 27, pp. 402-03.

[31] Banning Garrett, "US-China Relations in the Era of Globalisation and Terror: a Framework for Analysis", Journal of Contemporary China (United Kingdom), vol. 15(48), August 2006, p. 409.

[32] D.S. Rajan, "Chinese Perceptions of the US: Tactical Friendship and Strategic Suspicions", in Maharajakrishna Rasgotra (ed.), The New Asian Power Dynamic (New Delhi: Sage Publication in Connection with Observer Research Foundation, 2007), p. 83.

[33] Gary Ang, "Instituting Change in U.S. Foreign Policy Towards the Emerging Pacific Rim", in Karl P. Magyar (ed.), United States Post-Cold War Defence Interests: A Review of the First Decade (New York: Palgrave Mcmillan, 2004), p. 105.

[34] Jia Qinggua, n. 27, p. 407.

[35] See, "China, U.S. for Closer Cooperation", The Hindu (Hyderabad), 24 September 2009.

[36] Wednell Minnick, "U.S.-Taiwan Meeting Ends on F-16 Question", Defense News (United States), 5 October 2009, p. 60.

[37] Rajiv Sikri, Challenge and Strategy: Rethinking India's Foreign Policy (New Delhi: Sage Publications, 2009), p. 92.

[38] Alka Acharya, China and India: Politics of Incremental Engagement (New Delhi: Har-Anand Publications Pvt. Ltd., 2008), pp. 67-72.

[39] David Shambaugh, n. 20, pp. 146-47.

[40] C. Raja Mohan, "The Evolution of Sino-Indian Relations: Implications for the United States" in Alyssa Ayres and C. Raja Mohan (ed.), Power Realignments in Asia: China, India and United States (New Delhi: Sage Publications, 2009), pp. 277-78.

[41] P S Das, "India and China-A Relationship for the Future", U.S.I. Journal, vol. CXXXV(561), July-September 2005, p. 382.

[42] Manish Dabhade, "India and East Asia: A Region Rediscovered", in Harsh V. Pant (ed.), Indian Foreign Policy in a Unipolar World (New Delhi: Routledge, 2009), p. 317.

[43] See, "PM, Wen Avoid Arunachal Talk during Meeting", Times of India (Pune), 25 October 2009.

[44] Harry Harding, n. 28, p. 334.

[45] Rajiv Sikri, n. 37, pp. 94-97.

[46] See, "India, China Complement Each Other: People's Daily", Times of India (Pune), 6 August 2009.

[47] Annual Report 2008-09, Ministry of Defence, Government of India, pp. 5-6.

[48] Deepa M. Ollapally, "India and Russia: Renewing the Relationship", in Harsh V. Pant (ed.), Indian Foreign Policy in a Unipolar World (New Delhi: Routledge, 2009), p. 201.

[49] Lisa Curtis, "China's Military and Security Relationship with Pakistan", Testimony before the U.S.-China Economic and Security Review Commission, 20 May 2009.

[50] Kapil Kak, "India-China Relations: An Overview", Air Power Journal (New Delhi), vol. 3(3), Monsoon 2006, pp. 33-34 and Monika Chansoria, n. 21, pp. 269-70.

[51] Muhammad Ishaque Fani, "Pakistan-China Security Relations and Mutual Ventures", JRSP, vol. 46, No. 2, 2009, p. 81-6.

[52] Devki Nandan, "Sino-Pak Nuclear Nexus and India's Concerns", Issue Brief, Centre for Air Power Studies (New Delhi), 16 July 2010, pp. 1-2.

[53] Michael Chambers, "China's Military Rise to Great Power Status: Its Implications for the United States in Southeast Asia", in Evelyn Goh and Sheldon W. Simon (eds.), China, the United States and Southeast Asia: Contending Perspectives on Politico, Security and Economics (New York: London: Routledge, 2008), pp. 167-69.

[54] Jasjit Singh, "Trends in Defence Spending", in Jasjit Singh (ed.), Asian Defence Review 2006 (New Delhi: Knowledge World in Association Har-Anand Publications Pvt. Ltd. with the Centre for Air Power Studies, 2006), p. 99.

[55] "China's Defence Budget to Increase by 11.2 percent", in China Military Watch, vol. 1 (2), 16 March 2012.

[56] Andrew S. Erickson, "The Growth of China's Navy: Implications for Indian Ocean Security", Strategic Analysis, vol. 32(4), July 2008, pp. 657-58.

[57] D. S. Rajan, n. 32, pp. 98-99.

[58] David Shambaugh, n. 20, pp. 154-55.

[59] Zhang Guihong, n. 13, pp. 17-18.

[60] Walter K. Andersen, "India and the United States: A Different Kind of Relationship", Testimony before House Committee on Foreign Affairs: Subcommittee on the Middle East and South Asia United States House of Representatives, Washington, DC, 25 June 2008, p. 2, available at <http://foreignaffairs.house.gov/110/and062508.pdf>.

[61] Quoted from Gulshan Sachdeva, "India's Relations with Russia", in David Scott (ed.), *Handbook of India's* International Relations (London and New York: Routledge, 2011), p. 213.

[62] Ash Narain Roy, "Indo-US and India-Russia: Strategic Partners All?", Mainstream (New Delhi), vol. XLVIII(1), 26 December 2009, available at <http://www.mainstreamweekly.net/article1849.html>.

[63] See, "Growing India-US Ties will not Impact Russia: Envoy", available at <http://www.indiaenews.com/pdf/75271.pdf>.

[64] Satish Nambiar, "A Role for India in the Emerging World Order", U.S.I Journal, vol. CXXXVI(565), July-September 2006, p. 346.

[65] Masahiro Akiyama, "Development of the Japan-US Alliance after 11 September 2001 and the War in Iraq", U.S.I Journal, vol. CXXXIII(553), July-September 2003, pp. 352-61.

[66] Gurpreet S. Khurana, "Security of Sea Lines: Prospects for India-Japan Cooperation", Strategic Analysis, vol. 31(1), January-February 2007, pp. 140-41.

[67] Brahma Chellaney, Asian Juggerment: The Rise of China, India and Japan (New Delhi: Harper Collins Publishers in joint venture with The India Today Group, 2006), pp. 136-38.

[68] Mavara Inayat, "US-Indian Strategic Partnership: Implications for Asia and Beyond", Regional Studies (Islamabad), vol. XXIV(2), Spring 2006, p. 48.

[69] Mahendra Ved, "Indian Navy's Malabar and Other Exercises", India STRATEGIC (New Delhi), vol. 2(9), September 2007, pp. 10-12.

[70] Banning Garrett, n. 31, pp. 389-93.

[71] Ibid., pp. 402-03.

[72] Harry Harding, n. 28, pp. 348-49.

[73] C. Raja Mohan, "Balancing Interests and Values: India's Struggle with Democracy Promotion", Washington Quarterly, vol. 30(3), Summer 2007, p. 105.

[74] Amitabh Matto, "Shadow of the Dragon: Indo-US Relations and China", in Garry K. Bertsch, et. al., (eds.), Engaging India: US Strategic Relations with the World's Largest Democracies (New York: Routledge, 1999), pp. 213-14.

[75] Gary Ang, n. 33, p. 108.

[76] David Shambaugh, n. 20, p. 145.

INDIA-UNITED STATES CIVILIAN NUCLEAR COOPERATION

6.1 Introduction

The implementation of the long overdue civilian nuclear cooperation agreement between India and the United States has filled the space that remains unoccupied for expanding strategic relationship in the last two decades. Such a paradigm shift in the U.S. nuclear policy towards India is significant in terms of the growing strategic partnership between the two countries. Both India and the United States need each other in this competitive and challenging world. The civilian nuclear cooperation agreement is a reflection to the recognition of this on both sides. India on the one side, needs the support of the U.S. to allow civil nuclear commerce with the other supplier countries, while the U.S. need a partner like India that can help meet twenty-first century challenges and in particular to achieving the objectives of nuclear non-proliferation. That is why the former U.S. Administration was very quick to depart from the stand taken by the previous U.S. Presidents to acknowledge India as a responsible state with advanced nuclear technology. It also recognized the status of India as de facto nuclear weapon state.[1]

The civilian nuclear cooperation is a significant victory for Indian negotiators because under this agreement India will get the lost opportunity of getting to access to foreign nuclear fuel and reactors without being a member of the Nuclear non-proliferation Treaty (NPT). Unlike all others non-nuclear weapon states currently enjoying access to safeguarded nuclear fuel and technology only if they gave up their right to strategic nuclear weapons programme, India have not compromised its nuclear weapons programming.[2]

Unlike his predecessor, Mr. George W. Bush, former President of the U.S. seems to be very clear that unless the nuclear issue is resolved, the U.S. cannot have a deeper and closer strategic relationship with a stronger and reliable partner like India. Mr. Bush's decision was influenced by the fact that the then U.S. President Mr. Bill Clinton's policy of cap, freeze and rollback was neither successful in preventing India from exposing its nuclear capability nor was able to strengthen the relationship in a way that it should be. So, the civil nuclear initiative is part of the former U.S. President Mr. George W. Bush commitment to help India emerge as a major power in the twenty-first century. He strongly believes that if India has to become a strong, powerful and strategic partner of the U.S. in this century then a comparable courtesy must be extended to New Delhi. The motivating factors of civilian nuclear cooperation initiative should have been the common strategic objective that both countries share and the significant role that India has to play to achieving this objective and the economic benefits that would accrue out of this initiative.[3] The chapter argues that the paradigm shift in the U.S. nuclear policy has provided the much needed long-term opportunity for India to have access to advanced nuclear technology and fuel of the times that holds the key to India's growing energy needs and also in achieving its aspirations to become a major power in the world. It further argues that the agreement will not pose any hindrance to India's strategic nuclear weapons programme.

The foundation of the recently implemented civilian nuclear cooperation between India and the United States was laid during the Indian Prime Minister, Mr. Manmohan Singh visit to the U.S. in July 2005. It was during his visit both sides expressed their desire to expand cooperation in civilian nuclear and dual-use technology. It was after the July 18 agreement and in lieu to the international reactions, the U.S. President George W. Bush had said that as, "a responsible state with advanced nuclear technology, India should acquire the same benefits and advantages as other such countries." This statement seems to indirectly recognise India as a responsible nuclear power country. The U.S. President has assured the Indian Prime Minister Mr. Manmohan Singh that, "he will work to achieve full civil nuclear energy cooperation and trade with India as it realises its goals of achieving energy security." He further added that he would seek agreement from Congress to adjust U.S. laws and policies and would work with friends and allies to adjust international regimes to enable full civil nuclear energy cooperation and trade with India, including expeditious supply of fuel to safeguarded nuclear reactors at Tarapur but not limited to it. Moreover, the U.S. President also offered to facilitate India's inclusion in the international thermonuclear experiment reactor (ITER) project and in the Generation IV international forum.[4] This chapter would like to find answer to the following questions: What is the rationale behind this historic agreement? Whether the U.S. is really serious about helping India to meeting its 21st century energy security challenges? Is it a ploy to take India to signing the nuclear non-proliferation treaty? What would India gain out of this agreement? What are the strategic implications of the civilian nuclear deal? Will the civil nuclear cooperation agreement result to strengthening the international commitment to preventing the proliferation of nuclear weapons?

It must be noted that India had entered into this agreement without being a member of NPT. It is a great opportunity for

India to unlock larger global cooperation that was otherwise denied to India. If the civilian nuclear deal materialises then India would be recognized as a responsible de facto nuclear weapons state. Regarding the accusation made by other political parties, analysts and scientists that India has given away its sovereignty over the nuclear weapons, Prime Minister Mr. Manmohan Singh has assured the nation that, "it preserves our autonomy of the strategic weapons programme."

A dramatic shift in the U.S. nuclear non-proliferation policy towards India made it easier for the U.S. to extend such exception for India, knowing that India is not a signatory to NPT. The United States has come under pressure from other countries and Pakistan in particular was never in favor of the deal and even asked for the same facilities to them. But the U.S. President Mr. George W. Bush and his administration has declined Pakistan request to enter into such agreement with it. The reason may be due to its past record of getting involved in clandestine transfer of technology to a Non nuclear weapons state and even to a signatory of NPT.

The nuclear deal between India and the United States has to be seen broadly beyond the bilateral context to include other nuclear supplying countries. Many other countries have come out in support of the deal and agreed to provide Uranium to India.[5]

6.1.1 Historical Context

The significance of the civil nuclear cooperation agreement can be viewed by going few decades back and study India's denial to advanced technology of the time and its implications to India's nuclear programme. The time when India had exposed its nuclear weapons capability in 1974, it came under the pressure of the nuclear weapons states, resulting in the declaration of it as a peaceful nuclear weapons test. The test has given way too much of the United States nuclear nonproliferation policy that circumscribed the technological sharing between India and other countries. The nuclear and missile related technology control regimes that emerged after the Indian nuclear test includes Missile Technology Control Regime (MTCR) that aimed at limiting transfer of missile related technology, Nuclear suppliers group (NSG), Australia Group and Wassenaar arrangement. Through all these regimes what the U.S. was expecting was that India would come under their pressure and enter into the global nonproliferation regime. But India did not come under the pressure of the United States and instead went on adopting self reliance policy.[6]

India has been the target of these regimes because it is not a party to NPT of 1968. China, despite of being a signatory to the treaty and well known for its weak record of not abstaining from sharing its nuclear related advanced technology with states illegally seeking to acquire nuclear capability, was able to receive the U.S. technologies. The U.S. is well aware of the fact that India has so far not violated any international treaties, but has not been able to access to the U.S. advanced technology. The U.S. has not allowed India to share technologies with other countries. For instance, the U.S. has blocked the transfer of cryogenic engine technology to India from Russia. The main reason behind this whole issue is to bring India to signing the NPT. These U.S. inspired export control regimes posed a serious roadblock to India-U.S. relations in the past and continued till the end of the twentieth century.[7] This way the civilian nuclear cooperation initiative is one way of bringing an end to nuclear issue that in the past decades posed a serious hindrance to the expanding India-U.S. strategic relationship. This is not to say that India-U.S. relations would stop expanding if the initiative fails to materialise.

6.1.2 Underlying Rationale behind the Agreement

The need to study the underlying rationale behind the agreement arises because of the increasing concerns raised by the experts from both countries and other countries over the civilian nuclear agreement. The civilian nuclear cooperation agreement between India and the United States is good or bad would depend on how one look at it. Many have opposed and supported the agreement based on their respective perception. Many critics argue that the agreement is aimed at appeasing India to taking it into confidence vis-à-vis containment of the economic and military rising power, China. While many held the view that the agreement would undermine the international efforts to preventing the proliferation of weapons of mass destruction that pose a serious threat to the international peace and security at large.

On the Indian side, the opposition parties argue that the agreement would circumscribe India's strategic nuclear weapons programme and take India into signing the nuclear non-proliferation treaty that discriminates the world into have and have-nots. All of these questions and concerns were put up due the lack of actual clarity on the underlying rationale behind the agreement. 'The civil nuclear cooperation agreement between India and the United States is aimed at facilitating a substantive and clean energy sources to a fast emerging, huge energy deficient nation like India'.

The agreement is all about the civilian purpose, so no question arises about India making use of the imported materials for its nuclear weapons programme. Both India and the United States have committed strongly under this agreement to prevent the proliferation of nuclear weapons. The agreement does not result to undermining nuclear non-proliferation, instead the agreement would strengthen the nuclear non-proliferation objective.[8]

Prime Minister Mr. Manmohan Singh in his briefing to the Parliament on 29 July 2005 has made it very clear that, "India's quest for energy security as an essential component of our vision for our development was a significant theme of my talks."

He also underlined the needs for India to have unhindered access to all sources of energy, including nuclear energy, if we are to maintain and accelerate our rate of economic growth....It was in this context that we affirmed the importance of cooperation in the civilian nuclear energy sector."[9]

Today, India is facing a serious energy crisis that requires serious attention. Energy security has become one of the serious issues of India's foreign policy owing to certain factors such as growing energy demand, Carbon dioxide emissions and the issue of climate change, security of energy supplies and depleting fossil fuels. The situation is most likely to become worse due to the growing imbalance between the demand for energy and the supply from its indigenous sources. The civil nuclear between the two countries agreement is aimed at meeting India's increasing energy needs, when India's energy requirements are increasing day by day with increasing populations. Nuclear energy is seen as the key to India's faster economic growth. In 2002, in India, electricity generated by the nuclear power constitute only about 2 per cent, far less when compared to other countries like France with 78 per cent. In fiscal 2005, demand for nuclear energy has exceeded supply by 7.3 per cent.[10] This is further worsened by the fact that India is the sixth largest consumer of energy and the quantity will be doubled within few decades.[11] Also it is expected that by 2030, India would become the third largest energy consumer after the U.S., China and ahead of Russia and Japan.[12]

Contrary to earlier estimates that coal reserves of the country to last for over 200 years, a recent study done by the Central Mine Planning and Design Institute of India estimates that the coal reserves may last another four to five decades. At this critical juncture, India has to look for other alternative such as nuclear power that can help meet India's increasing energy challenges. Although at present its contribution may not be impressive, but nuclear power has the potential to offer India energy independence beyond 2050. The civil nuclear cooperation is the prerequisite for nuclear power developments.[13] Table 6.1 gives a statistical reason as to why India needs to expand its nuclear energy. As the agreement would release advanced technology that can utilized for the peaceful purpose of nuclear energy.

Table 6.1: India's Primary Commercial Energy Consumption Profile in 1996 and 2006 (Million tones oil equivalent).

Name of the Item	1996	2006	% increase (1995-2005)
Coal	154.4(56.87%)	237.7(56.17%)	53.95%
Oil	81.1(29.87%)	120.3(28.43%)	48.33%
Natural Gas	18.5(6.81%)	35.8(8.46%)	93.51%
Nuclear energy	1.9(0.70%)	4.0(0.95%)	110.53%
Hydroelectricity	15.6(5.75%)	25.4(6.00%)	62.82%
Total Primary Commercial Energy	271.5	432.2	55.87%

Source: Manjeet S. Pardesai and Sumit Ganguly, "India and Energy Security: A Foreign Policy Priority", in Harsh V. Pant (ed.), Indian Foreign Policy in a Unipolar World (New Delhi: Routledge, 2009), p. 105.

6.2 Civil Nuclear Deal and India's Energy Security

So far the contribution of nuclear power to generating electricity is very meager. About two-three per cent is what the nuclear power contributes. Given this fact, there are an increasing needs for civilian nuclear cooperation with other countries, thereby helping India to meet its large and growing energy needs. The civilian nuclear cooperation should be looked at it broadly in terms of India's growing energy deficit. Efforts has been made in the past to increase the contribution of nuclear power to generating electricity and meeting India's growing energy demands, but could not achieve as projected. The main reason was due to lack of adequate uranium available in the country owing to the lack of cooperation with the nuclear related materials supplier countries, resulted by India's nuclear isolation from the international community.

Despite of repeated commitments, currently India's nuclear power generation capability stands at around 3, 300 megawatts. With the successful implementation of the Civil nuclear initiative, the Indian nuclear power capacity is projected to generate 10, 000 MWs, 20,000 MWs, 150,000 MWs by 2010, 2020 and 2050 respectively. How India had planned to increase the level of nuclear power generation capability is shown in Table 6.2, 6.3 and 6.4. The more India cooperates with nuclear energy and fuel supplying countries, the easier will be for India to produce nuclear power to meet its growing energy security challenges.

The opponents of the nuclear initiative had said that, 'a realistic, safe and practical plan for partnership between India and the U.S. would be clean-coal cooperation, not a nuclear one'. But what the opponents failed to note is the fact that in addition to exchange of technology and fuel for nuclear power generation, both countries is most likely to cooperate for clean-coal.[14]

To raise the contribution of the nuclear power to energy generation, India plans to install 25-30 nuclear reactors in the next three decades that is expected to fulfill its plans for 65,000 MW energy. By 2020, India is expecting that the nuclear energy would account for eight per cent reflecting a five per cent increase and many more to come in the years to follow. This does not mean that nuclear energy would replace coal, but to some extent it would reduce the burning of fossil fuel and low quality coal, thereby reducing environmental deterioration.

Moreover, in the long run nuclear energy would be economical than any other alternatives.[15]

Table 6.2: Nuclear Reactors: Operational and Planned

Reactor Type	Capacity
18 reactors at 6 sites under operation: Tarapur, Rawatbhata, Kalpakkam, Narora, Kakrapar and Kaiga.	4, 340 MWe
4 PHWRs under construction at Kaiga (2x 220 MWe), Raps-5 & 6 (2x220 MWe) to be operational by March 2010	440 MWe
2 LWRs under construction at Kudankulam (2x1,000 MWe) to be operational during 2010-11	2,000 MWe
PFBR under construction at Kalpakkam (1x500 MWe) to be operational by 2012	500 MWe
Projects Planned till 2020	
PHWRs (8x700 Mwe), FBRs (4x500 Mwe), LWRs (6x1000 MWe) and AHWR (1x300 MWe)	13,900 MWe
Total by 2020	**21,180 MWe**

Source: "Raise Uranium Supply for Energy Security", Economic Times (Pune), 11 February 2010.

Table 6.3: India's Plan to Increase Nuclear Power Capacity

Year	Installed Capacity
2010	4,780 MW (20 reactors under operation) (3 %)
2012	7,280 MW
2017	10,080 MW
2020	20,000 MW (10 %)
2032	63,000 MW
2050	150,000 MW (26 %)

Source: Refer to "India Ranks Sixth in Nuclear Power Generation", available at <http://timesofindia.indiatimes.com/india/India-ranks-sixth-in-nuclear-power-generation/articleshow/7001693.cms>.

Table 6.4: India's Nuclear Power Reactors, Operating, Under Construction and Planned

Reactor	Type	Fuel	MWe net (each)	Completion/ target Year	Subject to IAEA Safeguard
		Operating			
Tarapur 1	BWR	light water, LEU & MOX	150	1969	Yes
Tarapur 2	BWR	light water, LEU	150	1969	Yes
Rawatbhata 1	PHWR	heavy water, natural U	90	1972	Yes
Rawatbhata 2	PHWR	heavy water, natural U	187	1980	Yes
Kalpakkam 1	PHWR	heavy water, natural U	155	1984	No
Kalpakkam 2	PHWR	heavy water, natural U	155	1986	No
Narora 1	PHWR	heavy water, natural U	202	1991	No
Narora 2	PHWR	heavy water, natural U	202	1992	No
Kakrapar 1	PHWR	heavy water, natural U	170	1993	No
Kakrapar 2	PHWR	heavy water, natural U	202	1995	No
Kaiga 1	PHWR	heavy water, natural U	202	1999	No
Rawatbhata 3	PHWR	heavy water, natural U	202	1999	No
Kaiga 2	PHWR	heavy water, natural U	202	2000	No
Rawatbhata 4	PHWR	heavy water, natural U	202	2000	No
Total Operating 14			2, 503		
		Under Construction			
Tarapur 3 & 4	PHWR	heavy water, natural U	490	2006-07	No
Kaiga 3 & 4	PHWR	heavy water, natural U	202	2007	No
Rawatbhata 5 & 6	PHWR	heavy water, natural U	202	2007-08	No
Kudankulam 1 & 2	VVER (PWR)	light water, LEU	953	2007-08	Yes
Kalpakkam PFBR	FBR	mixed oxide	470	2010	No
Total Under Construction - 9			3, 618		
		Planned			
Rawatbhata 7 & 8	PHWR	heavy water, Natural U	450	?	No

Source: Varun Sahni, "Limited Cooperation Between limited Allies: India's strategic Programs and India-US Strategic Trade", in Sumit Ganguly, et. al., (eds.), US-Indian Strategic Cooperation Into the 21st Century: More Than Words (London and New York: Routledge, 2006), p. 183.

Notes: BWR- boiling water reactor, FBR- fast breeder reactor, LEU- low-enriched uranium, MOX- mixed natural uranium and Plutonium oxide fuel, PHWR- pressurized heavy-water reactor, PWR- light-water pressurized reactor, VVER- light-water pressurized reactor.

6.3 Whether U.S. Exception to India is Justified

This is in response to what non-proliferation lobby in the U.S. and other countries has been claiming ever since India enters into a Civilian nuclear cooperation agreement with U.S. The United States under the able leadership of Bush has agreed to enter into Civilian nuclear agreement with India despite of its not being signatory to the Nonproliferation treaty. The joint statement issued on 18 July 2005 clearly mentioned India "as a responsible state with advanced nuclear technology, India should acquire the same benefits and advantages as other such states."

Also the agreement is in response to India's past records and the continuous strong commitment to preventing nuclear proliferation. India's commitment to preventing the proliferation of Weapons of Mass Destructions (WMDs) is justified by its impeccable record of not transferring any of its nuclear related technology and materials to the third countries. India has always acknowledged international efforts to curb the proliferation of WMDs. So far India has not violated any international commitments either in the making or testing of its nuclear weapons.

Unlike China, the U.S., India has desisted from assisting other countries seeking to gain nuclear weapon status. We have enough evidence to prove that China has assisted Pakistan and North Korea to become nuclear weapon states. China has provided Pakistan with nuclear related technology, materials and equipments. Same is the case with Pakistan, who had a very worse record of proliferating nuclear related technology and materials. To a large extent nuclear proliferation problems existing in this world are linked to Pakistan's weak export control regulation. Today, the whole world knows about Pakistan's alleged nuclear linkage with other states seeking to acquire nuclear weapons such as Libya, Iran, and North Korea, etc. It must also be noted that both Libya and Iran has imported centrifuge technology from the Pakistan based A. Q. Khan network. Unlike India, Pakistan is not a stable state where the possibility of nuclear weapons falling into the hands of terrorist cannot be rule out. It must be noted by those opposing from within and outside the country that India is not a proliferationist country to be feared for any wrongdoing. Instead, they should look at India's contribution to nuclear non-proliferation. India's inclusion will undoubtedly be of advantageous to the international community. Given this fact, one would say that India-U.S. civil nuclear cooperation agreement is highly justified.[16]

6.4 Significance of the Civilian Nuclear Cooperation Agreement

From the Indian point of view, the main points of significance of the recently successful conclusion of civilian nuclear cooperation agreement are as under:

1. the agreement sought to accommodate India to the global nuclear order.
2. bring an end to more than three and half decades of India's nuclear isolation.
3. the agreement is one of the most important step toward clearing the past misunderstanding and events relating to nuclear issues.
4. it opens up nuclear dialogues with other supplier countries.
5. it would open new vistas of cooperation, thereby strengthening the relationship between the two countries and the nuclear non-proliferation order.
6. it would ease restriction on transfer of fuel, dual use technology and weapons to India.[17]
7. it does not impose any restriction on India pursuing its nuclear and ballistic missile programmes.

6.5 India-U.S. Efforts to Reduce Divergence on Nuclear Proliferation

India and the United States created a history by entering into a landmark civilian nuclear cooperation agreement in the year 2005. The platform for such cooperation has been created much before July 2005 and started soon after May 1998 India's exposition of its nuclear capability. The understanding gained between the two countries since the end of cold war in general and the last term of Mr. Bill Clinton presidency in particular, was crucial in terms of reducing the divergence on nuclear issues, which brought the two countries apart for almost four decades. The last term of Clinton presidency witnessed the decline of nuclear issue as a factor to the expanding Indo-U.S relations.

India and the United States very soon after the former exposed its nuclear capability by carrying out a series of nuclear tests on 11 and 13 May 1998, engaged in a strategic dialogue to reduce the damage brought about by the tests. The dialogue between Mr. Jaswant Singh of India and Mr. Strobe Talbott of the U.S. was the longest ever dialogue in the history of India-U.S. relations. It was the first step toward reducing the differences on nuclear issue. Unlike Mr. Bill Clinton Administration, when Mr. George W. Bush became the president of the U.S., nuclear proliferation does not figure in the top-most priority lists. His low preference on nuclear proliferation issue was another factor. At the same time he was determined not to allow the nuclear issue to trouble the relationship. President Bush's stand seems to reflect both his eagerness and commitment to take the relationship to a much better level.

By the turn of the twenty first century, both India and the United States together have taken some significant number of steps to reduce the divergence on nuclear issue and open the way for civilian nuclear cooperation. The declaration of the "Next Step in Strategic Partnership (NSSP)" was one important step toward achieving this feat. Under the NSSP, the United States has agreed to have cooperation with India on a quartet of issues such as Civilian nuclear, civilian space, high-technology trade and missile defence. The NSSP initiative has clearly reflected the U.S. eagerness to make changes in its domestic and international law. This is a significant drift from the previous stand taken during the Clinton period.[18]

Before this, the conclusion of the High Technology Cooperation Group (HTCG) was also highly acknowledgeable. On its part, India had taken some very important initiative for nuclear non-proliferation. India had ratified the UN convention on nuclear safety and deposited the same at the IAEA on 31 March 2005.[19]

6.6 18 July 2005 Joint Statement- Reflection to India-U.S. Joint Commitments

Indian Prime Minister made a landmark visit to the United States in July 2005, where he met former U.S. President Mr. George W. Bush and agreed to sign an unexpected historic joint statement of civilian nuclear cooperation that has both economic and strategic significance. The strategic significance of this agreement lies in bringing an end to India's denial to access nuclear fuel, technology and reactors for its civilian reactors i.e. meant for power generation.

The July 18 joint statement reflects strong commitments by both the countries to take the relationship to a much better level. Former U.S. President George W. Bush became the first President of U.S. who held the view that India should acquire the same benefit and advantages as other such states. In response Indian Prime Mr. Minister Manmohan Singh had agreed to "assume the same responsibility and practices and acquire the same benefits and advantages as other leading countries with advanced nuclear technology such as the U.S., Russia, France, and China." Besides this, India has also agreed to separation of civilian facilities from that of the military facilities, thereby voluntarily placing all the civilian facilities under the IAEA safeguards in a phased manner by 2014. It has reaffirmed its existing commitments to continue a moratorium on nuclear testing and participate in multilateral negotiations on a Fissile Material Cut Off Treaty. It will also strengthen its export control mechanism including the reprocessing and enrichment technologies so as to ensure the international community that the technologies are not diverted to other countries.[20] (For more details on this issue, go to Appendix I).

The most important aspect of the Civilian nuclear cooperation initiative is the fact that both sides had agreed to make an adjustment to their respective policies without hurting each other interests. This clearly indicates the failures of the past the U.S. effort to insist India to cap, rollback its nuclear weapons programme. Unlike Mr. Bill Clinton, President George W. Bush has agreed to bring about a change in the three and half decades old domestic law and also convince the international community to amend its rules to facilitate full civilian nuclear cooperation agreement with India. The agreement does not amount to India giving up neither its nuclear status nor its nuclear weapons programme. At the same time, it sought to strengthen the nuclear non-proliferation objective. This way the interests of both countries and international community are preserved.[21]

6.6.1 Whether the Separation Process is in India's Interest

During his visit to India in March 2006, former U.S. President George W. Bush and Indian Prime Minister Mr. Manmohan Singh signed an agreement. Under this agreement, India voluntarily agreed to place 14 out of its 22 nuclear reactors under the IAEA safeguard in a phase manner by 2014. At the same time, India has also agreed to place 8 of its nuclear reactors outside the IAEA safeguard. The civilian nuclear facilities cannot be made use of for the military purposes. This way India's facilities under the IAEA safeguard has moved from 19 per cent to 65 per cent.

Many Indian scientists and experts are not happy with the way India has put 65 per cent of its facilities under the safeguard. This had raised the question from other sections over the separation process. Whether this step would seriously undermine India's national security interests. Whether this initiative would put a brake on India's nuclear weapons programme.

It must be noted that it was a significant diplomatic victory for India for not coming under the pressure of the U.S. to include all the reactors under safeguards. India resisted the pressure to bring the Fast Breeder Reactors (FBRs) under the civilian lists. The reason why India refused to place FBRs under safeguard is because of its strategic significance. The FBRs converts thorium 232 to uranium 233.[22] Keeping in mind, the huge gap between the shortage of natural uranium and the availability of vast thorium reserves, India have denied to include the FBRs in the civilian facilities for future energy needs.

The separation of the fourteen power reactors in operation, nine under construction and two planned in India into civilian (to be open to safeguards) and military (to remain unsafeguarded) categories as agreed by the two countries in March 2006 is shown in Table 6.4. Altogether there are fourteen safeguarded (4380 MWe) and eight military (2350 MWe). Moreover, India have excluded the Dhruva (100 MWth) and Cirus (40 MWth) Plutonium production reactors, the Fast Breeder Test Reactor (13 MWe), the Prototype Fast Breeder Reactor (PFBR) (500 MWe) and the Plutonium reprocessing plants at Trombay, Kalpakkam and Tarapur from coming under the safeguards.[23]

The decision on what to be included and what not to be included in the civilian lists has been decided in discussion with the head of India's Atomic Energy Commission Dr. Anil Kakodkar. Indian Prime Minister Mr. Manmohan Singh was quite right when he declared that, "we have made it clear that we cannot accept safeguards on our indigenous fast breeder program,' and he further added that "we have taken into account our current and future strategic needs and programs after careful deliberations of all relevant factors, consistent with our nuclear doctrines...there has been no erosion of the integrity of our nuclear doctrine, either in terms of current or future capabilities...it will be the autonomous Indian decision as to what is 'civilian' and what is 'military'..,the number of thermal nuclear reactors that India would agree to put under civilian list would be equal to 65 per cent of the total installed thermal nuclear power capability."[24]

Many have criticized for placing the civilian facilities under international safeguards at the ignorance of permanent fuel supplies and the right to reprocess foreign origin spent fuel. India form the very beginning was ready to place civilian facilities under international safeguards provided there are uninterrupted fuel supplies to India. This is important in terms of ensuring that the Tarapur incident does not repeat once again where the U.S. has suspended fuel supply due to India's nuclear test. If in case there is a repeat of such incidents, India reserves the right to take 'corrective measures'.[25] No way in this agreement India has given away its right to use for our own purposes our independent and indigenously developed nuclear facilities. India reserved the right to produce and utilize fissi e material for its current and future strategic needs.[26]

6.6.2 What are the Strategic Gains for India and United States after this Agreement?

What many people ignored about the civilian nuclear cooperation is the fact that the agreement is between India and United States, but it would open the way for the former to have nuclear commerce with other supplier countries. Unless India enters into such agreement, it cannot have any nuclear fuel and technological cooperation with other supplier countries such as France, Germany, Australia, etc. This agreement would allow India to share advanced technologies with the supplying countries. Since India concludes this historic agreement, many countries have shown its eagerness to share its nuclear fuel, energy and technology with India, once the agreement is finalised.

Given the advances made by France in this area, it would be advantageous for India to have cooperation with France. France eagerness to supply clean energy resources was reflected when its president Chirac had said that, "France would like to extend, within the non-proliferation framework and existing agreements, help India to achieve its energy needs."[27]

The importance of the deal can be smelled from what the Chairman of the Indian Atomic energy commission, Mr. Anil Kakodkar had said that 'if India cannot import fuel or reactors under the deal then it would have to burn 1.6 billion tones of imported coal per year by 2050. If India is to succeed expanding its nuclear power generating capacity from 3.8 per cent to 25 per cent by 2050, then it will have to transport uranium from other countries.' In this case nuclear deal will prove be effective in terms of meeting India's needs. This is because India has only just 1 per cent of the world's discovered uranium. He further added that, "the Pressurised Heavy Water Reactor (PHWR) will stall if Uranium and reactors cannot be imported to support an accelerated three stage programme and India will consequently suffer a severe 'energy gap'.

The deal has been concluded in the interests of both countries that would serve global interest too. It is a strategic gain for both countries. Given the expanding economic and trade relations, the cooperation agreement will broadened the level of economic and trade relations. It is being expected that by 2030, India would succeed China as the world's most populous state. In recent years India was successful in maintaining the economic growth rate between 7-9 per cent. It is important to note by the critics that India account for 17 per cent of the world population but consumes only just 4 per cent of its energy. With increasing population there will be an increase in the demand of energy and for a much better economic growth rate, clean energy is of dire need for India.[28] That is why many Indian and American economic analysts came out strongly in support of the n-deal because they foresightedly perceive the economic advantage that would accrue out of this agreement.

Under this agreement, the U.S. has agreed to supply nuclear reactors to India. It has been estimated that if the n-deal materializes then it will generate US $50 billion of new business in the United States. Because of this astounding amount and the future benefits, the U.S. Chamber of Commerce has strongly supported the n-deal.[29] This way the civilian nuclear cooperation agreement would generate more uranium resources that India needed most for its civilian reactors from the other supplying countries. This would result in higher economic growth rate by generating clean nuclear energy.[30]

6.7 Henry J. Hyde India-U.S. Peaceful Energy Co-operation Act, 2006

The Henry J. Hyde Act aroused serious opposition from within India because they feel this would undermine India's sovereignty and interests due to the presence of certain provisions that are contrary to the precedent agreement of July 2005 and March 2006. What the critics fails to recognize is the fact that the Hyde Act was signed by US Congress that would enable Washington to sign a bilateral agreement with India under the section 123 of the U.S. Atomic Energy Act 1954 (popularly known as the 123 Agreement).

The Hyde Act allows the U.S. Administration to engage in civil nuclear cooperation with India by waiving three permanent and unconditional provisions of the U.S. Atomic Energy Act of 1954. These waivers include:

a. that the partner country should not have exploded a nuclear explosive device in the past. This waiver is necessary because India had already exposed its nuclear capability by exploding a series of nuclear device way back in May 1998.

b. that the partner country must have all its nuclear facilities and activities under full-scope safeguards. This waiver becomes necessary because India has rejected to place its strategic nuclear programme to the international safeguards.

c. that the partner country is not currently engaged in the development and production of nuclear explosive devices. This waiver is required because there is no freeze or capping of India's strategic weapons programme. India will continue to carry out its nuclear weapons programme.

Prime Minister Special envoy Mr. Shyam Saran has made it very clear that if the US Congress considers the 123 Agreement currently drafted as being in contravention with their own understanding of the Hyde Act, the agreement would be voted down.[31] It is a domestic Act binding on the U.S. Administration alone, not on India. The agreement that is popularly known as the 123 agreement is binding on India. This is clarified by the fact that the 123 agreement did not find anything mention about the Hyde Act, not even a single. This is substantiated by the Article 5.6 (a) of the 123 Agreement that spelt out the U.S. commitment to seek agreement from the US Congress to amend its domestic laws, to ensure assured and full access to few Indian nuclear reactors. Above all, Article 6.4 says that, "This agreement shall be implemented in good faith and in accordance with the principles of International law." And Article 2.4 affirms that the Agreement will not affect the un-safeguarded nuclear activities of either party or interfere with nuclear military facilities built independent of the 123 Agreement for their own purposes.

Those whoever opposes the civilian nuclear deal for the presence of certain provisions that is not binding on India sends a clear message that they do not want the deal to be cleared? The U.S. President Mr. George W. Bush himself had stated that he was not bound by, "statement of policy" in Section 103, a provision that barred transfer to India of an item contrary to guidelines of the Nuclear Suppliers Group (NSG).[32]

By recognising India as a responsible nuclear power, the United States under the leadership of Mr. George W. Bush has made manifold commitment. It has agreed to amend its Section 123, 128 and 129 of the Atomic Energy Act, remove India-specific NPT-plus sanctions under the Nuclear Non-Proliferation Act 1978.[33] Thus, keeping in mind the changing international environment, the United States has finally shifted its nuclear policy from isolating India to that of engagement (including with other nuclear technology and fuel supplying countries).

6.8 Section 123 of the US Atomic Energy Act 1974

Why India need to enter into an agreement under Section 123 of the U.S. Atomic energy Act, 1954 with the United States. The reason behind this agreement is the fact that the Act prohibits the U.S. to have any nuclear commerce with a country who is not a member of Nuclear non-proliferation treaty (NPT). Section 123 of the U.S. Atomic energy Act, 1954 popularly known as 123 agreement is a necessary pre-requisite for India to have a civil nuclear cooperation with the U.S. and other nuclear technology, fuel and its related materials supplying countries. The agreement has set out the parameter of cooperation between India and the international community.[34]

Under this agreement, the United States has committed India to ensure uninterrupted fuel supplies to its reactors and help create strategic fuel reserves for the safeguarded nuclear reactors.[35]

6.8.1 Roadblocks to the Successful Conclusion of the Section 123 of the U.S. Atomic Energy Act Agreement

When the Henry J. Hyde Act was signed into law by the U.S. President George Bush in December 2006, there aroused serious concern in India by left parties, opposition party, Indian nuclear scientists and experts. They claimed that the Hyde Act is not in consistent with what has been promised by the Indian Prime Minister Mr. Manmohan Singh in his statement to Parliament. They further claimed that the Hyde Act lays down several 'procedures and conditions', the bilateral accord has to meet before it can win Congressional approval.[36] Dr. Anil Kakodkar, Chaiman of Atomic Energy Commission hold a meeting with the retired Indian scientists to discuss on these issues. The retired Indian scientists were trying to convince the Dr. Anil Kakodkar that once the Act is signed into law by U.S. President, all the further bilateral agreements with the U.S. will be required to be in consistent with this law.[37]

The successful implementation of the civilian nuclear cooperation agreement took more time than expected due to lack of consensus between India and the United States over the presence of provisions in the draft that was not acceptable to India. The main point of contention was over four provisions. They were as under:-

a. Cessation and termination in the event of an Indian nuclear tests.

b. Nuclear fuel supply assurances for India.

c. Full-scope safeguards.

d. Reprocessing of spent fuel by India of U.S. origin.

Now, we will discuss each one of these one by one so that one comes to know where the actual problem lies.

Cessation and Termination in the Event of an Indian Nuclear Tests

Right from the very beginning when both sides began discussion for this landmark agreement, India was never in a position to give away the sovereign right to carry out future nuclear test. Although the draft agreement does not clearly mention that the cooperation would come to an end once India conduct nuclear test. What the agreement stipulates is that the party seeking termination must have to give one year's notice to the other party, but before this both sides would discuss on the circumstances leading to test, whether it has resulted from a changed security environment or a response to similar activities by other states which would definitely have its impact on India's security. For instance, we need to keep the option alive in case should China or Pakistan conduct a nuclear tests in future.

Nuclear Fuel Supply Assurances for India

Under this agreement, India seeks to reserve the lifetime and uninterrupted fuel supply assurances for its civil nuclear reactors. In Art 5(6) b of the agreement, the U.S. undertakes to support an Indian effort to develop a strategic reserve of nuclear fuel to guard against any disruption of supply over the lifetime of India's reactors. In addition, it also pledges to help India find alternative sources of nuclear fuel in the event of a supply interruption by convening a group of friendly supplier countries such as Russia, France and the United Kingdom.

Safeguards

In Art 5(6) c, India pledges to place all the 14 civilian nuclear facilities under the India-specific IAEA safeguards. At the same time, India reserves the right to take corrective measures to ensure for the uninterrupted operation of its civilian nuclear reactors.

Reprocessing of Spent Fuel by India of U.S. Origin

The agreement has given the consent to India for reprocessing of the U.S. origin spent fuel. For reprocessing of the U.S. origin spent fuel what India required to do is to construct a new reprocessing facility under the IAEA safeguards. This should be followed by the building up of consensus on the 'arrangement and procedures' under which any Indian reprocessing of the U.S. origin spent fuel would occur.[38] With this, India became the fourth country after Japan, Switzerland and European Union to allow reprocessing of spent fuel by the U.S. It is totally incorrect, that this process will be inspected by the U.S. inspectors, but will be inspected by the IAEA.

The reason why India reserves the right to reprocessing of spent fuel is for the separation of plutonium which is extremely an important part in India's strategic nuclear weapons programme. The Indian nuclear fuel cycle is crucially dependent on pressurized heavy water reactors in the first phase, the use of Fast breeder reactors in the second stage and of thorium-based systems in the third stage which is yet to be developed. Separation of plutonium is essential for the eventual use of thorium as a nuclear fuel when India has the largest reserves of thorium.[39]

6.9 IAEA Safeguard Agreement with India

Safeguard agreement with the International Atomic Energy Agency is necessary before the civilian nuclear cooperation between the two countries is successfully completed. Since November 2007, both India and IAEA have concluded several rounds of consultation over the finalization of text of the safeguards agreement. The draft of India-specific safeguard agreement was circulated to Board Members on July 2008. On 1 August 2008, the IAEA Board of Governors approved by consensus a nuclear Safeguards Agreement with India, calling for application of IAEA safeguards to Indian civilian nuclear facilities.[40]

India's safeguard agreement with the Agency would serves three purposes- one that the agreement sends a clear message to the international community that the cooperation is not aimed at strengthening the former nuclear programme so that the countries should extend their support to strengthen India's civil nuclear programme. Secondly, to ensure that items classified under the safeguard is not used for development of nuclear explosive device. And lastly, it creates the necessary conditions for India to obtain reliable, uninterrupted and continuous access to fuel supplies and a strategic reserve of nuclear fuel to guard against any disruption of supply over the lifetime of India's reactors.[41]

IAEA Director General Mr. Mohamed ElBaradei had stated on the day of approval by the IAEA board of governors that, "The India Safeguards Agreement could have, if properly implemented, a lot of positive implications, development implications, security implications, non-proliferation implications, and arms control implications. I have been supporting the agreement from day one and am very happy today that I see that my judgment has been certified by the Board in approving the agreement by consensus." The above statement recognizes the role that India would play in the nuclear non-proliferation rather than proliferating it.[42]

6.9.1 India's Additional Protocol

The Additional Protocol is meant for safeguards. India must conclude an additional protocol consistent with IAEA principles, practices, and policies that would apply only to India's civil nuclear program, before the United States could engage in nuclear trade with India. On 3 March 2009, the IAEA approved an additional protocol to India's safeguards agreement, giving agency with greater authority to monitor India's civilian nuclear activities. India is not the first country to enter into such protocol. There are currently 90 countries with such protocols in effect.

The additional protocol is not against India's national security. According to a February 25 IAEA note to the agency's Board of Governors, "The provisions of the draft additional protocol with India are based on the text of those provisions in the Model Additional Protocol to which India has agreed." The note said that India sent a letter to the agency in September 2008 indicating the measures of the Model Additional Protocol that India was willing to accept and requesting that the agency prepare a draft protocol on the basis of those specifications.

Under the additional protocol, India only agreed to share information on nuclear-related exports. And as far as reporting provisions of the additional protocol is concerned, India will not report on the informational such as nuclear fuel-cycle-related research and development, nuclear-related imports, and uranium mining. Overall, the model additional protocol that India agreed to have nothing to do with India's strategic facilities. It does not provide any authority to the agency to inspect undeclared facilities. All those provisions that seek to detect India's undeclared nuclear facilities are excluded.[43]

6.10 Opposition to the Civilian Nuclear Cooperation Agreement

Where there is a support, there will also be opposition from both India and the United States. The opposition of the civilian nuclear cooperation from the U.S. is due to huge obsession with the objective of nuclear non-proliferation, while Indian opposition is a result from historical obsession with anti-American and the past experience. They are the one who are never in favor of the prospering India-U.S. relations that has a significant role to play in ensuring peace, security and stability in the international community. The Indian and American perceptions of opposing the nuclear deal diverge:

American Perception

From the American perspective, the nuclear deal has been opposed on the following grounds:

a. It would put a setback to achieving the objective of nuclear non-proliferation.

b. It would send wrong message to other nuclear supplier countries to extend the same to their close partner. For instance, Pakistan is asking for the same deal from China, who had in the past supplied nuclear technology to the former.

c. It would harness India's fissile materials production. The American critics point out that if the nuclear deal materializes then it would be able to procure fissile material for up to 50 weapons, far exceeding the present capacity.

Indian Perception

Indian political parties, nuclear scientists and scholars have opposed the deal on the following grounds:

a. It has limited India's nuclear deterrence. India's former Prime Minister Mr. A.B. Vajpayee held the view that it has compromised any "flexibility in determining the size of our nuclear deterrent.

b. The left parties have raised concerns over the n-deal fearing that such initiative compromises India's national interests. They are of the view that this would not allow India to adopt its own independent nuclear policy.

c. Many nuclear scientists and policy makers have opposed the agreement that the U.S. is not a reliable country. Their criticism stems from the bitter experiences of the U.S. not coming to the terms of agreement and in times of need withdrawing from the agreement when it doesn't satisfy its interest.

d. The agreement would pose a threat to or restricted India's fissile material production. Because under this agreement India had agreed to work together for FMCT.

It must be noted by the critics that the agreement is a civilian nuclear cooperation and has nothing to do with the India's nuclear programme. If India has agreed to separate the civilian nuclear facilities from military nuclear facilities, it is in keeping with national security interests. India did not come under the U.S. pressure to include Fast Breeder Reactors (FBRs) under the civilian facilities that would come under the IAEA safeguard. They have raised the question that the left out reactors would be sufficient enough to meet the need of the minimum nuclear deterrence or not.[44]

6.10.1 Support of the Civilian Nuclear Cooperation Agreement

Former U.S. Secretary of State Ms. Condollezza Rice, in her April 2006 testimony before the Senate Foreign Affairs Committee had argued in support of the deal that the deal will fully open the door to civil nuclear trade and create new business and market opportunities for American firms seeking to assist

India in the construction of new thermal power reactors. She also argued that participation in India's nuclear market will help make the American nuclear industry globally competitive, thereby benefiting our own domestic nuclear power sector. This deal will permit the U.S. companies to enter into the lucrative and growing Indian market-something they are currently prohibited from doing.

As against the concerns raised by the American experts that this deal would allow India to expand its nuclear arsenal significantly, she argued that, "This is not just the case. The initiative does not cap Indian nuclear weapons production, but nothing under this initiative will directly enhance its military capability or add to its military stockpile. India could already build additional weapons within the limits of its capabilities if it is so desired, with or without this deal. But the Indian government has repeatedly confirmed in public that it intends to expand its civil nuclear energy capability."[45]

Their criticism has been overshadowed by the support that has been extended by the diplomats and scholars. Mr. Karl Inderfurth, former Assistant Secretary of State during Mr. Bill Clinton's Second Administration supported the n-deal when he said that, "the first major restructuring of the nuclear non-proliferation in over 30 years..." He further added that it "breaks down what Indian officials have called nuclear apartheid of the current global non-proliferation regime." This is further strengthened by the support extended to by the Mr. Strobe Talbott, former U.S. deputy Secretary of State. He is of the view that India should not be denied any concession on sharing of nuclear technology for civilian energy generation. He further reacted by stating that India should grab the deal; nothing more it can hope to get.

Mr. Stanley A. Weiss, founder and chairman of Business executives for National Security, Washington, D.C. has come out very strongly in support of it and says, "If Washington shares nuclear technology with Beijing, the great nuclear proliferators, why not with India, with a solid record of preventing proliferation."[46]

Mr. Prem Shankar Jha, a columnist and journalist does not agree with the view of N. Prasad. Mr. Jha believes that, "this cost cannot be so high as to offset even the economic, let alone political benefits to be had from the inflow of cutting edge technology." He further added that "once European firms start taking advantage of President Mr. George W. Bush's green light for the sale of nuclear reactors to India, pressure from American translational will hasten the pace of legislation in the U.S. too."

As against the allegations made by the other political parties, Mr. C. Uday Bhaskar came out strongly in favor of the nuclear agreement when he says that, "The July 18, agreement does not compromise India in the nuclear domain in any manner. It has the potential to admit India into the global fold of nuclear commerce and strategic management and will advance India's overall national interests through the next few decades of the 21st century." These views clearly reflect the advantage that India would accrue out of this historic agreement and in no way India has compromised its long-term interest for sake of short-term interest.[47]

6.10.2 Political Crisis in India

The civil nuclear cooperation agreements arouse political crisis in India when left parties had threatened to withdraw its support to United Progressive Alliance (UPA) government led by Congress party. This comes in the backdrop of Indian government finalizing the negotiation with the IAEA Secretariat over the safeguard agreement.

Before India and IAEA entered into this negotiation, a UPA-Left committee had been set up to look at the matter of the agreements such as provisions of the Hyde Act, 123 agreements, etc. However the Congress led government in July 2008 went ahead to signed the 123 agreement with U.S. without any concerned about the approval of the UPA-Left Committee. Left parties was never happy with this step. Otherwise, the civilian nuclear deal has brought crisis in India start from the very beginning because of the lack of consensus among the political parties.[48] Not happy with the Government activities, Mr. Prakash Karat, General Secretary of the Left Front on 8 July 2008, announced that the party is withdrawing its support to the government over the decision by the government to go ahead with the United States-India Peaceful Atomic Energy Cooperation Act. This very lack of consensus had handicapped the UPA government for proceeding further steps before it is successfully implemented. Once the decision has been taken by the left party to withdraw its support, two options left out for the Indian government- one is to withdraw from this historic nuclear deal. With this the civilian nuclear deal would not take place. Secondly, ready for the early elections and if they want to really continue the negotiation for the success of the civil nuclear cooperation then they will have to win by a majority vote.

Prime Minister Mr. Manmohan Singh was ready to go for confidence vote to decide the fate of the nuclear deal. On 22 July 2008 the UPA faced its first confidence vote in the Lok Sabha where UPA emerged victory with 275 votes to the opposition's 256, (10 members abstained from the vote) to record a 19-vote victory. Thanks to Samajwadi party that came out at the right moment for the rescue of the UPA government to ensure that the deal is alive.[49]

6.11 Why Nuclear Supplier Groups Approval is Necessary and What It Means For India?

Since India is not officially recognized as the Nuclear weapon state nor a member of the NPT and also it is not a signatory to NSGs. Because of which, it is not possible for India to engage in nuclear commerce with the supplier countries. If it has to be made possible then NSG members must be ready to amends its rules and approve India specific exceptions through consensus. For which, United States has given an assurance to India that it would convince NSG members for such relaxation. The U.S. Administration is very much hopeful that it would successfully convince the members without abandoning NSG consensus rule or the full-scope safeguards conditions of supply.

Among the NSG members, France, U.K. and Russia have supported for such exception, while other members such as Sweden, Denmark, Austria and Ireland was fully committed to opposing such relaxation.[50]

It was on 6 September 2008, after a long battle India finally got the grant of waiver from the NSG to adjust its guidelines to enable full civil nuclear cooperation with the suppliers. The decision was a welcome development for India because it waives from the requirement of 'full-scope safeguards' as a precondition for the NSG members to export nuclear material and fuel for use in its safeguarded civilian nuclear facilities. It took so much of time due to the lack of consensus among the members of the group. Credit should go to both Indian and American negotiators and also the member of the group who have supported to achieve this feat. Indian Prime Minister Mr. Manmohan Singh and External Affairs Minister Mr. Pranab Mukherjee thanks the member countries of the Nuclear suppliers Group for the role they have played in ensuring this outcome. Indian External Affairs Minister expresses happiness over the final outcome that fully meets our expectation and is consistent with Government policy and the national consensus on disarmament and non-proliferation. He further added that the outcome is in accordance with the commitments given to parliament and the peoples of India, and is consistent with India's national interest.[51]

6.12 US Congress Approval

On 28 September 2008, the US House of Representatives passed the bill by 298 to 117 votes to approve the India-U.S. civil nuclear cooperation. This was followed by the US Senate passing the bill by 86-13 votes on 1 October 2008. Once the US Senate passed the bill, U.S. President Mr. George W. Bush had said that, "The legislation will strengthen our global nuclear nonproliferation efforts, protect the environment, create jobs and assist India in meeting its growing energy needs in a responsible manner." "I look forward to signing this bill into law and continuing to strengthen the U.S.-India strategic partnership." U.S. Secretary of State Ms. Condoleezza Rice said the agreement reflects a common commitment to share the benefits of the international system and also the burdens and responsibilities of maintaining, strengthening and defending it.[52] Some members of the US Congress expresses reservation over the final approval of civil nuclear cooperation as they want India to commit to strict limits on its strategic nuclear weapons program. This would enable India to pursue freely its nuclear weapons programme and undermine the NPT and the American efforts to Iran and North Korea nuclear ambitions. While the majority of the US Congress and the Senate was convinced that, "it will enable the United States to sell India nuclear reactors and an array of related equipment. It should also help cement an increasingly close strategic and diplomatic relationship with India."[53]

6.13 U.S. President Bush Signs Nuclear Bill into Law

It was on 10 October 2008, during a ceremony at the White House in Washington, former U.S. President Mr. George W. Bush signs the United States-India Nuclear Cooperation Approval and Nonproliferation Enhancement Act into law. After the signing of the bill, Mr. George W. Bush said, "the bill I sign today approves the 123 Agreement I submitted to Congress and establishes the legal framework for that agreement to come into effect." He also assured New Delhi that the new law made no changes in fuel supply commitments or the terms of the 123 agreement.[54]

6.14 International Reaction to the Agreement

The idea is to analyse the international reaction to the civil nuclear cooperation agreement between India and the United States. Many countries have come out in support of this agreement and many have opposed. It is always clear Pakistan never want any form of cooperation between India and its close allies the United States. One reason as to why Pakistan is not happy is the fact that the United States is moving closer to engaging India which would result to the United States tilting in favor of India. Pakistan Foreign Minister Mr. Khursheed Mehmood Kasuri has been quoted as saying, "the whole nuclear non-proliferation treaty will unravel. It's only a matter of time before other countries will act in the same way." The question of undermining nuclear non-proliferation arises when the co-operation is with India. Such question does not arise when they were proliferating nuclear related materials to other countries. Instead of raising such question they should ask themselves where they stand today.[55]

Russia is one country that has supported start from the very beginning. Russia has insisted for making an exception for India in NPT to give it access to civilian nuclear fuel and technology. According to Russian Foreign Minister Official, "we cannot ignore India's energy requirements. It is a rapidly developing country with a good non-proliferation record. We should probably make an exception in this case without adopting new norms that may erode the NPT regime."[56]

The initial indication of the Canada government was positive. It would be keen to engage in civilian nuclear cooperation should the agreement consummate. It was on 26 September, the Canadian Foreign Minister Mr. Pierre Pettigrew also announced that Canada was willing to resume trade with India in dual-use nuclear technologies without infringing on the rules of the NSG or the IAEA. An agreement to cooperate on nuclear safety measures was adopted.[57]

6.15 Outcome of the Civilian Nuclear Cooperation Agreement

Ever since India had earned the waiver from the Nuclear Supplier's Group (NSGs) on September 2008 to resume the nuclear commerce with the rest of the world, we have seen some unimaginable agreement between India and other countries. India and Kazakhstan signed the civilian nuclear cooperation agreement during the latter's President Visit to India on the eve of republic day on 24 January 2009. The agreement is in consonant with the increasing nuclear fuel demand to meet India's fuel starved nuclear power plants. With this Kazakhstan would be exporting Uranium to India. Kazakhstan became the fourth country with whom India had signed the civilian nuclear cooperation agreement. Before this, India had signed the same agreement with United States, France and Russia. The agreement is significant because Kazakhstan is the third largest producer of uranium, accounting for fifteen per cent of world production.[58] While Canada's Saskatchewan province is also readying a high profile delegation to pitch for nuclear sales to India as well.[59]

The successful completion of the historic agreement will only strengthen Indo-Russian cooperation in nuclear related technologies and reactors. India's isolation from nuclear cooperation has handicapped the possibility of cooperation between the two countries. With this, India can expect to receive critical nuclear related technology from Russia. The U.S. cannot object to Russia supplying fuel and reactors to India. This was even made clear by the U.S. Undersecretary of State for Political Affairs, Nicholas Burns that, "We think the proper sequencing would be that if India needs nuclear fuel for its reactors in Tarapur, then the proper way to do this would to have the US Congress Act, hopefully, change our laws, have the NSG Act and change NSG practices, then countries would be free to engage at that point in civil nuclear trade with India." This is one of the strategic advantages for India. This also gives a clear impression that the agreement is not just between India and the U.S.

Once India and the U.S. declare the joint statement for civil nuclear cooperation, Russian President Putin had offered to build four nuclear power plants in India.[60] Then India and Russia entered into a Uranium supply agreement for the second time on 11 February 2009, since NSGs lifted curbs on selling some nuclear fuel and equipment to India. The agreement was between Russia's leading nuclear company TVEL and India's Department of Atomic Energy. Both sides signed two contracts for supplying Uranium for Indian nuclear reactors. Under this agreement, TVEL will have a long-term supply of 2,000 tonnes of natural uranium pellets for India's pressurized heavy water reactors. Another contract was for the supply of about 60 tonnes of low-enriched uranium pellets for boiling water reactors units at Tarapur. Uranium imported from Russia will be used in the domestic pressurized heavy water reactors under IAEA safeguards.[61]

6.16 India and Nuclear Non-Proliferation

To meet the increasing challenges posed by nuclear proliferation, cooperation among the like-minded nations is necessary. The decision has been taken by the Bush Administration in keeping with the significant role that India has to play in meeting the challenges. It is time now that the U.S. project India as a role model for other countries seeking to acquiring nuclear weapons. In this case, Indian Foreign Secretary on October 2005 has made it clear to the international community that, "India is today a rapidly expanding industrial economy with a wide array of technologies that are relevant to proliferation. That in itself makes a case why our export controls and their effective implementation will matter more and more for global non-proliferation efforts."

Unlike other NPT members, India endorses a policy of non-transfer of enrichment and reprocessing technologies. In addition, India in the 18 July 2005 joint statement has agreed to separate civilian facilities from military facilities under IAEA safeguards, continue its unilateral moratorium on nuclear testing, work with U.S. and others to conclude multilateral Fissile Material Cut Off treaty (FMCT). Given India's impeccable record, India's civil nuclear cooperation agreement with the United States would only strengthen the international non-proliferation effort rather than undermining it. It will be an added advantage to states fighting for the horizontal prevention of proliferation.[62]

By entering into the civilian nuclear initiative, India's interests do not lies in undermining the non-proliferation regime, but to strengthen the regime. India has in the past and present shown its responsibilities to preventing the horizontal proliferation of nuclear weapons. It was during his address at the Golden jubilee function of the Department of Atomic Energy on 23 October 2004, Indian Prime Minister Mr. Manmohan Singh has stated that, "India is a responsible nuclear power. We are fully conscious of the immense responsibilities that come with the possession of advanced technologies, both civil and strategic. While we are determined to utilize our indigenous resources and capabilities to fulfill our national interests, we are doing so in a manner that is not contrary to the larger goals of nuclear non-proliferation." The Prime Minister's statement clearly reflects the fact that India is very clear about its responsibilities once India got the opportunity to share nuclear related materials with other countries.[63]

To ensure the safety of the nuclear related materials and equipments transferred or already available to India, it has put in place an effective and comprehensive system of national export controls, which has been constantly updated to meet the highest international standards. This is manifested in the enactment of the weapons of Mass Destruction and their Delivery systems Act in 2005. Above all, India has committed to adhere to the Missile Technology control Regime and Nuclear Suppliers Group. India also supports the international efforts to limit the spread of Enrichment and Reprocessing (ENR) equipment or technologies to states that do not have them. India urges the international community to work together to achieving the objective nuclear non-proliferation.[64]

6.17 Regional and Global Implications of the Civilian Nuclear Cooperation Agreement

It must be noted that India is not the first country to enter into such agreement with the United States. Before this many countries have concluded such agreement with the United States including China. Their agreement did not become an issue because they were official nuclear weapons states and also that they were signatory to NPT. But when India concludes the same agreement, this becomes an issue. The issue was more worsened by left parties and nuclear scientists of India opposing the agreement. Lack of consensus among the Indians have opened the way for others to strongly condemning the agreement.

This would give way to arms race in South Asia. It is quite interesting to note that the question of arms race arises when India had entered into a civilian nuclear cooperation with the United States, but such question doesn't arise when Pakistan was and continue to receive arms and equipment from the latter.

However, former U.S. Secretary of State, Ms. Condoleezza Rice in her testimony before the Senate Foreign Affaris Committee on 5 April 2006 had made it clear that the civil nuclear cooperation with India will not lead to arms race in South Asia. She further added that, "Nothing we are proposing would violate our NPT obligations that we not in any way assist India's nuclear weapons program." This is quite clear because the agreement is not about helping India's nuclear weapon's programme that would pose a threat to its neighboring countries. There is no reason why India's neighboring countries should be concerned about the India-U.S. civil nuclear initiative because it is fully civilian in nature.[65]

As far as Pakistan is concerned, if it had to go for enhancing its nuclear weapons programme then it would go even without this deal. There are many who claim that it would force Pakistan to go ahead for such cooperation with China, it would be a wrong claim and that they should go back to the history of Pakistan's nuclear weapons programme. India-U.S. civil nuclear cooperation should not become the guiding factor for Pakistan closer cooperation with China. That is one reason as to why the former U.S. President Mr. George W. Bush has declined to offer such opportunity to Pakistan, its close and long time partner.

India has not entered into this agreement to increase stockpile of its fissile material thereby strengthening its nuclear arsenal. It is a fake claim that the nuclear fuel and technology that would be supplied under this agreement would free India's indigenous uranium reserves to be used for its nuclear weapons programme. To ensure that this does not happen, India has put all the civilian facilities under the international safeguards. The Indian Prime Minister Mr. Manmohan Singh assurance during his address to the Indian parliament on 7 March that there will be no capping of our strategic program' should not be construed as directing towards increasing India's nuclear weapons programme.[66]

The reason as to why the civilian nuclear initiative between India and the United States has become a global issue is due to the fact that it is between the nuclear weapon state and non nuclear weapon state. Although India has exposed its nuclear capability, but it came after dateline for a country to be regarded a nuclear weapons state. Because of which, India is not ready to become a member of the NPT. What the critics say is that the nuclear cooperation between India and the United States is a violation of the international nuclear regime and violation of the international treaty. However the U.S. State Department has argued against this, "Nothing in the NPT, its negotiating history, or the practice of the parties supports the notion that fuel supply to safeguarded reactors for peaceful purposes could be construed as 'assisting in the manufacture of nuclear weapons' for the purposes of Article I." The civilian nuclear initiative is in no way aimed at helping India to acquire more nuclear arsenal. India and the United States are seriously concerned about the issue.

Nevertheless, the opponents of the deal are of the view that this would give the way for the other countries to follow the same footsteps. What is equally important is that the civilian nuclear initiative would no doubt strengthen the strategic relationship thereby deepening the level of strategic understanding on the global issues such as fighting the menace of terrorism, preventing the proliferation of nuclear weapons, etc, that remains the main determinant to the world peace, security and stability.[67]

However the response of Russia to the cooperation between India and Russia was positive. This is due to the fact that in the recent past the relations between Russia and the United States have improved significantly. This is further supported by Russia's eagerness to have a civil nuclear cooperation with India. Once the hurdled is cleared for India then Russia can really benefit from the supply of nuclear fuel and reactors to India. As a result of which, Russia has appreciated such developments. One of the renowned Russian scholar, Mr. Alexander Y. Borisov has said in Islamabad on 27 February 2006 that Russia had no objection to the U.S.-Indian agreement on civil nuclear research. He further added that Russia was "legalistic minded" and believed that the civil nuclear agreement should only become effective when certain preconditions were met.[68]

6.18 Conclusion

The India-U.S. civil nuclear cooperation initiative took more than three years to come to fruition, as it had to pass through several tough process, including amendment of the U.S. domestic law, a civil-military nuclear Separation Plan in India, an India specific IAEA safeguards agreement, waiver for India by the Nuclear Suppliers Group and finally the U.S. Congress approval. However the successful implementation of the initiative offers a great opportunity to India to get rid of the long standing nuclear dispute with United States that would also bring an end to more than three decades of India's nuclear isolation from the international community. If India is not able to capitalize on it then it would be a huge loss for India. India should take the advantage of this opportunity that is very hard to come in the near future. In this civilian nuclear initiative, India would gain more than what it would lose.

Unlike in the past, when the U.S. export control regimes posed a serious roadblock to India-United States relations, but today the transforming relations that witnessed since the cold war end, has given way to more understanding on the nuclear issue. This is evident from the fact since the start of the tenure of Bush Administration, India has been looked as the solution rather than problem to the nuclear proliferation.

Once India exposed its nuclear capability in 1998, the U.S. export control regimes started loosing its effectiveness, resulting in realization on the part of the U.S. the need to have more engagement rather than isolating it from international community by not sharing advanced technology of the supplying parties. India can play a crucial role in meeting the present and future challenges.[69]

This is also manifested by creating opportunities for Indian scientists to participate in the international exchange of scientific ideas and technical know-how and to contribute to the global effort to deal with the world-wide challenges of energy security. India's participation in the International Thermonuclear Research Reactor or ITER project as a full and equal member along with a handful of technologically advanced countries is a huge strategic gains for India.[70]

In this direction, the decision to conclude the civilian nuclear cooperation agreement between India and the United States is one of the most important decisions taken so far after the turn of the twenty-first century. That does not mean that the agreements signed before this is insignificant. The decision reflects commitment and understanding on the parts of the two countries on the need to work closely together in the changing world scenario. The civilian nuclear cooperation initiative is just one element of the transforming India-U.S. relations but has significant role to play in strengthening every aspects of the bilateral relations. This would also open the way for India to have closer engagement with other strong partners that was not possible before this breakthrough.

Endnotes

[1] Rajesh Kumar Mishra, "Indo-US Nuclear Deal and Non-proliferation", Strategic Analysis (New- Delhi), vol. 29(4), October-December 2005, p. 616.

[2] Ashley J. Tellis, India As a New Global Power: An Action Agenda For the United States (New Delhi: India Research Press, 2005), pp. 36-38.

[3] Ashley J. Tellis Testimony before the Senate Foreign Relations Committee on, "U.S.-India Atomic Energy Cooperation: Strategic and Nonproliferation Implications", 26 April 2006, p. 3.

[4] B.K. Shrivastava, "India

's Relations with the US: Vision of a Global Partnership", in V.D. Chopra (ed.), India's Foreign Policy in the 21st Century (New Delhi: Kalpaz Publications, 2006), pp. 103-04.

[5] P.M. Kamath, "Civilian Nuclear Cooperation: Turning Point in Indo-US Relations", India Quarterly (New Delhi) vol. LXII(3), July-September 2006, pp. 46-48.

[6] Manohar Thyagaraj and Raju G.C. Thomas, "The U.S.-Indian Nuclear Agreement: Balancing Energy Needs and Nonproliferation Goals", Orbis (Philadelphia, PA), vol. 50(2), Spring 2006, pp. 360-62.

[7] Brahma Challeney, "Technology Control Regimes: Dealing With Their Impact on India", India Quarterly, vol. LVIII(1), January-March 2002, pp. 27-31.

[8] Manpreet Sethi, "Indo-U.S. Cooperation No Threat to Proliferation", Nuclear Power, A Bimonthly Newsletter on Nuclear Energy, Centre for Strategic and International Studies, vol. 3(18), 15 June 2006, p. 1.

[9] Sudha Mahalingam, "Nuclear Power and the Mirage of Energy Security", The Hindu (Hyderabad), 16 March 2006.

[10] Manohar Thyagaraj and Raju G.C. Thomas, n. 6, pp. 356-58.

[11] Ashley J. Tellis, n. 2, p. 24.

[12] Deepa M. Ollapally, "India and Russia: Renewing the Relationship", in Harsh V. Pant (ed.), Indian Foreign Policy in a Uniplar World (New Delhi: Routledge, 2009), p. 198

[13] Manjeet S. Pardesai and Sumit Ganguly, "India and Energy Security: A Foreign Policy Priority", in Harsh V. Pant (ed.), Indian Foreign Policy in a Unipolar World (New Delhi: Routledge, 2009), pp. 106, 109.

[14] Adil Sultan Muhammad, "Indo-US Civilian Nuclear Cooperation Agreement: Implications on South Asian Security Environment", The Henry L. Stimson Center, July 2006, pp. 4-6.

[15] T.V. Paul, "The US-India Nuclear Accord: Implications for Nonproliferation Regime", International Journal (Canada), vol. LXII(4), Fall 2007, pp. 858-59.

[16] Rajesh Kumar Mishra, n. 1, pp. 616-18.

[17] C. Raja Mohan, "India and the Emerging Non-proliferation Order: The Second Nuclear Age", in Harsh V. Pant (ed.), Indian Foreign Policy in a Unipolar World (New Delhi: Routledge, 2009), pp. 43-44.

[18] Rajesh Rajagopalan, "Structural Imperatives and Asian Security", in R. R. Sharma (ed.), India and Emerging Asia (New Delhi: Thousand Oaks: London: Sage Publications, 2005), pp. 303-05.

[19] P. M. Kamath, n. 5, p. 28.

[20] See, India-United States Joint Statement, Washington, DC, 18 July 2005, Strategic Digest (New Delhi), vol. 35(8), August 2005.

[21] C. Raja Mohan, n. 17, pp. 43-44.

[22] Ibid., pp. 34-35.

[23] R. Rajaraman, "The India-US Nuclear Deal: the Perspective of a Non-governmental Nuclear Scientist", in Karthika Sasikumar and Wade L. Huntley (ed.), Canadian Policy on Nuclear Co-operation with India: Confronting New Dilemmas (Canada: Simons Centre for Disarmament and Non-Proliferation Research, 2007), pp. 58-59.

[24] Adil Sultan Muhammad, n. 14, pp. 6-7.

[25] Lecture by Prime Minister Special Envoy Shyam Saran on, India and the Nuclear Domain, 18 February 2008, available at <http://meaindia.nic.in/speech/2008/02/19ss01.htm>.

[26] See, Prime Minister Statement in the Lok Sabha on Civil Nuclear Energy Cooperation with the United States", Strategic Digest (New Delhi), vol. 37(9), September 2007, p. 1141.

[27] P. M. Kamath, n. 5, pp. 30-31

[28] Sandy Gordon, "An Australian Perspective on the Indo-US Nuclear Deal", South Asian Survey (New Delhi), vol. 16(1), January-April 2009, pp. 44-45.

[29] P. M. Kamath, n. 5, pp. 32-33.

[30] Ibid., pp. 40-41.

[31] Lecture by Shyam Saran, n. 25.

[32] Nalini Kant Jha, "Taking stock of India-US Deal on Civil Nuclear Cooperation", India Quarterly, vol. LXIII(4), October-December 2007, pp. 88-90.

[33] C. Vinodan, "Indo-US Nuclear Deal and South Asian Regional Security", International Journal of South Asian Studies (Pondicherry), vol. 1(2), July-December 2008, pp. 273-74.

[34] P. M. Kamath, n. 5, p. 28.

[35] See Agreed Text for, "Agreement for Cooperation between The Government of India and The Government of The United States of America Concerning Peaceful Uses of Nuclear Energy", 1 August 2007, available at <http://www.dae.gov.in/indous.pdf>.

[36] Brahma Chellaney, "We Cannot Hide from Hyde", Asian Age (Mumbai), 16 December 2006.

[37] See, "Top Scientists Rejected U.S. N-bill", Asian Age (Mumbai), 16 December 2006.

[38] 'On the Indian-US Civil Nuclear Cooperation Initiative', see Shannon N. Kile, "Nuclear Arms Control and Non-Proliferation", in SIPRI Yearbook 2008: Armaments, Disarmaments and International Security (New York: Oxford University Press, 2008), pp. 358-60.

[39] Nalini Kant Jha, n. 33, p. 92 and M. R. Srinivasan, "India May Lose Control of its Nuclear Future", The Hindu (Hyderabad), 11 December 2006.

[40] See, "Staff Reports on "IAEA Board Approves India-Safeguards Agreement", 1 August 2008, available at <http://www.iaea.org/NewsCenter/News/2008/board010808.html>.

[41] See, "Agreement between the Government of India and the International Atomic Energy Agency for the Application of Safeguards to Civilian Nuclear Facilities", 7 July 2008, available at <http://pmindia.nic.in/IaeaIndiaSGADrft.pdf>.

[42] See, "Staff Reports on IAEA Board Approves India-Safeguards Agreement", n. 39.

[43] Peter Crail, "IAEA Approves India Additional Protocol", available at <http://www.armscontrol.org/act/2009_04/IndiaProtocol>.

[44] P. M. Kamath, n. 5, pp. 38-43 and for Critics see Geoge Perkovich, "Faulty Promises", available at <http://www.carnegieendowment.org/files/po21.perkovich.pdf>.

[45] See, "Remarks of Secretary of State Condoleezza Rice at the Senate Foreign Relations Committee on the US-India Civil Nuclear Cooperation Initiative", 5 April 2006, pp. 10-11, 13, available at <http://foreign.senate.gov / testimony / 2006 / RiceTestimony 060405.pdf>.

[46] P.M. Kamath, n. 5, pp. 36-37.

[47] Y C Halan, "Manmohan Singh Visits the US: Towards Detente", South Asia Politics (New Delhi), vol. 4(4), August 2005, pp. 22-23.

[48] Rajiv Sikri, Challenge and Strategy: Rethinking India's Foreign Policy (New Delhi: Sage Publications, 2009), pp. 179-80.

[49] See, "Indo-US Civilian Nuclear Agreement", available at <http://en.wikipedia.org/wiki/United_States-India_Peaceful_Atomic_Energy_Cooperation_Act#Rationale_behind_the_agreement>.

[50] Adil Sultan Muhammad, n. 14, pp. 9-10.

[51] See, "Statement by the Prime Minister on the Final Outcome of the Meeting of the Nuclear Suppliers Group", New Delhi, 6 September 2008, Strategic Digest, vol. 38(10), October 2008, p. 1255 and also see, "Statement by Minister of External Affairs on the Final Outcome of the Meeting of the Nuclear Suppliers Group", New Delhi, 6 September 2008, Strategic Digest, vol. 38(10), October 2008, pp. 1255-1256.

[52] Merle D. Kellerhals Jr., "Congress Approves U.S.-India Civil Nuclear Accord", available at <http://www.america.gov/st/peacesec-english/2008/October/20081002094758dmslahrellek0.3916284.html>.

[53] Claudia Astarita, "China and India: Rivals or Partners? An Analysis of the Background of the Interactions between the two Major Emerging Asian Powers", Paper presented in 6th Pan-European International Relations Conference on Making Sense of Pluralist World, University of Turin, 12-15 September 2007, pp. 21-22, available at <http://turin.sgir.eu/uploads/Claudia-china_india_rivals_or_partners_claudia_astarita.pdf>.

[54] See, "Bush Signs India-U.S. Nuclear Bill into Law", available at <http://www.hindu.com/2008/10/10/stories/2008101060940100.htm>.

[55] See, "Pakistan Says Deal Will Encourage Proliferation", Times of India (Pune), 18 March 2006.

[56] See, "Russia Want NPT Exception for India", Times of India (Pune), 4 April 2006.

[57] Karthika Sasikumar, "India's Emergence as a 'Responsible' Nuclear Power", International Journal, vol. LXII(4), Fall 2007, p. 828.

[58] See, "India, Kazakhstan Ink for Uranium Supply", Indian Express (Pune), 25 January 2009.

[59] See, "India to Sign IAEA Pact on Feb 2", Times of India (Pune), 31 January 2009.

[60] Deepa M. Ollapally, n. 12, pp. 196-98.

[61] See, "India signs Uranium Deal with Russia", Asian Age (Mumbai), 12 February 2009.

[62] Rajesh Kumar Mishra, n. 1, pp. 623-25.

[63] See, "Prime Minister Address at the Golden Jubilee Function of the Department of Atomic Energy on 23 October 2004", available at <http://pmindia.nic.in/speech/content.asp?id=36>.

[64] See, "Statement by External Affairs Minister on the Civil Nuclear Initiative", New Delhi, 5 September 2008, available at <http://www.indianembassy.org/newsite/press_release/2008/Sep/3.asp>.

[65] See, Remarks of Secretary of State Condoleezza Rice, n. 45, p. 13.

[66] Adil Sultan Muhammad, n. 14, pp. 12-13.

[67] Karthika Sasikumar, n. 57, pp. 835-37.

[68] Mavara Inayat, "US-Indian Strategic Partnership: Implications for Asia and Beyond", Regional Studies (Islamabad), vol. XXIV(2), Spring 2006, pp. 46-47.

[69] Brahma Challeney, n. 7, p. 30.

[70] See, Prime Minister Statement in the Lok Sabha, n. 26, p. 1141.

Appendix-I

For Immediate Release

Office of the Press Secretary July 18, 2005

Joint Statement between President George W. Bush and Prime Minister Manmohan Singh

Prime Minister Manmohan Singh and President Bush today declare their resolve to transform the relationship between their countries and establish a global partnership. As leaders of nations committed to the values of human freedom, democracy and rule of law, the new relationship between India and the United States will promote stability, democracy, prosperity and peace throughout the world. It will enhance our ability to work together to provide global leadership in areas of mutual concern and interest.

Building on their common values and interests, the two leaders resolve:

- To create an international environment conducive to promotion of democratic values, and to strengthen democratic practices in societies which wish to become more open and pluralistic.
- To combat terrorism relentlessly. They applaud the active and vigorous counterterrorism cooperation between the two countries and support more international efforts in this direction. Terrorism is a global scourge and the one we will fight everywhere. The two leaders

strongly affirm their commitment to the conclusion by September of a UN comprehensive convention against international terrorism.

The Prime Minister's visit coincides with the completion of the Next Steps in Strategic Partnership (NSSP) initiative, launched in January 2004. The two leaders agree that this provides the basis for expanding bilateral activities and commerce in space, civil nuclear energy and dual-use technology.

Drawing on their mutual vision for the U.S.-India relationship, and our joint objectives as strong long-standing democracies, the two leaders agree on the following:

FOR THE ECONOMY

Revitalize the U.S.-India Economic Dialogue and launch a CEO Forum to harness private sector energy and ideas to deepen the bilateral economic relationship.

- Support and accelerate economic growth in both countries through greater trade, investment, and technology collaboration.
- Promote modernization of India's infrastructure as a prerequisite for the continued growth of the Indian economy. As India enhances its investment climate, opportunities for investment will increase.
- Launch a U.S.-India Knowledge Initiative on Agriculture focused on promoting teaching, research, service and commercial linkages.

FOR ENERGY AND THE ENVIRONMENT

- Strengthen energy security and promote the development of stable and efficient energy markets in India with a view to ensuring adequate, affordable energy supplies and conscious of the need for sustainable development. These issues will be addressed through the U.S.-India Energy Dialogue.

- Agree on the need to promote the imperatives of development and safeguarding the environment, commit to developing and deploying cleaner, more efficient, affordable, and diversified energy technologies.

FOR DEMOCRACY AND DEVELOPMENT

- Develop and support, through the new U.S.-India Global Democracy Initiative in countries that seek such assistance, institutions and resources that strengthen the foundations that make democracies credible and effective. India and the U.S. will work together to strengthen democratic practices and capacities and contribute to the new U.N. Democracy Fund.
- Commit to strengthen cooperation and combat HIV/AIDs at a global level through an initiative that mobilizes private sector and government resources, knowledge, and expertise.

FOR NON-PROLIFERATION AND SECURITY

- Express satisfaction at the New Framework for the U.S.-India Defense Relationship as a basis for future cooperation, including in the field of defense technology.
- Commit to play a leading role in international efforts to prevent the proliferation of Weapons of Mass Destruction. The U.S. welcomed the adoption by India of legislation on WMD (Prevention of Unlawful Activities Bill).
- Launch a new U.S.-India Disaster Relief Initiative that builds on the experience of the Tsunami Core Group, to strengthen cooperation to prepare for and conduct disaster relief operations.

FOR HIGH-TECHNOLOGY AND SPACE

- Sign a Science and Technology Framework Agreement, building on the U.S.-India High-Technology Cooperation Group (HTCG), to provide for joint research and training, and the establishment of public-private partnerships.

- Build closer ties in space exploration, satellite navigation and launch, and in the commercial space arena through mechanisms such as the U.S.-India Working Group on Civil Space Cooperation.
- Building on the strengthened nonproliferation commitments undertaken in the NSSP, to remove certain Indian organizations from the Department of Commerce's Entity List.

Recognizing the significance of civilian nuclear energy for meeting growing global energy demands in a cleaner and more efficient manner, the two leaders discussed India's plans to develop its civilian nuclear energy program.

President Bush conveyed his appreciation to the Prime Minister over India's strong commitment to preventing WMD proliferation and stated that as a responsible state with advanced nuclear technology, India should acquire the same benefits and advantages as other such states. The President told the Prime Minister that he will work to achieve full civil nuclear energy cooperation with India as it realizes its goals of promoting nuclear power and achieving energy security. The President would also seek agreement from Congress to adjust U.S. laws and policies, and the United States will work with friends and allies to adjust international regimes to enable full civil nuclear energy cooperation and trade with India, including but not limited to expeditious consideration of fuel supplies for safeguarded nuclear reactors at Tarapur. In the meantime, the United States will encourage its partners to also consider this request expeditiously. India has expressed its interest in ITER and a willingness to contribute. The United States will consult with its partners considering India's participation. The United

States will consult with the other participants in the Generation IV International Forum with a view toward India's inclusion.

The Prime Minister conveyed that for his part, India would reciprocally agree that it would be ready to assume the same responsibilities and practices and acquire the same benefits and advantages as other leading countries with advanced nuclear technology, such as the United States. These responsibilities and practices consist of identifying and separating civilian and military nuclear facilities and programs in a phased manner and filing a declaration regarding its civilians facilities with the International Atomic Energy Agency (IAEA); taking a decision to place voluntarily its civilian nuclear facilities under IAEA safeguards; signing and adhering to an Additional Protocol with respect to civilian nuclear facilities; continuing India's unilateral moratorium on nuclear testing; working with the United States for the conclusion of a multilateral Fissile Material Cut Off Treaty; refraining from transfer of enrichment and reprocessing technologies to states that do not have them and supporting international efforts to limit their spread; and ensuring that the necessary steps have been taken to secure nuclear materials and technology through comprehensive export control legislation and through harmonization and adherence to Missile Technology Control Regime (MTCR) and Nuclear Suppliers Group (NSG) guidelines.

The President welcomed the Prime Minister's assurance. The two leaders agreed to establish a working group to undertake on a phased basis in the months ahead the necessary actions mentioned above to fulfill these commitments. The President and Prime Minister also agreed that they would review this progress when the President visits India in 2006.

The two leaders also reiterated their commitment that their countries would play a leading role in international efforts to prevent the proliferation of weapons of mass destruction, including nuclear, chemical, biological and radiological weapons.

In light of this closer relationship, and the recognition of India's growing role in enhancing regional and global security, the Prime Minister and the President agree that international institutions must fully reflect changes in the global scenario that have taken place since 1945. The President reiterated his view that international institutions are going to have to adapt to reflect India's central and growing role. The two leaders state their expectations that India and the United States will strengthen their cooperation in global forums.

Prime Minister Manmohan Singh thanks President Bush for the warmth of his reception and the generosity of his hospitality. He extends an invitation to President Bush to visit India at his convenience and the President accepts that invitation.

Appendix-II

NEW FRAMEWORK FOR THE U.S.-INDIA DEFENSE RELATIONSHIP

Signed on June 28, 2005 in Washington DC by Minister of Defense of India, Mr. Pranab Mukherjee & Secretary of Defense of the United States, Mr. Donald Rumsfeld

1. The United States and India have entered a new era. We are transforming our relationship to reflect our common principles and shared national interests. As the world's two largest democracies, the United States and India agree on the vital importance of political and economic freedom, democratic institutions, the rule of law, security, and opportunity around the world. The leaders of our two countries are building a U.S.-India strategic partnership in pursuit of these principles and interests.

2. Ten years ago, in January 1995, the Agreed Minute on Defense Relations between the United States and India was signed. Since then, changes in the international security environment have challenged our countries in ways unforeseen ten years ago. The U.S.-India defense relationship has advanced in a short time to unprecedented levels of cooperation unimaginable in 1995. Today, we agree on a new Framework that builds on past successes, seizes new opportunities, and charts a

course for the U.S.-India defense relationship for the next ten years. This defense relationship will support, and will be an element of, the broader U.S.-India strategic partnership.

3. The U.S.-India defense relationship derives from a common belief in freedom, democracy, and the rule of law, and seeks to advance shared security interests. These interests include:
   - maintaining security and stability;
   - defeating terrorism and violent religious extremism;
   - preventing the spread of weapons of mass destruction and associated materials, data, and technologies; and
   - protecting the free flow of commerce via land, air and sea lanes.
4. In pursuit of this shared vision of an expanded and deeper U.S.-India strategic relationship, our defense establishments shall:

   A. conduct joint and combined exercises and exchanges;

   B. collaborate in multinational operations when it is in their common interest;

   C. strengthen the capabilities of our militaries to promote security and defeat terrorism;

   D. expand interaction with other nations in ways that promote regional and global peace and stability;

   E. enhance capabilities to combat the proliferation of weapons of mass destruction;

   F. in the context of our strategic relationship, expand two-way defense trade between our countries. The

United States and India will work to conclude defense transactions, not solely as ends in and of themselves, but as a means to strengthen our countries' security, reinforce our strategic partnership, achieve greater interaction between our armed forces, and build greater understanding between our defense establishments;

G. in the context of defense trade and a framework of technology security safeguards, increase opportunities for technology transfer, collaboration, co-production, and research and development;

H. expand collaboration relating to missile defense;

I. strengthen the abilities of our militaries to respond quickly to disaster situations, including in combined operations;

J. assist in building worldwide capacity to conduct successful peacekeeping operations, with a focus on enabling other countries to field trained, capable forces for these operations;

K. conduct exchanges on defense strategy and defense transformation;

L. increase exchanges of intelligence; and

M. continue strategic-level discussions by senior leadership from the U.S. Department of Defense and India's Ministry of Defence, in which the two sides exchange perspectives on international security issues of common interest, with the aim of increasing mutual understanding, promoting shared objectives, and developing common approaches.

5. The Defense Policy Group shall continue to serve as the primary mechanism to guide the U.S.-India strategic defense relationship. The Defense Policy Group will

make appropriate adjustments to the structure and frequency of its meetings and of its subgroups, when agreed to by the Defense Policy Group co-chairs, to ensure that it remains an effective mechanism to advance U.S.-India defense cooperation.

6. In recognition of the growing breadth and depth of the U.S.-India strategic defense relationship, we hereby establish the Defense Procurement and Production Group and institute a Joint Working Group for mid-year review of work overseen by the Defense Policy Group.
   - The Defense Procurement and Production Group will oversee defense trade, as well as prospects for co-production and technology collaboration, broadening the scope of its predecessor subgroup the Security Cooperation Group.
   - The Defense Joint Working Group will be subordinate to the Defense Policy Group and will meet at least once per year to perform a midyear review of work overseen by the Defense Policy Group and its subgroups (the Defense Procurement and Production Group, the Joint Technical Group, the Military Cooperation Group, and the Senior Technology Security Group), and to prepare issues for the annual meeting of the Defense Policy Group.
7. The Defense Policy Group and its subgroups will rely upon this Framework for guidance on the principles and objectives of the U.S.-India strategic relationship, and will strive to achieve those objectives.

Signed in Arlington, Virginia, USA, on June 28, 2005.

Appendix-III

Chronology of India-U.S. Relations, 1991-Present

April 1991	Mr. Claude Kickleighter, a former Commander of the U.S. Army in the Pacific visited India and made several proposals that were aimed at strengthening the level of defence co-operation between the two countries.
October 1991	Admiral Charles Larson, Commander in Chief of the U.S. Pacific Command visited India in an effort to expand military cooperation.
7 October 1991	The U.S. Trade Representative Ms. Carla Hills visited India where she says that India should change patent laws for drugs and pharmaceuticals in its own interests. However, she rejected India's plea that there should be free access of professionals and technical manpower to the United States market as immigration is not covered by GATT.
November 1991	The Director General of the International Atomic Energy Agency (IAEA) visited India and holds talks with officials.
January 1992	Naval officers from both countries established the groundwork for a long-term 'forces to forces' level relationship.

11 January 1992	The United States Senator Mr. Larry Pressler visited India where he says that he is against the extension of the Pressler Amendment to India.
31 January 1992	Prime Minister Mr. Narasimha Rao had a meeting with the U.S. President George Bush at New York.
January 1992	Senator Larry Pressler, General Johonen Corus of the U.S. Army and Admiral Frank Kelso, Chief of the Operations of the the U.S. Navy visited India.
February 1992	For the first time in the history of India-U.S. relations, a joint training exercise named Teak Iroquois was conducted whereby the army and air force para-troopers of the two countries participated.
5-9 April 1992	Defence Minister of India visited the U.S. at the invitation of U.S Defence Secretary.
29 April 1992	The United States withdraws duty benefits under the Generalised System of Preferences (GSP) to Indian Pharmaceutical for inadequate protection of patents in Indian Pharmaceutical markets.
May 1992	The U.S. Army Chief, Gen. Sullivan Gordon visited India and holds talks with the Indian military leadership in which the latter had declined to have a direct Army-to-Army exchange beyond training.
11 May 1992	The U.S. imposed a two year ban on American trade and technological transfer with the Indian Space Research Organisation (ISRO) and Glavkosmos of Russia over the deal of the supply of cryo-

	genic rocket engines to India.
29 May 1992	India-U.S. naval exercises were held off the Western seaboard.
12 June 1992	The U.S. Congress Committee rejects a move to link American aid to India with the issue of nuclear non-proliferation.
April 1993	The U.S. State Department's Annual Report on Terrorism 1992, which was made public in April 1993 find mention of official Pakistani backing to Khalistani and Kashmiri terrorists.
30 April 1993	Mr. Bill Clinton Administration places India on the priority watch list under the Super 301 for failing to protect Intellectual Property Rights.
15 July 1993	Mr. Bill Clinton Administration accepts that Pakistan supports terrorism in Punjab and Kashmir, but was not ready to place the country on the list of state sponsoring terrorism.
16 July 1993	Under the pressure of the U.S., Russia suspends the transfer of technology including Cryogenic engines to India.
September 1993	The U.S. States Department of Commerce designated India as one of the Big Emerging Markets.
24 October 1993	Indian Home Minister Mr. S.B. Chavan accuses the U.S. of helping Pakistan in aiding and abetting terrorist and anti-social activities in India.
25 October 1993	Assistant Secretary of State Ms. Robin Raphel says that the United States does not accept the Instrument of Accession

	and views Jammu and Kashmir as a disputed territory. This statement had no doubt angered India because it came at the time when the relationship is steadily improving.
9-13 Dec. 1993	The U.S. Senators, Thad Cochran, Larry Pressler and Hank Brown, visited India for discussions with Government on security related issues.
February 1994	Ms. Robin Raphel, Assistant Secretary of State, visited India to remove some misunderstanding and work to place India-U.S. relations on a sound footing.
6-10 April 1994	The U.S. Deputy Secretary of State, Mr. Strobe Talbott visited India.
14-20 May 1994	Indian Prime Minister Mr. Narasimha Rao visited the U.S. for discussion on a wide range of global issues of common concern.
17 May 1994	The U.S. Ambassador to India Mr. Frank Wisner says that the U.S. does not want India as a Permanent member of the United Nations Security Council as it could undermine cohesion in the council.
27-28 April 1994	India and the U.S. held a further round of discussions on nonproliferation, regional security and disarmament in London.
30 June 1994	Mr. Bill Clinton Administration finally decided not to take action against India under the Super 301 trade law and says that it prefers to enter into negotiations

	with India on strengthening its provisions dealing with intellectual property laws.
13-27 August 1994	Air Chief Marshal, Mr. S K Kaul visited the U.S. that was aimed at strengthening the bilateral relations between the two countries.
19-29 Sept. 1994	Chief of Army Staff, late General B C Joshi visited the U.S.
8-13 Dec. 1994	Admiral Richard Macke, Commander-in-Chief of the U.S. Pacific Command visited India.
January 1995	The U.S. Defence Secretary Mr. William Perry visited India and met his Indian counterpart where both sides signed the landmark agreement named "Agreed Minutes on Defence Relations."
3 January 1995	The U.S. Assistant Secretary of State Ms. Robin Raphel says that India's relation with Pakistan over Kashmir is a deterrent for its entry into the UNSC.
14 February 1995	Indian Home Minister Mr. S.B. Chavan says that a third party was complicating the situation in Kashmir.
12 April 1995	On the occasion of the introduction of the draft resolution on indefinite extension of the NPT in UNSC, India made it very clear that it will not sign the discriminatory treaty.
9 May 1995	Indian Minister of State for Defence Mr. Mallikarjun says that the Government will not cap its Prithvi programmes under the pressure of the U.S. or any other country.

May-June 1995	Military units from both the countries conducted joint exercises on Land and at Sea.
19-21 Oct. 1995	The U.S. Department of State Coordinator for Counter-Terrorism, Mr. Philip Wilcox led a delegation of counter-terrorism experts to India for discussion on the potential for greater counter- terrorism cooperation.
7 December 1995	The U.S. Assistant Secretary for South Asia, Ms. Robin Raphel says that the United States is reluctant to transfer of arms to India as it might alter the existing military balance in the region. She also says that the United States no longer thinks a plebiscite is possible to settle the Kashmir issue.
27 January 1996	India successfully test fires advanced version of Prithvi. The U.S. terms the test a mistake.
25 March 1996	A joint naval exercises named Malabar-96 was carried out between India and the United States off the Kerala coast.
30 April 1996	The United States placed India on the priority watch list under the Special 301 tráde law and decides to invoke the dispute settlement procedure of the World Trade Organisation (WTO).
20 May 1996	The U.S. President Mr. Bill Clinton says that Kashmir is one of the world's two most dangerous flash points.
20 June 1996	India made it very clear that it will not sign the Comprehensive Test Ban Treaty

	(CTBT) unless it calls for universal nuclear disarmament and also it reflects India's security interests.
10 August 1996	The U.S. Secretary of State Mr. Warren Christopher says that the U.S. is determined not to allow a single nation to prevent from reaching a test ban treaty and terms India's demand for setting up a time table for the elimination of nuclear arsenals not possible.
September 1996	Chief of Army Staff General Shankar Roychowdhury visited the U.S. in September 1996.
4 October 1996	The United States State Department rejected the Pakistan Prime Minister Ms. Benazir Bhutto's call for an international conference on Kashmir.
13 December 1996	The U.S. Assistant Secretary of State, Ms. Robin Raphel says that 'the election in Kashmir is not going to resolve the underlying question of Kashmir as a disputed territory.
2 January 1997	India asks two diplomats in the U.S. Embassy in New Delhi to leave the country for their alleged espionage activities.
8 March 1997	Former U.S. Secretary of State Mr. Henry Kissinger on a visit to India supported India's claim for a permanent seat in the UNSC.
9-12 January 1997	The Commander-in-Chief of the U.S. Pacific Command Admiral Joseph W Prusher led a delegation to India.

April 1997	The U.S. demands the abolition of the United Nations military Observer's Group in Kashmir as a condition for paying its arrears to the UN.
1 May 1997	The U.S. places India on its priority watch list under Super 301.
25 June 1997	India and the United States sign a bilateral extradition treaty committing their Governments to eradicate the scourge of terrorism in all its manifestations.
August 1997	Mr. George Pickart, Senior Advisor to the State Department's South Asia bureau says that the U.S. believes that J&K is a disputed territory, and is an issue to be resolved between India and Pakistan taking the desires of the Kashmiri people into account.
16 October 1997	The U.S. Under Secretary of State, Mr. Thomas Pickering, on a visit to India says that his country will support India's claim for a permanent seat in the UNSC if it is backed by all Asian countries. While India expresses unhappiness with such U.S. stand.
22 September 1997	Indian Prime Minister Mr. Inder Kumar Gujral meets the U.S. President, Mr. Bill Clinton in which the latter assures India that its country will be careful not to interfere in any way on India-Pakistan issues.
7 November 1997	The U.S. Senate passes an amendment imposing sanctions on the export of relatively low performance computers to India and 49 other countries.

19 November 1997	The U.S. Secretary of State, Mr. Madeline Albright visits India where both sides agree on a mechanism to discuss all outstanding issues including nuclear cooperation.
25 November 1997	The Pentagon's report on Proliferation lists India among 25 nations whose nuclear, biological and chemical weapons programmes may pose a threat to the United States.
16 December 1997	India and the U.S. sign a memorandum of understanding on joint space exploration.
20 February 1998	India rejected a formal request from the U.S. to use Indian air space to attack Iraq.
11 May 1998	India successfully conducted three nuclear explosions near Pokhran. While the U.S. State Department says that we are deeply disturbed by this announcement.
12 May 1998	On the very next day, U.S. President Mr. Bill Clinton says that he intends to implement fully sanctions against India.
13 May 1998	India further conducted two more nuclear tests.
14 May 1998	The UNSC strongly condemn the Indian nuclear explosion and appeals to India to sign the NPT and the CTBT without delay and without any conditions.
21 May 1998	Indian Prime Minister Principal Secretary, Mr. Brajesh Mishra, announces the Government's decision on a voluntary moratorium on further nuclear tests.

June 1998	India and Russia inks a deal worth $2.6 billion for the construction of two atomic reactors at Koodan Kulam. Despite of the fact that these reactors will be under the IAEA inspection, the U.S. opposes the deal on the ground that it is inconsistent with Russia's commitment as a member of the Nuclear Supplier Group.
4 June 1998	Indian Prime Minister Mr. A.B. Vajpayee rules out signing the Comprehensive Test Ban Treaty (CTBT) in its present form.
12 June 1998	The U.S. Deputy Secretary of State, Mr. Strobe Talbott meets Mr. Jaswant Singh, Special Emissary of the Indian Prime Minister in Washington. The first round of India-United States talks on nuclear issues was successfully concluded.
18 June 1998	Mr. Bill Clinton Administration announces the sanctions it will put on India, which includes termination of new commitments of the U.S. Government, investment and agricultural credits and ban on export of all nuclear or missile related dual used items. The U.S. Government estimates the total direct impact on India at $2.5 billion.
9-10 July 1998	Indian External Affairs Minister, Mr. Jaswant Singh and the United States Deputy Secretary of State, Mr. Strobe Talbott meet in Frankfurt, Germany and hold second round of talks on nuclear issues.

16 July 1998	The U.S. Congress empowers the President with the authority to waive trade sanctions against India and Pakistan.
21 July 1998	The third round of talks was held between Mr. Strobe Talbott and Mr. Jaswant Singh in New Delhi.
24 August 1998	The fourth round of talks on the nuclear issue was held in Washington.
26 August 1998	The U.S. Under Secretary of State, Mr. Thomas Pickering cautions India against following hot pursuit in Kashmir.
24 September 1998	Indian Prime Minister, A.B. Vajpayee, speaking in the United Nations General Assembly, expresses India's readiness to sign the CTBT subject to other countries adhering to it without conditions.
21 October 1998	The U.S. Congress approves the Brownback Amendment giving the authority to waive sanctions.
20 November 1998	The seventh round of talks on nuclear issue was concluded between the representatives of the two countries in Rome.
January 1999	The representative of India and United States concluded the eighth round of talks in New Delhi over the nuclear issue.
4 February 1999	The U.S. Ambassador to India, Richard Celeste, says that India should specify its requirements of nuclear deterrence so that it is not seen as an open ended threat to its neighbours.
5 February 1999	India rejects the United States suggestion to specify its requirements for minimum nuclear deterrence.

14 June 1999	The U.S. President Mr. Bill Clinton calls India's Prime Minister A.B. Vajpayee on the telephone and says he appreciated India's restraint in Kargil.
29 May 1999	The U.S. admits that infiltrators from Pakistan have occupied positions inside Indian Territory in Kargil.
September 1999	India's national security advisor, Mr. Brajesh Mishra visited Washington.
24 December 1999	An Indian Airlines plane IC 814 was hijacked.
28 December 1999	The U.S strongly condemns the hijack and demands the immediate safe release of hostages.
5 January 2000	The U.S. President Mr. Bill Clinton in his address to the U.S. Congress says that easing of tensions between India and Pakistan and fighting weapons proliferation, terrorism and the nexus between them are on top of his agenda.
20-24 March 2000	The U.S. President Mr. Bill Clinton accompanied by high level dignitaries including Commerce Secretary Ms. William Daley and Ambassador Susan Esserman visited India.
21 March 2000	President Bill Clinton and Prime Minister Mr. A.B. Vajpayee issued a joint statement outlining a vision for India-U.S. relations for the 21st century.
	President Bill Clinton announced easing of economic sanctions against India to restart the $25 million Financial Institutions Reform and Expansion (FIRE).

23 March 2000	The U.S. Commerce Secretary Mr. William Daley and Minister of Commerce and Industry of India, Mr. Murasoli Maran signed the 'Formation of and Terms of Reference for the India-U.S. Commercial Dialogue'.
24 March 2000	The U.S. President Mr. Bill Clinton announced that over $4 billion worth business agreements were signed during the visit.
13-17 Sept. 2000	Indian Prime Minister Mr. A.B. Vajpayee paid a five day official visit to Washington D.C. where he met U.S. President Clinton and Vice President Mr. Al Gore.
July 2001	Indian Minister for Commerce and Industry, Shri Murasoli Maran, accompanied by Shri Prabir Sengupta, Commerce Secretary and other senior officials visited Washington D.C.
	Chairman of the U.S. Joint Chiefs of Staff, General Henry Shelton visited India.
August 2001	The United States Trade Representative visited India for three days on the invitation of Indian Minister for Commerce an 1 Industry.
8-10 August 2001	A U.S. delegation comprising the U.S. search and rescue core group visited New Delhi and held discussion with representative from Ministry of Defence, Indian Army, Indian Navy, Air force and Coast Guard over the structure and capabilities of the search and rescue organisations.

5 November 2001	The U.S. Defence Secretary, Mr. Donald Rumsfeld visits New Delhi where he meet Indian Defence Minister, Mr. George Fernandes and discuss on how to strengthen the level of military and defence ties between the two countries.
January 2002	Former Indian Defence Minister, Mr. George Fernandes visits United States in which both countries signed a U.S.-India Bilateral General Security on Military Information Agreement.
17-18 Feb. 2002	General Richard B. Myers, Chairman of the U.S. Joint Chief of Staff visited India.
April 2002	During the Operation enduring freedom, Indian Navy ships Sharda and Sukanya escorted the U.S. ships in the Straits of Malacca.
17 April 2002	India and the United States entered into a first major defence deal for the purchase of eight advanced radars worth approximately $146 million.
June 2002	Indian experts participated in a missile defense exercise in Colorado.
September 2002	The Indian Chief of Naval Staff visits the U.S.
December 2002	Former Indian National Security Advisor Mr. Brajesh Mishra visited United States to discuss on matters relating to cooperation on high-technology, civilian nuclear, etc.
February 2003	Joint U.S.-India Army peacekeeping exercise named 'Shantipath' driven by latest computer war-gaming simulation was

	held at United Service Institution, New Delhi. The U.S. Army Chief also visited to India.
June-July 2003	Indian and the U.S. forces participated in the exercises at Guam.
July 2003	Chairman of the Joint Chiefs of Staff General Myers visited India.
September 2003	Indian and the U.S. forces participated in another exercises at Leh in Jammu and Kashmir.
October 2003	Chief of Air Staff, Air Marshal S. Krishnaswamy attended the 'Global Air Chiefs' conference in Washington D.C. Admiral Vernon Clark, Chief of Naval Operations, U.S. Navy had visited India.
January 2004	Both India and the United States signed the significant "Next Step in Strategic Partnership."
February 2004	The U.S. and Indian air forces also participated in the first bilateral Dissimilar Air Combat Exercise (DACT) at Gwalior with their fighter aircraft. A Master Information Exchange Agreement facilitating exchange of defence research and development information was signed by the U.S. Secretary of State, Mr. Donald Rumsfeld and Defence Minister of India, Mr. George Fernandes. A senior defence technology security group met in Washington.

March 2004	Indian Chief of Army Staff General N.C. Vij visited U.S.
	The 6th meeting of the Joint Technical Group on R&D cooperation met in Delhi.
13-14 July 2004	The U.S. Deputy Secretary of State, Mr. Richard Armitage visited New Delhi to reconfirm U.S. commitment to continued expansion of India-U.S. ties.
October 2004	Admiral Raman Puri, the Chief of Integrated Defence Staff visited the U.S.
14-15 Nov. 2004	India-U.S. eighth Executive Steering Group (ESG) meeting was held at Guam in USA.
8-9 December 2004	The U.S. Secretary for Defence, Mr. Donald Rumsfeld visits India and had discussions with the External Affairs Minister, Defence Minister as well as the National Security Advisor.
March 2005	The U.S. Secretary of State, Condoleezza Rice visits India.
19-28 March 2005	Indian Admiral Arun Prakash went for an official visit to United States. During which he met Deputy Secretary of Defense Mr. Paul Wolfowitz, Under Secretary of Defense for Policy Mr. Douglas Feith, the Secretary of the Navy Mr. Gordon England, the Chairman Joint Chiefs of Staff General Richard Myers, Chief of Naval Operations Admiral Vernon Clark and Commandant Marine Corps General Michael Hagee.
April 2005	The then External Affairs Minister of India, Mr. Natwar Singh visits the United

	States where he meets Mr. George W. Bush, former President of the U.S. and held discussion on the need to strengthen the growing India-U.S. relations.
16-19 May 2005	Mr. Shyam Sharan, Foreign Secretary of India visited the U.S. to attend the meeting of India-U.S. Global Issues Forum.
27-30 June 2005	Indian Defence Minister, Mr. Pranab Mukherjee visited the U.S. at the invitation of U.S. Secretary of Defence, Mr. Donald Rumsfeld.
	Indian Defence Minister, Mr. Pranab Mukherjee and U.S. Defence Secretary, Mr. Donald Rumsfeld signed a ten year Defence framework agreement.
18 July 2005	President Mr. George W. Bush and Prime Minister Mr. Manmohan Singh first announce their intention to enter into a nuclear agreement in Washington.
19 July 2005	Prime Minister Mr. Manmohan Singh addressing the Joint meeting of the U.S. Congress at Great Hall, House of Representatives, Capitol Hill in Washington.
25 Sept.-5 Oct. 2005	The Malabar 2005 exercise was the largest naval exercise India had with any other country. It was for the first time that India had introduced its aircraft carrier INS Viraat, while U.S. introduced its aircraft carrier Nimitz.
1 March 2006	Mr. George W. Bush visits India for the first time.
3 March 2006	Ms. George W. Bush of U.S. and Mr. Manmohan Singh of India issue a joint

	statement on their growing strategic partnership, emphasizing their agreement on civil nuclear cooperation.
26 July 2006	The U.S. House of Representatives passes the 'Henry J Hyde United States-India Peaceful Atomic Energy Cooperation Act of 2006,' which stipulates that Washington will cooperate with New Delhi on nuclear issues and exempt it from signing the Nuclear Nonproliferation Treaty.
28 July 2006	In India, the Left parties demand threadbare discussion on the issue in Parliament.
15-16 Nov. 2006	The U.S. Under Secretary of Defence for Policy visited New Delhi to attend the eighth meeting of the India-U.S. Defence Policy Group (DPG).
16 November 2006	The U.S. Senate passes the 'United States-India Peaceful Atomic Energy Cooperation and U.S. Additional Protocol Implementation Act' to "exempt from certain requirements of the Atomic Energy Act of 1954 United States exports of nuclear materials, equipment, and technology to India."
18 December 2006	President Mr. George W. Bush signs into law congressional legislation on Indian atomic energy.
10 April 2007	First Meeting of India-U.S. Defence Joint Working Group was held in New Delhi.

The Ninth Meeting of the Joint Technology Group was held in Washington.

30-31 May 2007	A Delegation led by Director General of Acquisition had visited USA to attend

fourth India-U.S. Defence Procurement and Production Group (DPPG) meeting.

June 2007 India and the U.S. signed a Memorandum of Understanding (MoU) to establish the India-U.S. Aviation Cooperation Programme (ACP), a public-private partnership between Ministry of Civil Aviation of India and U.S. Trade Development Agency (USTDA) and Federal Aviation Agency (FAA).

Commerce and Industry Minister, Mr. Kamal Nath visited Washington D.C. in to participate in the "Global India Summit."

27 July 2007 India and the United States conclude the negotiations on the agreement for cooperation between the Indian Government and the Government of United States of America concerning peaceful uses of nuclear energy (popularly known as 123 Agreement).

3 August 2007 The text of the 'Agreement for Cooperation between the Government of the United States of America and the Government of India concerning peaceful uses of nuclear energy' was released by both governments.

13 Aug 2007 Prime Minister, Mr. Manmohan Singh makes a suo motu statement on the deal in Parliament.

17 August 2007 The CPI (M) General Secretary, Mr. Prakash Karat says the 'honeymoon (with government) may be over but the marriage can go on'.

September 2007	After a long gap of almost 36 years, the U.S. 7th fleet was back in the Bay of Bengal.
4 September 2007	In India, the UPA-Left committee to discuss nuclear deal set up.
19 November 2007	The second Meeting of Defence Joint Working Group was held in the U.S.
27 November 2007	The fourth meeting of India-USA Senior Technology Security Group was held in New Delhi.
11-13 Dec. 2007	A delegation from India visited USA to attend eighth India-U.S. Military Cooperation Group (MCG).
15-16 January 2008	The fifth meeting of the Defence production and procurement group was held in Washington.
16-17 January 2008	The Ninth Meeting of the India-U.S. Defence Policy Group (DPG) took place in Washington.
February 2008	The U.S. Secretary of Defence Mr. Robert Gates came to India and held discussion over the India-U.S. nuclear deal and to pitch for a Rs. 450 billion multi-role combat aircraft contract.
25 February 2008	Left parties in India say the ruling party would have to choose between the deal and its government's stability.
3-6 March 2008	Left parties warn of 'serious consequences' if the nuclear deal is operationalised and set a deadline asking the government to make it clear by March 15 whether it intended to proceed with the nuclear deal or drop it.

7-14 March 2008	The CPI writes to the Prime Minister Mr. Manmohan Singh warns of withdrawal of support if government goes ahead with the deal and puts political pressure on the Mr. Manmohan Singh government not to go with the deal.
March 2008	The U.S. Secretary of the Navy, Donald C. Winter visited India for three days where he meets India's Chief of Naval Staff Admiral Sureesh Mehta at Naval Headquarters.
April 2008	The U.S. Chief of Naval Operations visited India.
23 April 2008	The Indian Government says it will seek the sense of the House on the 123 Agreement before it is taken up for ratification by the American Congress.
17 June 2008	External Affairs Minister, Mr. Pranab Mukherjee meets Mr. Prakash Karat, asks the Left to allow the government to go ahead with International Atomic Energy Agency (IAEA) safeguards agreement.
30 June 2008	The Indian Prime Minister Mr. Manmohan Singh says his government prepared to face Parliament before operationalising the deal.
8 July 2008	Left parties in India withdraw support to government.
9 July 2008	The draft India-specific safeguards accord with the IAEA circulated to IAEA's Board of Governors for approval.
10 July 2008	Prime Minister Mr. Manmohan Singh calls for a vote of confidence in Parliament.

14 July 2008	The IAEA says it will meet on 1 August to consider the India-specific safeguards agreement.
18 July 2008	Foreign Secretary Mr. Shivshankar Menon briefs the IAEA Board of Governors and some NSG countries in Vienna on the safeguards agreement.
22 July 2008	Government is willing to look at "possible amendments" to the Atomic Energy Act to ensure that the country's strategic autonomy will never be compromised, says Prime Minister Manmohan Singh.
	The UPA government lead by Mr. Manmohan Singh wins trust vote in the Lok Sabha in India.
24 July 2008	India dismisses warning by Pakistan that the deal will accelerate an atomic arms race in the sub-continent. Also India launches full blast lobbying among the 45-nation NSG for an exemption for nuclear commerce.
25 July 2008	IAEA secretariat briefs member states on India-specific safeguards agreement.
1 August 2008	IAEA Board of Governors approved India-specific safeguards agreement unanimously.
21-22 August 2008	The NSG meet to consider an India waiver ends inconclusively amid reservations by some countries.
4-6 September 2008	The NSG meets for the second time on the issue after the U.S. comes up with a revised draft and grants waiver to India after marathon parleys.

7-10 Sept. 2008	A delegation led by Defence Minister visited United States of America and discuss issues on defence cooperation activities and regional security.
9 September 2008	Indian defence Minister, Mr. A K Anthony is on a four-day visit to Washington, D.C. that was aimed at strengthening defence and strategic ties between the two countries.
11 September 2008	President Bush sends the text of the 123 Agreement to the U.S. Congress for final approval.
12 September 2008	The U.S. remains silent over the controversy in India triggered by President Mr. George W. Bush's assertions that nuclear fuel supply assurances to New Delhi under the deal were only political commitments and not legally binding.
13 September 2008	The State Department issues a fact sheet on the nuclear deal saying the initiative will help meet India's growing energy requirements and strengthen the non-proliferation regime by welcoming New Delhi into globally accepted nonproliferation standards and practices.
18 September 2008	The Senate Foreign Relations Committee kicks off a crucial hearing on the India-U.S. nuclear deal.
19 September 2008	America's nuclear fuel supply assurances to India are a "political commitment" and the government cannot "legally compel" the U.S. firms to sell a "given product" to

	New Delhi, top officials tells Congressional panel.
26 September 2008	Indian Prime Minister Manmohan Singh meets the U.S. President Mr. George W. Bush at the White House, but was not able to sign the nuclear deal as the Congress did not approve it.
27 September 2008	House of Representatives approves the India-U.S. nuclear deal. 298 members voted for the Bill while 117 voted against.
1 October 2008	Senate approves the India-U.S. civil nuclear deal with 86 votes for and 13 against.
4 October 2008	The U.S. Secretary of State, Ms. Condoleezza Rice visits Delhi. India and the U.S. unable to ink the nuclear agreement with New Delhi insisting that it would do so only after President Mr. George W. Bush signs it into a law, an occasion when it expects certain misgivings to be cleared. White House announces that President Mr. George W. Bush will sign the legislation on the India-U.S. nuclear deal into a law on 8 October.
8 October 2008	President Mr. George W. Bush signs legislation to enact the landmark U.S.-India civilian nuclear agreement.
10 October 2008	The 123 Agreement between India and U.S. is finally operationalized between the two countries after the deal is signed by External Affairs Minister, Mr. Pranab Mukherjee and his counterpart Secretary

	of State, Ms. Condoleezza Rice in Washington D C.
16-18 October 2008	The U.S. Chief of Army Staff General George W Casey visited India for three days where he had discussions with Defence Minister Mr. A K Antony, and General Deepak Kapoor on ways to further enhance bilateral military relations between New Delhi and Washington.
4 December 2008	Admiral Michael Mullen, Chairman, Joint Chiefs of Staff Committee of the U.S. visited India and met Defence Minister of India.
10 March 2009	In the first high level contact with the Mr. Barack Obama Administration, Foreign Secretary, Mr. Shivshankar Menon held discussion with Secretary of State, Ms. Hillary Clinton and other U.S. Officials regarding Mumbai terror attacks and the security situation in South Asian region.
8 April 2009	The U.S. Special Envoy, Mr. Richard Holbrooke and Adm. Michael Mullen, chairman of the Joints Chiefs of Staff, visits India.
13-15 May 2009	Admiral Timothy Keating, Commander, the U.S. Pacific Command visited India to discuss with Government of India on issues related to the regional security situation, terrorism, and maritime security. He met Foreign Secretary, National Security Adviser and Chief of Naval Staff.

2 April 2009	Prime Minister Mr. Manmohan Singh met the U.S. President Mr. Barack Obama at the G-20 Summit in London.
10-13 June 2009	The U.S. Under Secretary of State, Mr. William Burns visits India to prepare for Secretary of State, Ms. Hillary Clinton's July visit and meets Foreign Secretary, Mr. Shivshankar Menon and External Affairs Minister, Mr. S.M. Krishna.
16-19 June 2009	Commerce and Industry Minister Shri Anand Sharma visited Washington to attend the 34th anniversary of the U.S.-India Business Council. During which he met with his U.S. counterpart U.S. Trade Representative, Ambassador Ron Kirk with whom he discussed India-U.S. trade relations.
26 June 2009	The U.S. National Security, Mr. Advisor James Jones meets Indian counterpart M.K. Narayanan in New Delhi and called on Prime Minister Dr. Manmohan Singh and Defence Minister Shri A. K. Antony.
17-21 July 2009	U.S. Secretary of State, Ms. Hillary Clinton visited India where both countries jointly announced a new agenda for India-U.S. relations. Two agreements - Technology Safeguards Agreement (Space) and an India-U.S. Science and Technology Endowment Fund and Board Agreement were signed during the visit.
20-24 July 2009	Indian Army Chief General Deepak Kapoor went for week long visit to U.S. where he will meet American counterpart.

11-12 August 2009	The first round of India-U.S. negotiations on a Bilateral Investment Treaty was held in New Delhi.
11-13 August 2009	The U.S. Deputy Trade Representative, Ambassador Demetrios Marantis visited India to attend the India-U.S. Trade Policy Forum meeting.
3-4 September 2009	Ambassador Ron Kirk, the U.S. Trade Representative visited New Delhi to attend the informal ministerial meeting of the Doha Round hosted by India.
8-10 Sept. 2009	Indian Home Minister, Mr. P. Chidambaram visited USA in a bid to strengthen India's bilateral partnership with the USA in the field of counter-terrorism and to identify areas for mutual cooperation with focus on procurement of advanced technology and sharing of information and best practices in investigation and prevention of terrorist attacks.
21 September 2009	Indian Foreign Secretary Smt. Nirupama Rao visits U.S. where she met Mr. William Burns, Under Secretary for Political Affairs, Ms. Maria Otero, Under Secretary for Democracy and Global Affairs, the U.S. State Department and discussed the agenda and issues identified for co-operation in the India-U.S. Global Issues Forum.
25-29 October 2009	National Security Advisor, Shri M. K. Narayanan visited USA where he met with his U.S. counterpart, Gen. James Jones, Defence Secretary, Secretary

	Homeland Security, Director, FBI and several Senators and Congressmen. Later, he also visited the National Counter Terrorism Centre.
12-29 October 2009	India-U.S. Joint Exercise YUDH ABHYAS 09 is being conducted at Babina during this period under the aegis of HQ Southern Command. The aim of this exercise is to conduct a joint India-U.S. training exercise under the framework of agreed joint training programme for sharing useful experience in Peace Keeping operations and humanitarian in the disaster relief situations.
15-16 October 2009	The Under Secretary, Mr. Burns visits India to assess progress on the new India-U.S. Strategic Dialogue announced during Secretary Clinton's visit and to discuss substantive issues related to Prime Minister Singh's November visit to the U.S.
15-25 October 2009	India-U.S. Joint Exercise named Cope India (Air Force) was held in Agra.
25-31 October 2009	Minister for Human Resource Development Shri Kapil Sibal visited New York and Washington. During which he met with the U.S. Education Secretary and visited several universities in both the cities.
26 October 2009	A meeting of the India-U.S. Trade Policy Forum was held in New Delhi.
3-4 November 2009	The India-U.S. Defence Procurement and Production Group meeting was held in

	New Delhi which was co-chaired by Vice Admiral Jeffrey Wierenga and Director General (Acquisition), Ministry of Defence.
5-6 November 2009	A meeting of the India-U.S. Defence Policy Group co-chaired by Indian Defence Secretary and Mr. William Lynn, Deputy Secretary, U.S. Department of Defence took place in New Delhi.
11-13 Nov. 2009	The U.S. Under Secretary of State for Arms Control and Nonproliferation Ellen Tauscher visits India for talks with Foreign Secretary Nirupama Rao. They reaffirm a commitment to the timely and full implementation of the U.S.-India civil nuclear agreement.
22-24 Nov. 2009	It was during the visit of Indian Prime Minister Manmohan Singh to U.S., both sides launched a new phase in the India-U.S. partnership, describing it as a 'global strategic partnership'.
2-5 December 2009	The U.S. Pacific Command (PACOM) Admiral Robert F Willard visited India. He called on National Security Advisor, Shri M. K. Narayanan and Chief of Army Staff Gen. Deepak Kapoor and exchanged views on issues related to defence cooperation & regional security situation
6-11 Dec. 2009	A 55-member Civil Nuclear Trade Mission from the U.S. led by the U.S.-India Business Council and the Nuclear Energy Institute, Washington visited New Delhi and Mumbai and interacted with Indian

	public and private power sector companies and FICCI and CII.
18 January 2010	Ambassador Richard Holbrooke, the U.S. Special Envoy for Afghanistan and Pakistan visited India to consult Government of India and seek our assessment about the current situation in Afghanistan and Pakistan. He met with Foreign Secretary Smt. Nirupama Rao, National Security Adviser Shri M. K. Narayanan, and called on External Affairs Minister Shri S. M. Krishna and Prime Minister Dr. Manmohan Singh.
19-20 January 2010	The U.S. Defence Secretary, Mr. Robert Gates visited India where he holds substantive talks with India's Prime Minister Manmohan Singh, External Affairs Minister S.M. Krishna and Defence Minister, Mr. A.K. Anthony on expanding the defence and security cooperation and on the security situation in South Asia.
28-29 January 2010	India-USA Joint Technical Group held its 12th meeting in Delhi which was co-chaired by the Chief Controller Defence Research and Development in DRDO and his U.S. counterpart Mr. Alfred Volkman, Director of International Cooperation in U.S. Department of Defence.
11 April 2010	The U.S. Navy Chief Admiral Gary Roughead visits India for six days where he meets Chief of the Navy, Army and Air force as well as Defence Secretary Pradeep Kumar. This visit was aimed at

	exploring ways to bolster naval cooperation between the two countries.
3 June 2010	The U.S. Secretary of State, Ms. Hillary Rodham Clinton and India's External Affairs Minister, Mr. S.M. Krishna, met in Washington for the inaugural meeting of the "India-U.S. Strategic Dialogue.
23 July 2010	India and the United States signed the India-U.S. Counter Terrorism Initiative, the text of which was initialed during the visit of the Prime Minister Mr. Manmohan Singh of India to the U.S. in November 2009.
6-9 Nov. 2010	The U.S. President Barack Obama visits India and held discussions on the prospects of expanding bilateral relations and also discusses on the regional and global issues of concern to both sides. During this visit both sides issued a joint statement.
April 2011	India-U.S. bilateral exercise MALABAR-11 was held off Okinawa. The US Navy units USS Sterett, Stethem and Preble, Ronald Reagan, Chancellorsville, Santa Fe, Blue Ridge, Carl Brashear and IN ships Delhi, Ranvir, Ranvijay and Jyoti participated in this exercise.
28 April 2011	The U.S. President Obama announced the nomination of *Panetta* as the *United States Secretary of Defense.*
18 July 2011	The United States Secretary of State Hillary Clinton was on official three day visit to India where she meet Indian offi-

	cial and discusses regional and global issues of concerns.
12 Dec. 2011	The U.S. Deputy Secretary William Burns visits India and held discussion with Foreign Secretary Ranjan Mathai, National Security Adviser Shivshankar Menon, External Affairs Minister S.M. Krishna, Finance Minister Pranab Mukherjee, and Prime Minister Manmohan Singh.
June 2012	Indian External Affairs Minister, S.M Krishna visit the U.S. where he met U.S. Secretary of State Rodham Clinton and had discussions on a wide range of bilateral, regional, and global issues.
5 June 2012	The U.S. Secretary of Defense Leon Panetta's visits India in which both sides discussed on the scope of expanding the defence ties and in particular to defence trade.
July 2012	The U.S. Deputy Secretary of Defense Ashton Carter visited India to discuss matters concerning defence trade and cooperation.
7 Nov. 2012	President Barack Obama has been reelected to a second term, defeating Republican challenger Mitt Romney.

Bibliography

Primary Sources

Agreed Text for, Agreement for Cooperation between The Government of India and The Government of The United States of America Concerning Peaceful Uses of Nuclear Energy, 1 August 2007.

Agreement between the Government of India and the International Atomic Energy Agency for the Application of Safeguards to Civilian Nuclear Facilities, 7 July 2008.

Andersen, Walter K., India and the United States: A Different Kind of Relationship, Testimony before House Committee on Foreign Affairs: Subcommittee on the Middle East and South Asia United States House of Representatives, Washington, D.C., 25 June 2008.

Annual Report 1991-2009, Ministry of Defence, Government of India.

Annual Report 2001-2009, Ministry of External Affairs, Government of India.

Burns, R. Nicholas, The U.S. and India: An Emerging Entente?, Testimony to the House International Relations Committee, 8 September 2005.

Bush, George W., The National Security Strategy of the United States of America, The White House, Washington, September 2002.

______________, National Security Strategy of the United States of America, The White House, Washington, March 2006.

Clinton, Bill, Speech to Joint Session of Parliament, New Delhi, 22 March 2000.

Clinton, William and Atal Bihari Vajpayee, India-U.S. Relations: A Vision for the 21st Century, New Delhi, 21 March 2000.

Curtis, Lisa, China's Military and Security Relationship with Pakistan, Testimony before the U.S.-China Economic and Security Review Commission, 20 May 2009.

India-United States Joint Statement, Washington, DC, 18 July 2005, Strategic Digest (New Delhi), vol. 35(8), August 2005.

Indo-American Cooperation Documents on Prime Minister's Visit to USA, Strategic Digest, vol. 24(7), July 1994.

Joint Statement on Strategic Partnership between India and the United States, Washington, DC, 17 September 2004.

Joint Statement on US-India on High Technology Commerce, Strategic Digest, vol. 35(12), December 2005.

Lecture by Prime Minister Special Envoy Shyam Saran on, India and the Nuclear Domain, 18 February 2008.

Mapping the Global Future, Report of the National Intelligence Council's 2020 Project, December 2004.

Minister of External Affairs, Pranab Mukherjee Statement on the Civil Nuclear Initiative, New Delhi, 5 September 2008.

Minister of External Affairs, Pranab Mukherjee Statement on the Final Outcome of the Meeting of the Nuclear Suppliers Group, New Delhi, 6 September 2008, Strategic Digest, vol. 38(10), October 2008.

New Framework for the U.S.-India Defence Relationship, Washington, DC, 28 June 2005.

President George W. Bush Address before the Asia Society on India and Pakistan, Mandarin Oriental Hotel, Washington, DC, 22 February 2006.

Prime Minister Manmohan Singh Address at the Golden Jubilee Function of the Department of Atomic Energy on 23 October 2004.

Prime Minister Manmohan Singh Address to Joint Session of the Congress, Washington, DC, 19 July 2005, Strategic Digest, vol. 35(8), August 2005.

Prime Minister Manmohan Singh Statement in the Lok Sabha on Civil Nuclear Cooperation, Strategic Digest, vol. 37(9), September 2007.

Prime Minister Manmohan Singh Statement on the Final Outcome of the Meeting of the Nuclear Suppliers Group, New Delhi, 6 September 2008, Strategic Digest, vol. 38(10), October 2008.

Quadrennial Defense Review Report, Washington: Department of Defense, February 2010.

Remarks by Alan Larson, Under Secretary for Economic, Business and Agricultural Affairs on Raising the Bar: U.S.-India Economic Relations, at the Delegation of the Indo-American Chamber of Commerce, Mumbai, India, 16 September 2004.

Remarks by Carlos M. Gutierrez, Secretary of Commerce, to the U.S.-India Business Council, Washington, DC.

Remarks by Condoleezza Rice, Secretary of State at the Senate Foreign Relations Committee on the, US-India Civil Nuclear Cooperation Initiative, 5 April 2006.

Remarks by David C. Mulford on, Building Strong Partnerships, at the 4th Indo-U.S. Economic Summit, 18 September 2007.

____________on ,U.S. and India: Building Global Partnership, at the Federation of Indian Chambers of Commerce and Industry and American Chamber of Commerce, Mumbai, India, 21 April 2004.

Remarks by Karl F. Inderfurth, Assistant Secretary of State for South Asian Affairs at the Confederation of Indian Industry, 3 September 1997, Strategic Digest, vol. 27(7), October 1997.

Remarks by Richard A. Boucher, Assistant Secretary for South and Central Asian Affairs on, The U.S.-India Friendship: Where we Were and Where We're Going at the Confederation of Indian Industry, New Delhi, India.

Remarks by Robert O. Blake, Charge d' Affairs, U.S. Embassy in India on, Expanding U.S.-Indian Economic Co-operation at the 13th Annual meeting of the American Chamber of Commerce, New Delhi, 28 April 2005.

______________on, IPR Enforcement and Its Tangible Benefits, New Delhi, 26 April 2006.

Standards and Conformance Cooperation Programme on 1st Indo-US Summit on Standards in Trade, Background Paper Prepared in collaboration between Ministry of Commerce & Industry, Government of India, Confederation of Indian Industry, American National Standards Institute and US Trade and Development Agency, 16 February 2010, New Delhi.

Tellis, Ashley J., Lessons from Mumbai, Testimony Presented before Committee on Homeland Security and Governmental Affairs, United States Senate, 28 January 2009.

______________, U.S.-India Atomic Energy Cooperation: Strategic and Nonproliferation Implications, Testimony before the Senate Foreign Relations Committee, 26 April 2006.

Vajpayee, A B, Next Step in Strategic Partnership with USA New Delhi, 13 January 2004.

SECONDARY SOURCES

A. Books

Acharya, Alka, China and India: Politics of Incremental Engagement (New-Delhi: Har-Anand Publications Pvt. Ltd., 2008).

Alam, Aftab, US Policy Towards South Asia: Special Reference to Indo-Pak Relations (Delhi: Raj Publications, 1998).

Ayres, Alyssa and C. Raja Mohan (eds.), Power Realignment in Asia: China, India and the United States (New Delhi: Sage Publication, 2009).

Bajpai, kanti, India-US Foreign Policy Concerns, Cooperation and Conflict (Delhi: Lancer Publications, 1998).

Bajpai, kanti and Amitabh Mattoo (eds.), Engaged Democracies: India-US Relations in the 21st Century (New Delhi: Har-Anand Publications Pvt. Ltd., 2000).

Banerjee, Pranab K., Issues in Indo-US Trade and Economic Cooperation (New Delhi: Kanishka Publishers, Distributors, 1996).

Baranwal, Jayant (ed.), SP's Military Yearbook Since 1965: 2003-2004 (New Delhi: SP Guide Publications Pvt. Ltd., 2003).

____________, SP's Military Yearbook Since 1965: 2007-2008 (New Delhi: SP Guide Publications Pvt. Ltd., 2007).

Bertsch, Garry K., et. al., (eds.), Engaging India: US Strategic Relations with the World's Largest Democracies (New York: Routledge, 1999).

Bhandari, M C, Solving Kashmir (New Delhi: Lancer Publishers and Distributors, 2006).

Bhonsle, Rahul, et. al., (ed.), Indo-U.S. Civil Nuclear Deal (New Delhi: Atlantic Publishers and Distributors Pvt. Ltd., 2007).

Blank, Stephen, J., Natural allies? Regional Security in Asia and Prospects for Indo-American Strategic Cooperation (Carlisle, PA: Strategic Studies Institute, US Army War College, September 2005).

Chadha, Vivek, Indo-US Relations: Divergence to Convergence (New Delhi: Macmillan India Ltd., 2008).

Chait, Anil, From Estrangement to Engagement: Threats and Opportunities in Indo-U.S. Relations and the Roles of their Armed Forces (Carlisle, PA: Strategic Studies Institute, U.S. Army War College, February 2006).

Chellany, Brahma, Asian Juggerment: The Rise of China, India and Japan (New Delhi: Harper Collins Publishers in joint venture with The India Today Group, 2006).

Chopra, V.D. (ed.), India's Foreign Policy in the 21st Century (New Delhi: Kalpaz Publications, 2006).

Cohen, Stephen, P., India Emerging Power (New Delhi: Oxford University Press, 2002).

__________, The Idea of Pakistan (New Delhi: Oxford University Press, 2005).

Das, P.K., New Heights in Indo-US Relations (Jaipur: Raj Publishing House, 2005).

Dash, P.L. (ed.), India-Russia Relations: The Post Cold War Era (Mumbai: Nehru Centre, 2011).

Datta-Ray, Sunanda k., Waiting for America: India and US in the New Millennium (New Delhi: Harper Collins Publishers, 2002).

Deepak, B. R., India & China 1904-2004: A Century of Peace and Conflict (New Delhi: Manak Publications Pvt. Ltd., 2005).

Deshpande, G.P. and Alka Acharya (eds.), Crossing a Bridge of Dreams: 50 years of India China (New Delhi: Tulika Publishers, 2001).

Dixit, J.N., India and Regional Developments: Through the Prism of Indo-Pak Relations (New Delhi: Gyan Publishing House, 2004).

__________, India's Foreign Policy Challenge of Terrorism: Fashioning New Interstate Equations (New Delhi: Gyan Publishing House, 2002).

Dossani, Rafiq and Henry S. Rowen (eds.), Prospects for Peace in South Asia (Hyderabad: Orient Longman Pvt. Ltd., 2006).

Forsythe, David P., et. al., (eds.), American Foreign Policy in a Globalized World (New York: London: Routledge, 2006).

Frankel, Francine, R. and Harry Harding (eds.), The India-China Relationship: Rivalry and Engagement (New Delhi: Oxford University Press, 2004).

Gaan, Narottam, India and United States: From Estrangement to Engagement, (Delhi: Kalpaz Publications, 2007).

Ganguly, Sumit and Devin T. Hagerty, Fearful symmetry: India-Pakistan Crisis in the Shadow of Nuclear Weapons (New Delhi: Oxford University Press, 2005).

Ganguly, Sumit, Brian Shoup, et. al., (eds.), US-India Strategic Cooperation into the 21st Century (London and New York: Routledge, 2006).

Gehlot, N.S. and Anu Satsangi, Indo-Pak Relations: Twists and Turns from Partition to Agra Summit and Beyond (New Delhi: Deep and Deep Publications, 2004).

Goh, Evelyn and Sheldon W. Simon (eds.), China, the United States and Southeast Asia: Contending Perspectives on Politics, Security and Economics (New York and London: Routledge, 2008).

Gould, Harold A. and Sumit Ganguly (ed.), The Hope and the Reality: U.S.-Indian Relations from Roosevelt to Reagan (New Delhi: Oxford and IBH Publishing Co. Pvt. Ltd., 1993).

Gupta, Amit, The US-India Relationship: Strategic Partnership or Complementary Interests? (Carlisle, PA: Strategic Studies Institute, US Army War College, February 2005).

Gupta, Arvind (ed.), India in a Changing Global Nuclear Order (New Delhi: IDSA-Pugwash Publication, 2009).

Guruswamy, Mohan (ed.), Emerging Trends in India-China Relations (Gurgaon: Hope India Publications, 2006).

Harshe, Rajen and KM Sethi (eds.), Engaging with the World: Critical Reflections on India's Foreign Policy (New Delhi: Orient Longmans Pvt. Ltd., 2005).

Iqbal, Badar Alam, Indo-U.S. Economic Relations: Then and Now (Hyderabad: Icfai University Press, 2005)

Jain B.M (ed.), International System and Great Power Relationship (Jaipur: INA Shree Publishers, 2008).

Jain, Rashmi (ed.), United States and India, 1947-2006: A Documentary Study (New Delhi: Radiant Publishers, 2007).

Jha, Nalini Kant (ed.), India's Foreign Policy in a Changing World (New Delhi: South Asian Publishers, 2000).

Kapur, Ashok and Y.K.Malik, et. al., (eds.), India and United States in a Changing World (New Delhi: Sage Publication, 2002).

Karat, Prakash, Subordinate Ally-The Nuclear Deal and India-US Strategic Relations (New Delhi: Left Word Books, 2007).

Karve, Abhay R., Indo-US Strategic Relations: Moving from Estrangement to Engagement, Paper submitted to the National War College, National Defense University.

Kidwai, Saleem (ed.), US Policy Towards South Asia: Focus on Sixty Years (Delhi: Academic Excellence, 2008).

Kiesow, Ingolf and Nicklas Norling, The Rise of India: Problems and Opportunities, (Sweden: Central Asia-Caucasus Institute and Silk Road Studies Program, 2007).

Kux, Dennix, Estranged Democracies: India and the United States, 1941-1991 (New- Delhi: Sage Publication, 1993).

Magyar, Karl P. (ed.), United States Post-Cold War Defence Interests: A Review of the First Decade (New York: Palgrave Mcmillan, 2004).

Mahapatra, Chintamani, Indo-US Relations in the 21st Century (New Delhi: Knowledge World in Association with the Institute for Defence Studies and Analysis, 1998).

Malhotra, Vinay Kumar and K.S. Purushothaman (ed.), India and the USA: Economic Relations and Literature (New Delhi: Anmol Publications Pvt. Ltd., 1998).

Malik, Hafeez, US Relations with Afghanistan and Pakistan: The Imperial Dimension (Karachi: Oxford University Press, 2008).

Mann, Poonam, India's Foreign Policy in the Post Cold War Era (New Delhi: Harman Publishing House, 2000).

Mohan, C. Raja, Crossing the Rubicon: The Shaping of India's New Foreign Policy (New Delhi: Viking, 2003).

______________, Impossible Allies: Nuclear India, United States and the Global Order (New Delhi: India Research Press, 2006).

Muni, S.D. (ed.), Asian Strategic Review 2007 (New Delhi: Academic Foundation, 2008).

Muthanna, K A, Enabling Military-to-Military Cooperation as a Foreign Policy Tool: Options for India (New Delhi: Knowledge World, 2006).

Nayar, Baldev Raj and T. V. Paul, India in the World Order: Searching for Major-Power Status (New Delhi: Cambridge University Press, 2004).

Palmer, Norman, D., The United States and India: The Dimensions of Influence (New York: Philadelphia: Praeger Publishers, 1984).

Panagariya, Arvind, India: The Emerging Giant (New York: Oxford University Press, 2008).

Pant, Harsh V., Indian Foreign Policy in a Unipolar World (New Delhi: Routledge, 2009).

Paul, T.V. (ed.), The India-Pakistan Conflict: An Enduring Rivalry (New York: Cambridge University Press, 2005).

People, Progress, Partnership: The Transformation of U.S.-Indian Relations (New Delhi: Public Affairs Section, Embassy of the United States of America, n.d.).

Raghavan, V.R. (ed.), Asian Security Dynamic: US, Japan and the Rising Powers (New Delhi: Promilla and Co. Publishers in Association with Bibliophile South Asia, 2006).

Rajagopalan, Swarna (ed.), Security in South Asia: Ideas, Institutions and Initiatives (London: New York: New Delhi, 2006).

Raju, A. Subramanyam, Democracies at Loggerheads: Security Aspects of US-India Relations (New Delhi: South Asian Publishers, 2001).

Rao, V. Nagendra and Mohammad Monir Alam, Central Asia: Present Challenges and Future Prospects (New Delhi: Knowledge World, 2005).

Rasgotra, Maharajkrishna (ed.), The New Asian Power Dynamic (New Delhi: Sage Publication in Connection with Observer Research Foundation, 2007).

Santhanam, K. and Srikanth Kondapalli (eds.), Asian Security and China 2000-2010 (New Delhi: Shipra Publications, 2004).

Sasikumar, Karthika and Wade L. Huntley (ed.), Canadian Policy on Nuclear Co-operation with India: Confronting New Dilemmas (Canada: Simons Centre for Disarmament and Non-Proliferation Research, 2007).

Scott, David (ed.), Handbook of India's International Relations (London and New York: Routledge, 2011).

__________, China Stands Up: The PRC and the International System (London and New York: Routledge, 2007).

Sharma, R.R, India and Emerging Asia (New Delhi: Thousand Oaks: London: Sage Publications, 2005).

Shukla, Subhash, Foreign Policy of India (New Delhi: Anamika Publishers, 2007).

Sikri, Rajiv, Challenge and Strategy: Rethinking India's Foreign Policy (New Delhi: Sage Publications, 2009).

Singh, Anil Kumar, India's Security Concerns in the Indian Ocean Region (New Delhi:, 2003).

Singh, Daljit, Political and Security Dynamics of South and Southeast Asia (Singapore: Institute of Southeast Asian Studies, 2007).

Singh, Jasjit (ed.), Asian Defence Review 2006 (New Delhi: Knowledge World in Association Har-Anand Publications Pvt. Ltd.with the Centre for Air Power Studies, 2006).

__________, Asian Strategic Review (1993-94) (New Delhi: Institute for Defence Studies and Analyses, 1994).

__________, Indo-US Relations in a Changing World: Proceedings of the Indo-US Strategic Symposium (New Delhi: Institute for Defence Studies and Analyses, 1992).

Singh, R. K. Jasbir (ed.), Indian Defence Yearbook 2004 (New Delhi: Natraj Publication, 2004).

__________, Indian Defence Yearbook 2005 (New Delhi: Natraj Publication, 2005).

Singh, Swaran (ed.), China-Pakistan Strategic Cooperation: Indian Perspectives (New Delhi: Manohar Publishers, 2007).

Sinha, Atish and Madhup Mohta (ed.), Indian Foreign Policy: Challenges and Opportunities (New Delhi: Academic Foundation, 2007).

SIPRI Yearbook 2008: Armaments, Disarmament and International Security (New York: Oxford University Press, 2008).

Sisodia, N.S and C Uday Bhaskar (eds.), Emerging India: Security and Foreign Policy Perspectives (New Delhi: IDSA, Promila and Co. in Association with Bibliophile South Asia, 2005).

Smith, David, The Dragon and the Elephant-India and the World Order (London: Profile Books Ltd, 2007).

Sudan, Falendra K. (ed.), Globalisation and Liberalization: Nature and consequences (New Delhi: Serials Publications, 2005).

Synnott, Hilary, Transforming Pakistan: Ways Out of Instability (London: Routledge, 2009).

Tellis, Ashley, J., India and a New Global Power: An Action Agenda for the United States (New Delhi: India Research Press, 2005).

Thakur, Ramesh, The Politics and Economics of India's Foreign Policy (New Delhi: Oxford University Press, 1995).

The Asia Foundation, America's Role in Asia: Asian and American Views (San Francisco, 2008).

The International Institute of Strategic Studies, The Military Balance 2009: The Annual Assessment of Global and Military Capabilities and Defence Economics (London: Routledge, 2009).

Vijayalakshmi, K.P., et. al., (eds.), Report on the National Workshop on Changing Contours of Indo-US Relations (Bangalore: International Strategic and Security Studies Programme and National Institute of Advanced Studies, 2006).

Wisner, Frank G., et. al., New Priorities in South Asia: US Policy Toward India, Pakistan and Afghanistan (New York: Council on Foreign Relations, 2003).

B. Articles in Journals and Periodicals

Advani, L.K., "Indo-US Relations in a Strategic Partnership", ICWA Foreign Affairs Reports (New Delhi), vol. 2(5-6), May-June 2003.

Akiyama, Masahiro, "Development of the Japan-US Alliance after 11 September 2001 and the War in Iraq", U.S.I Journal (New Delhi), vol. CXXXIII(553), July-September 2003.

Bajpai, Kanti, "Where are India and the US Heading?", Economic and Political Weekly (Mumbai), vol. XL(32), 6 August 2005.

Balachandran, G., "Indo-US Relations: Perception and Reality", Strategic Analysis (New Delhi), vol. 29(2), April-June 2005.

Banerjeee, Dipanker, "Defining Indo-US Defence Relations", Peace and Conflict (New Delhi), Article no. 1779, 1 July 2005.

Bertsch, Gary K. and Anupam Srivastava, "U.S.-India Strategic Relations: Issues Before the New Administration", Bharat Rakshak Monitor (New Delhi), Vol. 3(4), January-February 2001.

Blackwill, Robert D., "A Friend Indeed", National Interest (Washington, DC), May/June 2007.

Blank, Stephen, "The Geo-Strategic Implications of the Indo-American Strategic Partnership", India Review, vol. 6(1), January 2007.

Burns, Nicholas R., "America's Strategic Opportunity with India", Foreign Affairs (New York), November/December 2007.

Carter, Ashton B., "America's New Strategic Partner", Foreign Affairs, vol. 85 (4), July/August 2006.

Chansoria, Monika, "Indo-US Relations: Assessing the China Factor", World Focus (New Delhi), vol. XXIX(7), July 2008.

Chari, P. R., "Indo-US Strategic Cooperation: Constraints and Limitations", Peace and Conflict, Article no. 1789, 13 July, 2005.

Chawla, Shalini, "Pakistan's Conventional Arms Acquisitions: Priorities and Prospects", Air Power Journal (New Delhi), vol. 3(1), Spring 2006.

Chellaney, Brahma, "An Indian Critique of U.S. Export Controls". Orbis (Philadelphia, PA), vol. 38(3), Summer 1994.

____________, "Technology Control Regimes: Dealing with their Impact on India", India Quarterly (New Delhi), vol. LVIII(1), January-March 2002.

Chenoy, Kamal Mitra and Anuradha M Chenoy, "India's Foreign Policy Shifts and the Calculus of Power", Economic and Political Weekly, vol. XLII (35), 1-7 September 2007.

Chowdhury, Shankar Roy, "Beyond the 123- IS there A plan B?", U.S.I. Journal, vol. XXXVI(567), January-March 2007.

Curtis, Lisa, "After Mumbai: Time to Strengthen U.S.-India Counterterrorism Cooperation", The Heritage Foundation, No. 2217 (Washington, DC), 9 December 2008.

____________, "U.S.-India: An Enduring Partnership in Uncertain Times", Heritage Foundation No. 2708, 24 November 2009.

Das, P S., "India and China-A Relationship for the Future", U.S.I. Journal, vol. CXXXV(561), July-September 2005.

Dehua, Wang, "Economic Reforms, Opening-Up and Attraction of FDI-India: Can it Be a Benchmark for China?", The Atlantic Journal of World Affairs (New- Delhi), vol.1(1), October-December 2005

Delury, John, "China and U.S. Collaborate, Confront", Far Eastern Economic Review (Hong Kong), vol. 172(1), January-February 2009.

Dubey, Ajit K., "Progressing Partnership: India Exercises Once Again with the US During COPEINDIA 05", Force (New Delhi), vol. 3(4), December 2005.

Erickson, Andrew S., "The Growth of China's Navy: Implications for Indian Ocean Security", Strategic Analysis, vol. 32(4), July 2008.

Fair, C. Christine, "Time for Sober Realism: Renegotiating U.S. Relations with Pakistan", Washington Quarterly (Washington, DC), vol. 32(2), April 2009.

______________, "US–Indian Army-to-Army Relations: Prospects for Future Coalition Operations", Asian Security, vol. 1(2), April 2005.

Foran, Virgina, "The Case for Indo-US High-Technology Cooperation", Survival (United Kingdom), vol. 40(2), Summer 1998.

Frankel, Francine, R., "Indo-US Relations: Changing Perceptions", Centre for Security Analysis (Chennai), Bulletin No.10, October 2006.

Gaan, Narottam, "India and the United States Spinning a Strategic Engagement: Convergences and Divergences", BIISS Journal (Dhaka), vol. 27(4), October 2006.

Gaan, Narottam and Sudhansubala Das, "Indo-US Relation Toward a Rapprochement- From Post Cold War to Post September 11", India Quarterly, vol. LVIII(3&4), July-December 2002.

Ganguly, Sumit, "America and India at a Turning Point", Current History (Philadelphia, PA), vol. 104(680), March 2005.

____________, "The Start of a Beautiful Friendship? The United States and India", World Policy Journal, vol. XX(1), Spring 2003.

Ganguly, Sumit and Andrew Scobell, "India and US: Forging a Security Partnership" World Policy Journal, vol. XXII(2), Summer, 2005.

Garrett, Banning, "US-China Relations in the Era of Globalisation and Terror: A Framework For Analysis", Journal of Contemporary China (United-Kingdom), vol. 15(48), August 2006.

Garver, John W., "The China-India-U.S. Triangles: Strategic Relations in the Post Cold War Era", The National Bureau of Asian Research (NBR) Analysis (Washington), vol. 13(5), October 2002.

Ghosh, R.N. and M.A.B. Siddique, "A view of Indo-Australian Economic Relations: Trade, Investment and Aid", The Atlantic Journal of World Affairs, vol. 1(1), October-December 2005.

Ghosh, Samarjit, "Two Decades of Indo-Pak CBMs: A Critique from India", IPCS Issue Brief 132, September 2009.

Ghosh, Sekhar, "Indo-U.S. Relations: The New Vistas", India Quarterly, vol. LVIII(1), January-March 2002.

Gopalakrishnan, A., "Indo-US Nuclear Cooperation: A Non-Starter?", Economic and Political Weekly, 2 July 2005.

____________, "Some Concerns on Indo-US Deal", Economic and Political Weekly, 27 August 2005.

Gordon, Sandy, "An Australian Perspective on the Indo-US Nuclear Deal", South Asian Survey (New Delhi), vol. 16(1), January-April 2009.

Guihong, Zhang, "US-India Strategic Partnership: Implications for China", International Studies (New Delhi), vol. 42(3&4), July-December 2005.

____________, "U.S. Security Policy toward South Asia and its Implications for China: A Chinese Perspective", Paper presented at The Henry L. Stimson Center, January 2003.

Halan, Y C, "Manmohan Singh Visits the US: Towards Detente", South Asia Politics (New Delhi), vol. 4(4), August 2005

Haq, M. Emdadul, "Indo-US Nuclear Agreement: Regional Concerns", BIISS Journal, vol. 27(2), April 2006.

Harrison, S., "The United States and South Asia: Trapped by the Past?", Current History, vol. 96(614), 1997.

Hiranandani, G M, "Indo-US Naval Cooperation", Indian Defence Review (New Delhi), vol. 17(1), January-March 2002.

____________, "The Indo-US Strategic Partnership", Indian Defence Review, vol. 17 (3), July-September 2002.

Hussain, Touqir, "US-Pakistan Engagement: the War on Terrorism and Beyond", Regional Studies (Islamabad), vol. XXIV(1), Winter 2005-06.

Inayat, Mavara, "US-Indian Strategic Partnership: Implications for Asia and Beyond", Regional Studies, vol. XXIV(2), Spring 2006.

Inderfurth, Karl F., "South Asia is a Region of True Importance", Span, Vol. XXXVIII(5), September/October 1997.

Jaspal, Zafar Nawaz, "Enhanced Defence Cooperation Between United States and Pakistan", Strategic Insights (Monterey, CA), vol. VI(4), June 2007.

Jha, Nalini Kant, "Reviving US-India Friendship in a Changing International Order", Asian Survey (Berkeley, CA), vol. 34(12), December 1994.

__________, "Taking Stock of India-US Deal on Civil Nuclear Cooperation", India Quarterly, vol. LXIII(4), October-December 2007.

Kak, Kapil, "India-China Relations: An Overview", Air Power Journal, vol. 3(3), Monsoon 2006.

Kamath, P.M., "Civilian Nuclear Deal: Turning Point in Indo-US Relations", India Quarterly, vol. LXII(3), July-September 2006.

Kapila, Subhash, "India-USA Strategic Partnership-The Advent of the Inevitable", South Asia Analysis Group (Noida), Paper no.120, 22.04.2000.

__________, "United States Obsession with the Kashmir Issue: An Analysis", South Asia Analysis Group, Paper no. 403, 30.01.2002.

Kapoor, V. K., "India-US Relationship on an Ascending Trajectory", in U.S.I. Journal, vol. CXXXVI(565), July-September 2006.

Karamat, Jehangir, "General Trends, Global Futures, and U.S.-Pakistan Relations", Strategic Insights, vol. VI(4), June 2007.

Karat, Prakash, "Vajpayee Government Covertly Forging Military Ties with US", People's Democracy (New Delhi), vol. XXV(48), 2 December 2001.

__________, "Growing Military Nexus with US", People's Democracy, vol. XXV(30), 29 July 2001.

Khurana, Gurpreet S., "Security of Sea Lines: Prospects for India-Japan Cooperation", Strategic Analysis, vol. 31(1), January-February 2007.

Koithara, Verghese, "India-US Defence Cooperation: Expectations and Prospects", Economic and Political Weekly, vol. XL(32), 6 August 2005.

Krishnan, Natarajan, "Indo-US Relations–A Strategic Partnership", U.S.I. Journal, vol. CXXXVI(564), April-June 2006.

Kumar, Arun, "US to Sell India Six Hercules Planes for $1 billion", India STRATEGIC (New Delhi), vol. 2(6), June 2007.

Kumar, Ashwin, "Indo-US Nuclear Deal: Seperation of Civilian and Military Facilities", Economic and Political Weekly, vol. XL(53), 31 December 2005.

Kumar, Dinesh, "Defence in Indo-US Relations", Occasional Paper, Institute for Defence Studies and Analyses, August 1997.

Kumar, Ranjit, "Malabar Exercise and its Fallout: PSI Dilemma", Strategic Affairs (New Delhi), vol. 2(13), 15 September-15 October 2007.

Lavoy, Peter R. and Adam Radin, "U.S.-Pakistan Relations in the Twenty-First Century", Strategic Insights, vol. VI(4), June 2007.

Limaye, Satu, P., "Mediating: A Bridge Too Far", Washington Quarterly, vol. 26(1), 2002.

____________, "The Changing Place of Pakistan in US-Indian Relations", Contemporary South Asia, vol. 1(1), 1992.

Lodhi, Iftikhar A., "India-US Strategic Partnership, the Asian Balance of Power and the Greater Middle East", Indian Foreign Affairs Journal (New Delhi), vol. 3(4), October-December 2008.

Luthra, Gulshal, "US will Sell Aegis to India-Just Please Ask", India STRATEGIC, vol. 2(1), January 2007.

Mahapatra, A B, "Implications of MNNA Status for Pakistan and the Subcontinent", Defence Digest (New Delhi), vol. 3(6), May-June 2004.

Mahapatra, Chintamani, "India and the US Evolving Economic Ties", Strategic Analysis, vol. XXI(2), March 1998.

____________, "Pakistan Factor in Indo-American Relations", Strategic Analysis, vol. 19(7), October1996.

____________, "The US in South Asia: An Overview", World Focus, vol. XXVIII(8), August 2007.

____________, "US Factor and the Kashmir Issue", Journal of Peace Studies (New Delhi), vol. 8(4), July-August 2001.

Maitra, Ramtanu, "India-U.S. Relations in the Shadow of an Uncertain Nuclear Deal", AAKROSH-Asian Journal on Terrorism and Internal Conflicts, vol. 11(41), October 2008.

Malik, Mohan, "India-China Relations: Giants, Stir, Cooperative and Compete", Asia Pacific Center for Security Studies, October 2004.

Mansingh, Lalit, "Indo-US Strategic Partnership: Are We There Yet?", Institute of Peace and Conflict Studies, Issue brief 39, October 2006.

Mansingh, Surjit, "How the US Perceives China and India", World Affairs (New Delhi), vol. 1(4), October-December 1997.

Mansingh, Surjit, "Indo-US Relations: a Closer Relationship?", Economic and Political Weekly (Mumbai), 18 May-4 June 2005.

Mattoo, Amitabh, "Is the United States Mediating in Kashmir?", World Focus, vol. 21(6-7), June-July 2000.

Mazumdar, Mrityunjoy and Rupak Chattopadhyay, "India-U.S. Naval Exercises Bearing Fruit", US Naval Institute Proceedings (Annapolis, MD), vol. 132(7), July 2006.

____________, "Malabar 2005", Indian Defence Review, vol. 20(4), October-December 2005.

Milhollin, Gary, "The US-India Nuclear Pact: Bad for Security", Current History, vol. 105(694), November 2006.

Mishra, Bhabani, "India-US Relations: A Paradigm Shift", Strategic Analysis, vol. 29(1), January-March 2005.

Mistry, Dinshaw, "Tempering Optimism About Nuclear Deterrence in South Asia", Security Studies (Philadelphia, PA), vol. 18(1), January-March 2009.

Mistry, Dinshaw and Sumit Ganguly, "The US-India Nuclear Pact: A Good Deal", Current History, vol. 105(694), November 2006.

Mitra, Pramit and John Ryan, "Gathering Stream: India and the United States Extend Military Ties", South Asia Monitor, Centre for Strategic and International Studies, Washington, DC, No. 99, 2 October 2006.

Mohan, C. Raja, "A Paradigm Shift Toward South Asia", Washington Quarterly, vol. 26(1), Winter 2002-03.

____________, "Balancing Interests and Values: India's Struggle with Democracy Promotion", Washington Quarterly, vol. 30(3), Summer 2007.

____________, "India and the Balance of Power", Foreign Affairs, vol. 85(4), July-August 2006.

____________, "India's Quest for Continuity in the Face of Change", Washington Quarterly, vol. 31(4), Autumn 2008.

Mohan, C. Raja and Parag Khanna, "Getting India Right: Mutual Interests and Democratic Affinity", Policy Review No.135 (Stanford, CA), February and March 2006.

Mohanty, Sanjay, "US-Pakistan Relations", World Focus, vol. 28(8) August 2007.

Muhammad, Adil Sultan, "Indo-US Civilian Nuclear Cooperation Agreement: Implications on South Asian Security Environment", The Henry L. Stimson Center, July 2006.

Muni, S.D. and C. Raja Mohan, "Emerging Asia: India's Options", International Studies, vol. 41(3), July-Sept, 2004.

Mustafa, Malik Qasim, "Indo-US Civilian Nuclear Cooperation Agreement: Implications for International Nuclear Non-Proliferation Regime", Strategic Studies (Islamabad), vol. XXVI(4), Winter 2006.

Nair, Anirudha and Rudra Dev, "Prospects for Indo-US Partnership", Strategic Research Review (New Delhi), vol. 2(2), 2006.

Nambiar, Satish, "A Role for India in the Emerging World Order", U.S.I Journal, vol. CXXXVI(565), July-September 2006

____________, "The Security Dimensions of Emerging Indo-US Relations", World Focus, vol. 21(6-7), June-July 2000.

Nandan, Devki, "Sino-Pak Nuclear Nexus and India's Concerns", Issue Brief, Centre for Air Power Studies (New Delhi), 16 July 2010.

Nayak, Polly, "U.S. Security Policy on South Asia since 9/11—Challenges and Implications for the Future", Occasional Paper Series, Asia Pacific Centre for Security Studies, February 2005.

Palit, Parama Sinha, "India, China and US-Key Variables in Indian Ocean", Journal of Indian Ocean Studies (New Delhi), vol. 14(3), December 2006.

Paul, T.V., "The US-India Nuclear Accord: Implications for the Nonproliferation Regime", International Journal (Canada), vol. LXII(4), Fall 2007.

____________, "Why has the India-Pakistan Rivalry Been So Enduring? Power Asymmetry and an Intractable Conflict", Security Studies, vol. 15(4), October-December 2006.

Paul, T. V. and Mahesh Shankar, "Why the US-India Nuclear Accord is a Good Deal", Survival, vol. 49(4), Winter 2007-08

Pradhan, Radhe Gopal, "India and the Chinese Dimensions", South Asia Politics (New Delhi), vol. 6(1), May 2007.

_______________, "The Nuclear Agreement: Through the Chinese Prisms", South Asia Politics, vol. 6(8), December 2007.

Qingguo, Jia, "Learning to Live with the Hegemon: Evolution of China's Policy Toward the US Since the End of the Cold War", Journal of Contemporary China, vol. 14(44), August 2005.

Raghavan, V R, "Indo-US Strategic Partnership: China as a Factor", U.S.I. Journal (New Delhi), vol. CXXXVII(570), October-December 2007

Raj, Christopher S. and Chintamani Mahapatra, "US Strategic Response to Emerging Problems in Asia", International Studies, vol. 41(3), July-September 2004.

Ram, Uday, "India-US Relationship: A US Perspective, Peace and Conflict, Article no.1792, 14 July 2005.

Roy, Ash Narain, "Indo-US and India-Russia: Strategic Partners All?", Mainstream (New Delhi), vol. XLVIII(1), 26 December 2009.

Sagar, Rahul, "What's in a Name? India and America in the Twenty-First Century", Survival, vol. 46(3), Autumn 2004.

Saileja, "Indo-US Defence Co-operation", World Focus, vol. XXIX(7), July 2008.

Sakhuja, Vijay, "From Malabar to Malacca Post Cold War Indo-US Naval Relations", Indian Defence Review, vol. 17(2), April-June 2002.

Samuel, Cherian, "Indo-US Defence Cooperation and the Emerging Strategic Relationship", Strategic Analysis, vol. 31(2), March, 2007.

Sasikumar, Karthika, "India's Emergence as a Responsible Nuclear Power", International Journal, vol. LXII (4), Fall 2007.

Sawhney, Pravin and Ghazala Wahab, "Beyond Borders", Force, vol. 5(1), September, 2007.

Schaffer, Teresita C., "Building a New Partnership with India", Washington Quarterly, vol. 25(2), Spring 2002.

_____________, "The US-India Policy Options in Asia", U.S.I. Journal, vol. CXXXV(560), April-June 2005.

Sengupta, S. Prasun K., "In Tandem: Indian Lessons for American Pilots at Cope India 06", Force, vol. 3(4), December 2005.

Sethi, Manpreet, "Indo-U.S. Cooperation No Threat to Proliferation", Nuclear Power, A Bimonthly Newsletter on Nuclear Energy, Centre for Strategic and International Studies, vol. 3(18), 15 June 2006.

Sharma, Ashok, "Growing Influence of Indian American Lobbying on Indo-US Relations", World Focus, vol. XXIX(7), July 2008.

___________, "Indo-U.S. Strategic Convergence: An Overview of Defence and Military Cooperation", Claws Paper no. 2, New Delhi, Knowledge World in Association with the Centre for Land Warfare Studies, 2008.

Sharma, Bobby, "Deepening Indo-US military Relations", Peace and Conflict, vol. 7(4), April 2004.

Shrivastava, B. K., "Indo-American Relations Since September 11", World Focus, vol. 23(7&8), July-August 2002.

Shrivastava, B. K. and Manmohan Agarwal, "India and the US: Natural allies?", South Asian Survey, vol. 12(2), July-December 2005.

Sidhu, Waheguru Pal Singh, "Enhancing Indo-US Strategic Cooperation", Adelphi Paper 313, November 1997.

Srinivasan, M.R., "Challenges and Opportunity", Economic and Political Weekly, 27 August 2005.

Srivastava, Anupam and Gary k. Bertsch, "Issues Before the New Administration- US-India Strategic Relations", Indian Defence Review, vol. 16(1), January-March 2001.

Subrahmanyam, K., "Indo-US Relations in a Changing World", Air Power Journal, vol. 2 (3), Monsoon, July-September 2005.

___________, "Indo-US Relations in the Coming Decades", U.S.I. Journal, vol. CXXXV(561), July-September 2005.

___________, "Partnership, Not Alliance" in a debate on Indo-US Strategic Partnership, Indian Foreign Affairs Journal, vol. 1(1), January-March 2006.

Tellis, Ashley J., "Natural Born Partners", Force, vol. 1(12), August 2004.

___________, "The Merits of Dehyphenation: Explaining U.S. Success in Engaging India and Pakistan", Washington Quarterly, vol. 31(4), Autumn 2008.

Thyagaraj, Manohar and Raju G.C. Thomas, "The U.S.-Indian Nuclear Agreement: Balancing Energy Needs and Nonproliferation Goals", Orbis, vol. 50(2), Spring 2006.

Tomar, Ravi, "India-US Relations in the Changing Strategic Environment", Research Paper No. 20, Department of Parliamentary Libnrary, Australian Parliament, 25 June 2002.

Tourangbham, Monish, "The Pakistan Factor in India-US Relations: Is it Finally Muted?", World Focus, vol. XXIX(7), July 2008

Ved, Mahendra, "Exercise Malabar Moves from Bilateral to Multilateralism", Asia Defence News, vol. III(10), 15 October, 2007.

________________, "Indian Navy's Malabar and Other Exercises", India STRATEGIC, vol. 2(9), September 2007.

C. Reports

Adhikari, Gautam, "U.S.-India Relations: Reports on AEI's Roundtable Discussions", American Enterprise Institute for Public Policy Research (AEI) Working Paper #112, 22 June 2005.

"Charting New Frontiers: Enhancing India-U.S. Cooperation in the Global Innovation Economy", Report of a Joint Task Force between Pacific Council on International Policy and the Federation of Indian Chambers of Commerce, 2009.

Choudhury, Upendra, "The Indo-USA Nuclear Deal and its Impact on India's Ballistic Missile Programme", South Asian Strategic Studies Institute Research Report 17, June 2008.

Garver, John W., "The China-India-U.S. Triangles: Strategic Relations in the Post Cold War Era", The National Bureau of Asian Research (NBR) Analysis (Washington), vol. 13(5), October 2002.

"India/Pak Relations and Kashmir: Steps Toward Peace", International Crisis Group Asia, Report No. 79, 24 June 2004.

"India-USA Economic Relations: The Next Decade", Confederation of Indian Industry, June 2009.

Jaspal, Zafar Nawaz, "The Indo-US Strategic Relationship and Pakistan's Security", South Asian Strategic Studies Institute Research Report 9, December 2007.

Kumar, Rajiv, et. al., "Indian Economic Outlook 2008-09 and 2009-10", Indian Council for Research on International Economic Relations (ICRIER) Working Paper no. 234, March 2009.

Martin, Michael F. and K. Alan Kronstadt, "India-U.S. Economic and Trade Relations", CRS Report for Congress, RL34161, 31 August 2007.

Morrison, Wayne and Alan Kronstadt, "India-U.S. Economic Relations", CRS Report for Congress, Code RS21502, Updated on 25 February 2004.

Rajagopalan, Rajeswari Pillai, "Indo-US Nuclear Deal: Implications for India and the Global N-Regime", IPCS Special Report, No. 62, December 2008.

D. Seminar Paper and Conference Paper

Astarita, Claudia, "China and India: Rivals or Partners? An Analysis of the Background of the Interactions between the two Major Emerging Asian Powers", Paper presented in 6th Pan-European International Relations Conference on Making Sense of Pluralist World, University of Turin, 12-15 September 2007, available at <http://turin.sgir.eu/uploads/Claudia-china_india_rivals_or_partners_claudia_astarita.pdf>.

Chopra, R K, "Indo-US Economic Relations", Paper Presented in a seminar on Indo-US Relations: The Changing Perspective, at Yashwantrao Chavan Academy of Development Administration, Organised by Centre for Advanced Strategic Studies, Pune, 22nd October 2008.

Ghosh, P K, "Maritime Security Challenges in South Asia and the Indian Ocean: Response Strategies", Paper Presented at the Conference on Maritime Security in Asia, Honolulu, Hawaii, 18-20 January 2004, available at <http://www.southchinasea.org/docs/ghosh,%20maritime%20security%20challenges%20in%20SAsia%20&%20Indian%20Ocean.pdf>.

Mansingh, Surjit, "Improving Relations with the United States", in a Seminar Proceedings on Perspective on National Security, National Defence College, New Delhi, 23-26 November 1998.

E. Newspaper

1. Times of India, Pune.
2. Indian Express, Pune.
3. The Hindu, Hyderabad.

4. Asian Age, Pune.

5. Financial Time, Pune.

F. Websites

1. http://www.mod.nic.in
2. http://mealib.nic.in
3. www.yaleglobal.yale.edu
2. www.pinr.com
3. www.brookings .org
4. www.iiss.org